BBC

DOCTOR WHO

THE ELEVENTH DOCTOR

VOL 4: THE THEN AND THE NOW

"Amazing! It hit all the right notes, and got the Doctor perfect! 9/10"
COMIC BOOK CAST

"Mind-bending and impressive."
BENJAMIN HERMAN

"Balances out the serious with well-placed humor, slapstick included."
WHATCHA READING

"A fun read with some great characterization and a sense of adventure. 9 out of 10!"
COMICS VERSE

"An enjoyable romp."
FLICKERING MYTH

"9.5 out of 10!"
NERDS UNCHAINED

"Does a splendid job of capturing Matt Smith's expressions."
GEEK WITH CURVES

"The tone of the Eleventh Doctor is strong in this one."
WARPED FACTOR

"A fantastic Eleventh Doctor adventure! 9 out of 10!"
NEWSARAMA

"A great job creating a companion who can keep up with the Doctor. 10 out of 10!"
PROJECT FANDOM

"Nails the tone and spirit right out of the gate. 4 out of 5!"
COMIC BOOK RESOURCES

"A great continuation of a fabulous series. The character depth, dramatic arc and suspenseful flow make it a gripping read."
UNLEASH THE FANBOY

"Excellent script with great artwork. I've become a fan of Alice Obiefune – what a character she has become!"
TM STASH

"Compelling art."
BLEEDING COOL

"Well-written with great art!"
COMIC BASTARDS

TITAN COMICS

EDITOR
Andrew James

ASSISTANT EDITORS
Jessica Burton
Gabriela Houston

DESIGNER
Rob Williams

SENIOR EDITOR
Steve White

TITAN COMICS EDITORIAL
Lizzie Kaye, Tom Williams

PRODUCTION ASSISTANT
Peter James

PRODUCTION SUPERVISORS
Maria Pearson, Jackie Flook

PRODUCTION MANAGER
Obi Onuora

STUDIO MANAGER
Emma Smith

CIRCULATION MANAGER
Steve Tothill

SENIOR MARKETING & PRESS OFFICER
Owen Johnson

MARKETING MANAGER
Ricky Claydon

ADVERTISING MANAGER
Michelle Fairlamb

PUBLISHING MANAGER
Darryl Tothill

PUBLISHING DIRECTOR
Chris Teather

OPERATIONS DIRECTOR
Leigh Baulch

EXECUTIVE DIRECTOR
Vivian Cheung

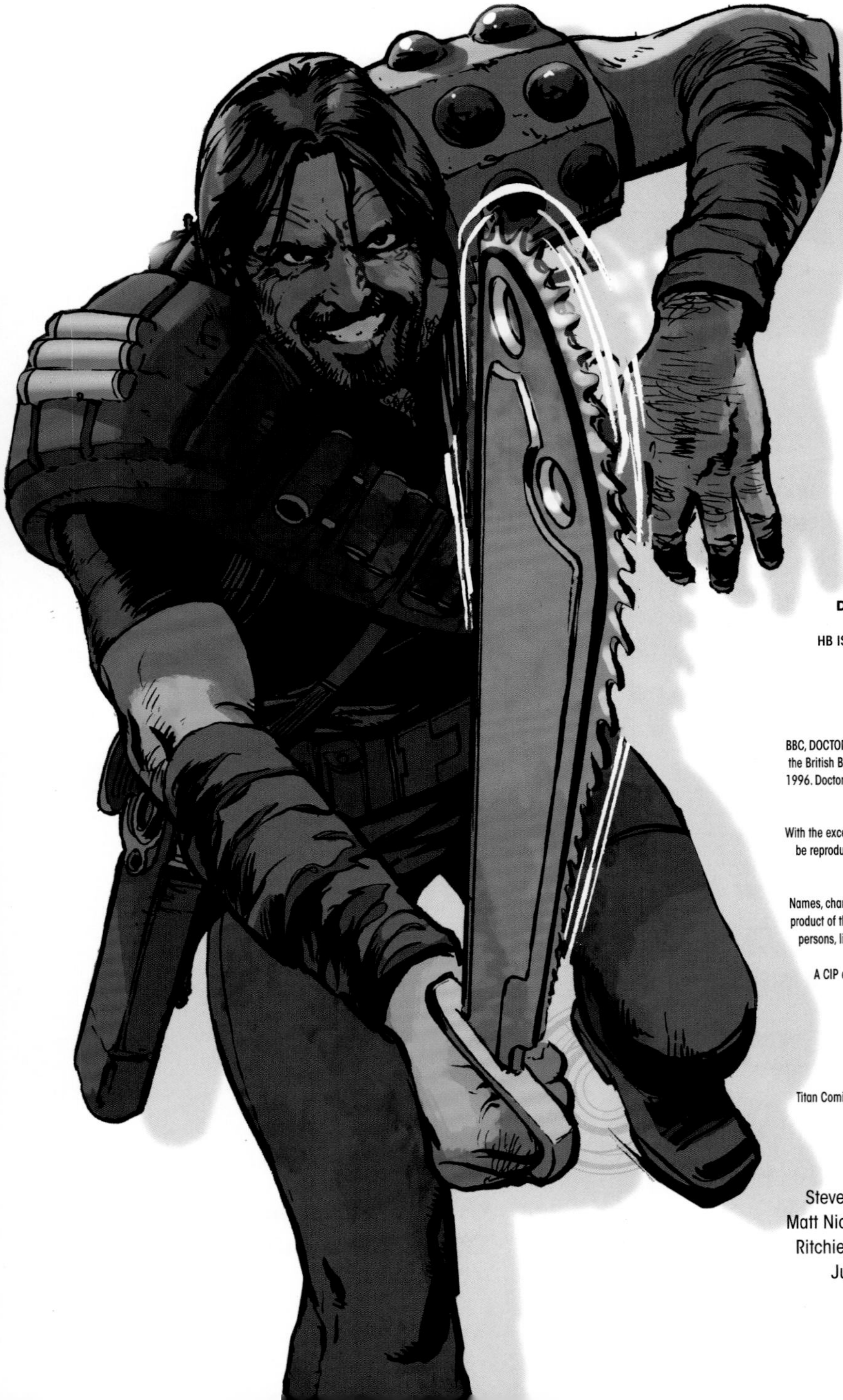

BBC WORLDWIDE

DIRECTOR OF EDITORIAL GOVERNANCE
Nicolas Brett

DIRECTOR OF CONSUMERPRODUCTS AND PUBLISHING
Andrew Moultrie

HEAD OF UK PUBLISHING
Chris Kerwin

PUBLISHER
Mandy Thwaites

PUBLISHING CO-ORDINATOR
Eva Abramik

DOCTOR WHO: THE ELEVENTH DOCTOR VOL 4
HB ISBN: 9781782767466 SB ISBN: 9781782767428

Published by Titan Comics, a division of Titan Publishing Group, Ltd. 144 Southwark Street, London, SE1 0UP.

A CIP catalogue record for this title is available from the British Library.
First edition: June 2016.

10 9 8 7 6 5 4 3 2 1

Printed in China. TC0929.

Special thanks to
Steven Moffat, Brian Minchin, Mandy Thwaites, Matt Nicholls, James Dudley, Edward Russell, Derek Ritchie, Scott Handcock, Kirsty Mullan, Kate Bush, Julia Nocciolino and Ed Casey for their invaluable assistance.

DOCTOR WHO
THE ELEVENTH DOCTOR

VOL 4: THE THEN AND THE NOW

WRITERS:
SI SPURRIER & ROB WILLIAMS

ARTISTS:
SIMON FRASER
WARREN PLEECE

COLORISTS:
GARY CALDWELL
HI-FI

LETTERS: RICHARD STARKINGS
AND COMICRAFT'S
JIMMY BETANCOURT

ABSLOM DAAK CREATED BY STEVE MOORE AND STEVE DILLON

ABSLOM DAAK APPEARS COURTESY OF **PANINI COMICS**
WITH THANKS TO THE AMAZING TEAM AT **DOCTOR WHO MAGAZINE**.
VISIT **DOCTORWHOMAGAZINE.COM** TO SUBSCRIBE AND FIND OUT MORE.

www.titan-comics.com

Titan
COMICS

BBC

DOCTOR WHO

THE ELEVENTH DOCTOR

POLICE PUBLIC CALL BOX
POLICE TELEPHONE
FREE
FOR USE OF
PUBLIC
PULL TO OPEN

ALICE OBIEFUNE

Former Library Assistant Alice Obiefune felt like her life was falling apart – then she met the Doctor! Now she's determined to see all the beauty and strangeness of the universe as she travels with him in the TARDIS!

THE DOCTOR

The last of the Time Lords of Gallifrey, the Eleventh Doctor is an old soul in the body of a boy professor. Though he makes mistakes – and often! – he *never* runs away from the consequences. Apart from days like today, when running seems like the best idea!

THE TARDIS

'Time and Relative Dimension in Space'. Bigger on the inside, this unassuming blue box is your ticket to unforgettable adventure! The Doctor likes to think he's in control, but often the TARDIS takes him where and when he needs to be...

PREVIOUSLY...

Alice first met the Doctor when she helped save London from a rainbow-colored alien dog.

From an evil, shapeshifting wish-granter to a sentient corporation, the pair have already experienced great dangers – and astounding wonders! – on their travels through time and space.

But their greatest adventures, and most taxing perils, are yet to come!

When you've finished reading the collection, please email your thoughts to doctorwhocomic@titanemail.com

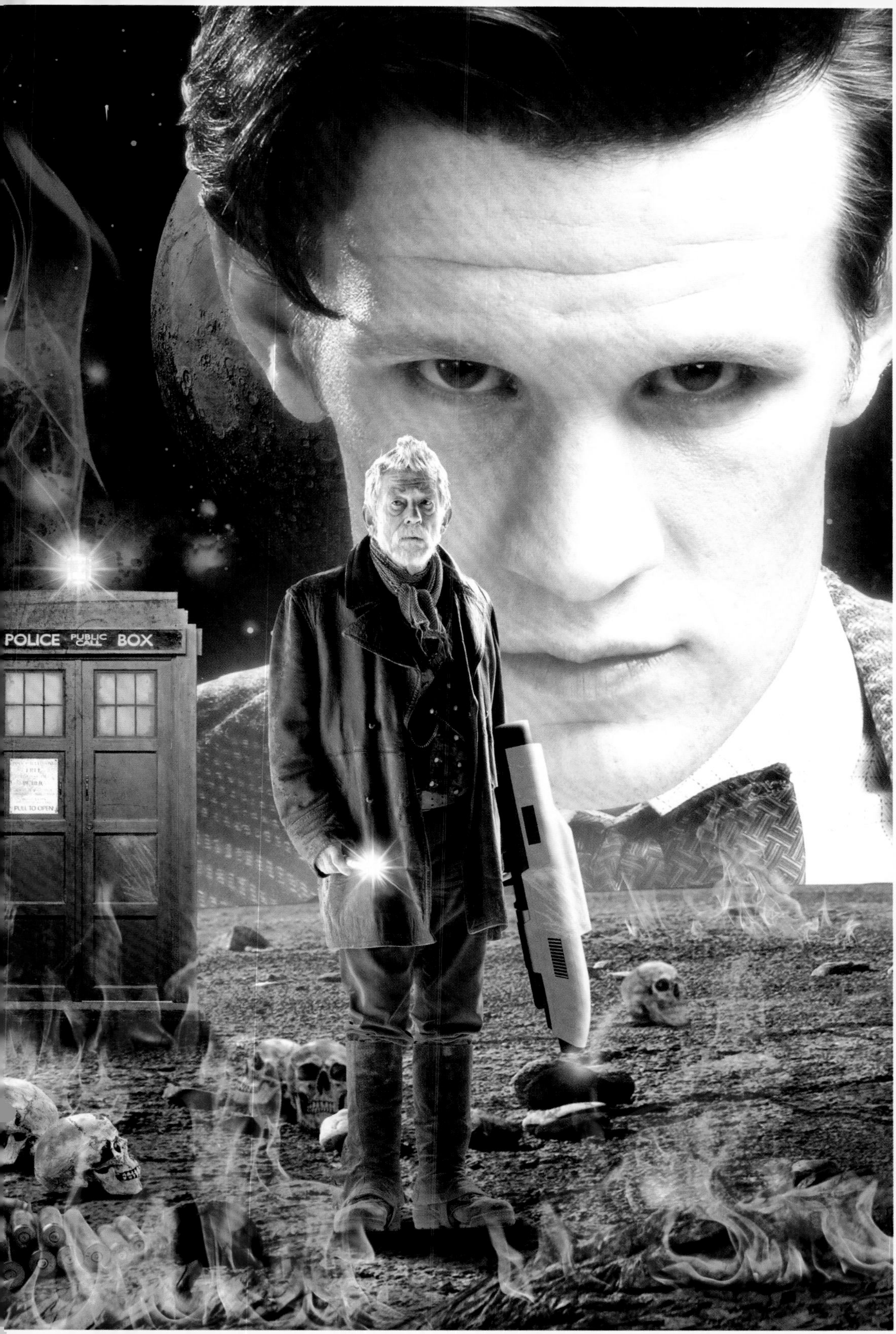
POLICE PUBLIC CALL BOX
PULL TO OPEN

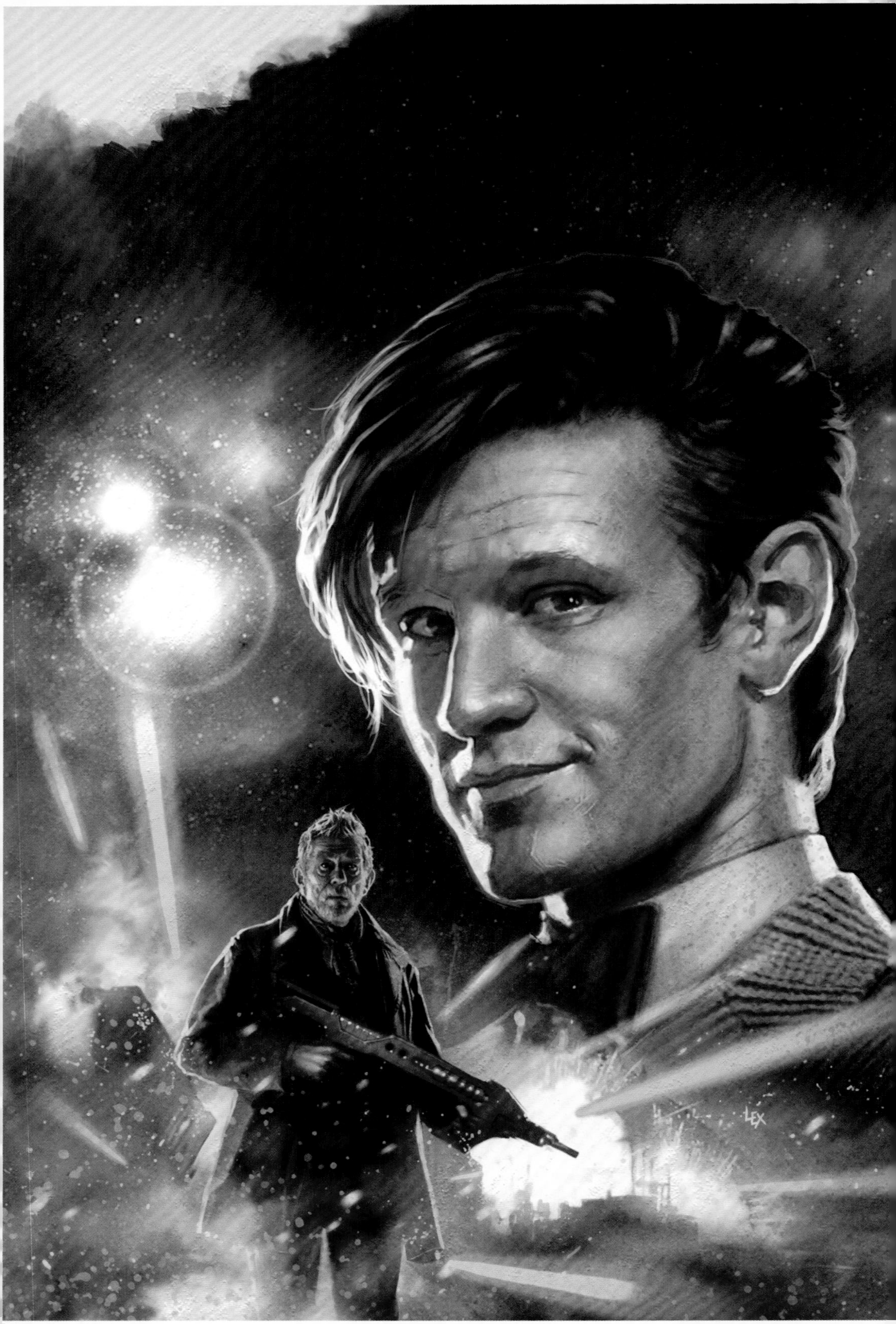
LEX

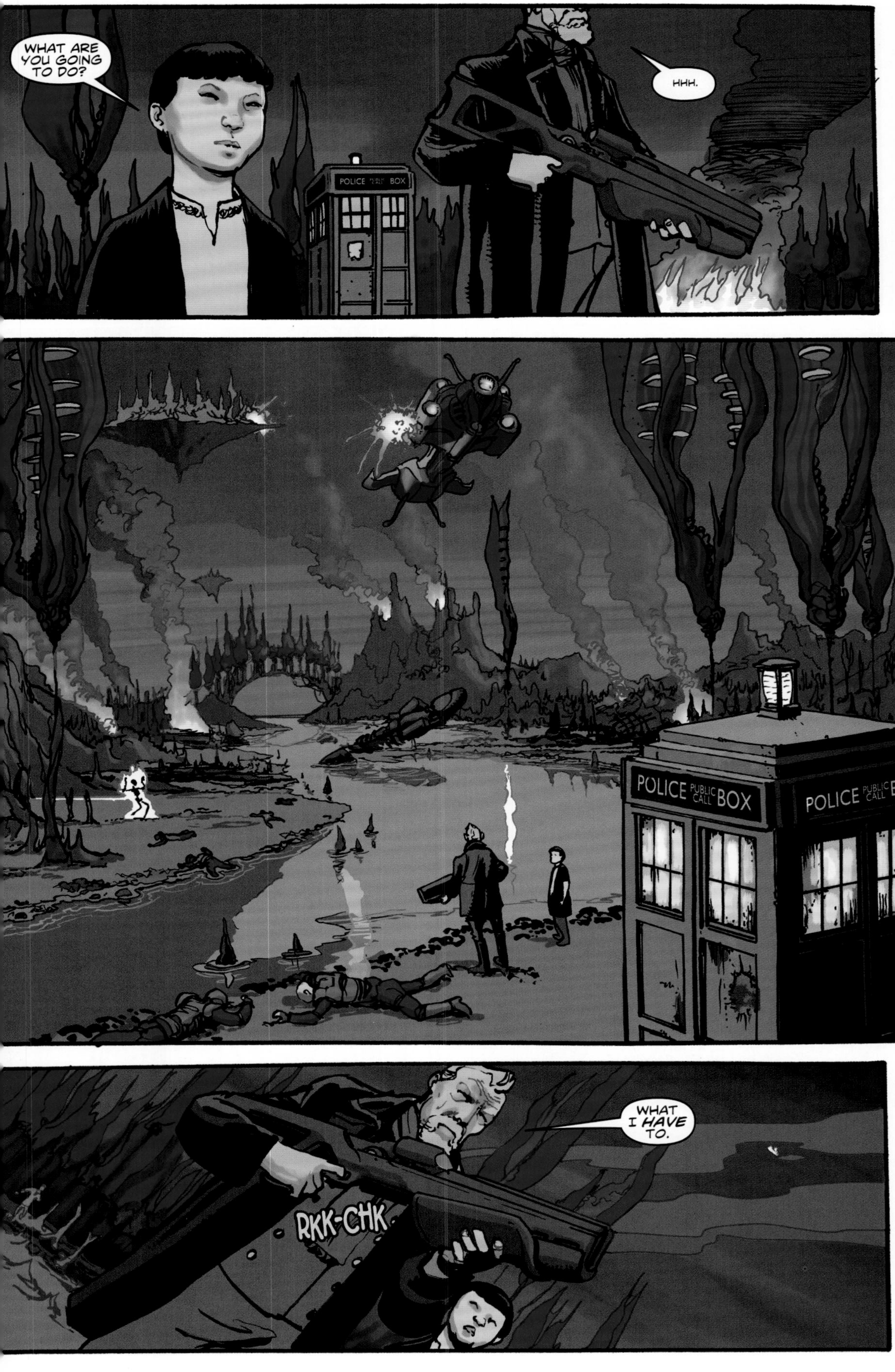
WHAT ARE YOU GOING TO DO?
HHH.
POLICE BOX
POLICE PUBLIC CALL BOX
POLICE PUBLIC CALL BO
WHAT I *HAVE* TO.
RKK-CHK

YOU JUST *HAD* TO, DIDN'T YOU?

UM.

THE THEN AND THE NOW

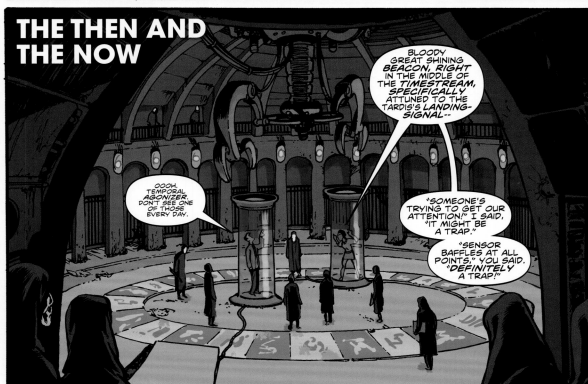

BLOODY GREAT SHINING *BEACON*, RIGHT IN THE MIDDLE OF THE *TIMESTREAM, SPECIFICALLY* ATTUNED TO THE *TARDIS'S LANDING-SIGNAL*--

OOOH. TEMPORAL *AGONIZER.* DON'T SEE ONE OF THOSE EVERY DAY.

"SOMEONE'S TRYING TO GET OUR *ATTENTION!*" I SAID, "IT MIGHT BE A *TRAP.*"

"*SENSOR BAFFLES* AT ALL POINTS," YOU SAID. "*DEFINITELY* A *TRAP!*"

WHILST. *LANDING.*

LOOK, CURIOSITY NEVER HURT *ANYONE.* PRETTY SURE YOU EARTH-TYPES HAVE A SAYING ABOUT THAT, DON'T YOU?

WAIT. STOP. BACK UP.

DID YOU SAY *"TEMPORAL AGONIZER"*?

I'M AFRAID HE *DID.*

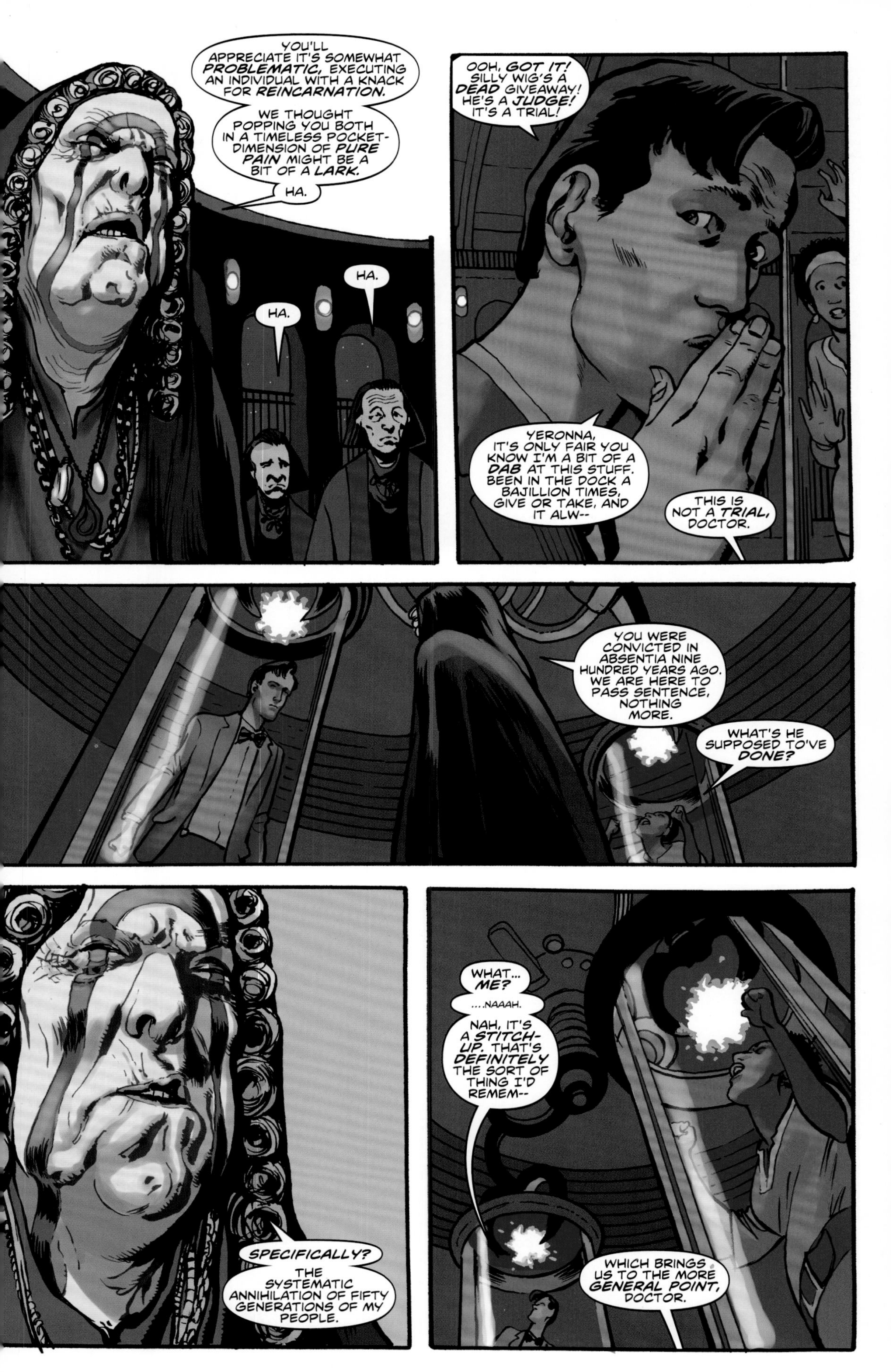
YOU'LL APPRECIATE IT'S SOMEWHAT PROBLEMATIC, EXECUTING AN INDIVIDUAL WITH A KNACK FOR REINCARNATION.
WE THOUGHT POPPING YOU BOTH IN A TIMELESS POCKET-DIMENSION OF PURE PAIN MIGHT BE A BIT OF A LARK.
HA.
HA.
HA.
OOH, GOT IT! SILLY WIG'S A DEAD GIVEAWAY! HE'S A JUDGE! IT'S A TRIAL!
YERONNA, IT'S ONLY FAIR YOU KNOW I'M A BIT OF A DAB AT THIS STUFF. BEEN IN THE DOCK A BAJILLION TIMES, GIVE OR TAKE, AND IT ALW--
THIS IS NOT A TRIAL, DOCTOR.
YOU WERE CONVICTED IN ABSENTIA NINE HUNDRED YEARS AGO. WE ARE HERE TO PASS SENTENCE, NOTHING MORE.
WHAT'S HE SUPPOSED TO'VE DONE?
SPECIFICALLY?
THE SYSTEMATIC ANNIHILATION OF FIFTY GENERATIONS OF MY PEOPLE.
WHAT... ME?
....NAAAH.
NAH, IT'S A STITCH-UP. THAT'S DEFINITELY THE SORT OF THING I'D REMEM--
WHICH BRINGS US TO THE MORE GENERAL POINT, DOCTOR.

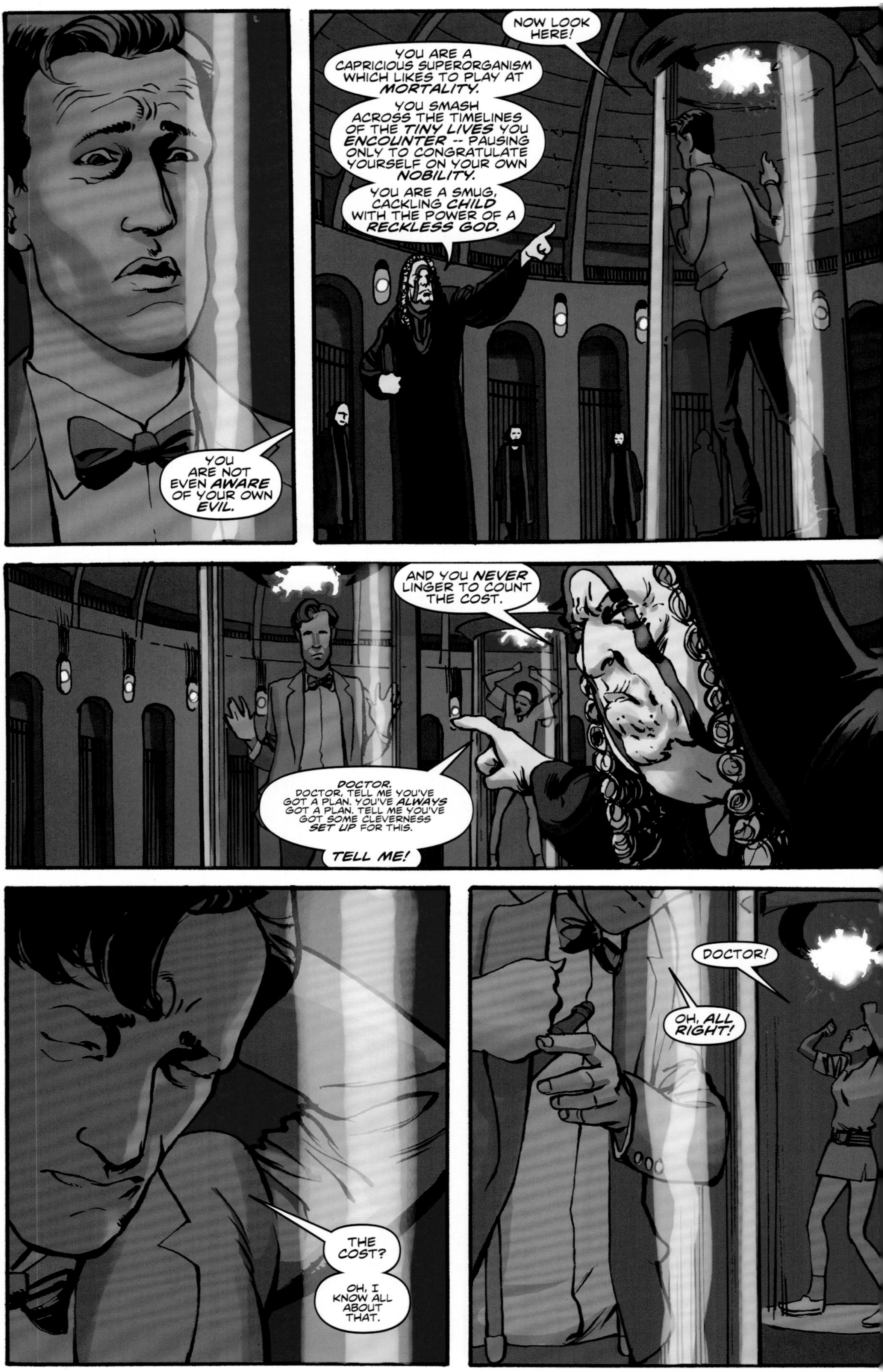
YOU ARE NOT EVEN AWARE OF YOUR OWN EVIL.
NOW LOOK HERE!
YOU ARE A CAPRICIOUS SUPERORGANISM WHICH LIKES TO PLAY AT MORTALITY.
YOU SMASH ACROSS THE TIMELINES OF THE TINY LIVES YOU ENCOUNTER -- PAUSING ONLY TO CONGRATULATE YOURSELF ON YOUR OWN NOBILITY.
YOU ARE A SMUG, CACKLING CHILD WITH THE POWER OF A RECKLESS GOD.
AND YOU NEVER LINGER TO COUNT THE COST.
DOCTOR.
DOCTOR, TELL ME YOU'VE GOT A PLAN. YOU'VE ALWAYS GOT A PLAN. TELL ME YOU'VE GOT SOME CLEVERNESS SET UP FOR THIS.
TELL ME!
THE COST?
OH, I KNOW ALL ABOUT THAT.
DOCTOR!
OH, ALL RIGHT!

BOOM BOOM BOOM

ZWOOOOORB

PSYCHIC MODERATORS. NOTICED THEM ON THE *WAY IN*. PROBABLY WHY *CHUCKLES* AND CO ARE SO *GLUM* THE WHOLE TIME.

VERY SUSCEPTIBLE TO A DOSE OF THE OLD *NEURO-TACHYONS*.

AND LOOK, SEE? EVERYONE'S MOSTLY *FINE!* NOTHING RECKLESS *HERE!*

I AM LINGERING TO COUNT THE COST AND IT IS MINIMAL!

AND NOW I'M OFF.

TO THE *TARDIS*, FAITHFUL COMPANION!

HOW DO YOU KNOW WHERE IT IS? THEY *BLINDFOLDED* US!

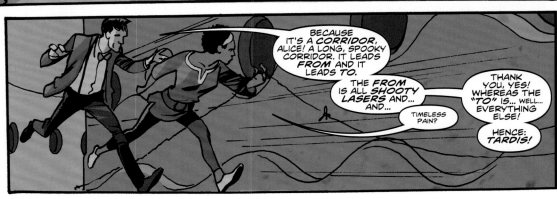

BECAUSE IT'S A *CORRIDOR*, ALICE! A LONG, SPOOKY CORRIDOR. IT LEADS *FROM* AND IT LEADS *TO*.

THE *FROM* IS ALL *SHOOTY LASERS* AND... AND...

TIMELESS PAIN?

THANK YOU, YES! WHEREAS THE "*TO*" IS... WELL... EVERYTHING ELSE!

HENCE: *TARDIS!*

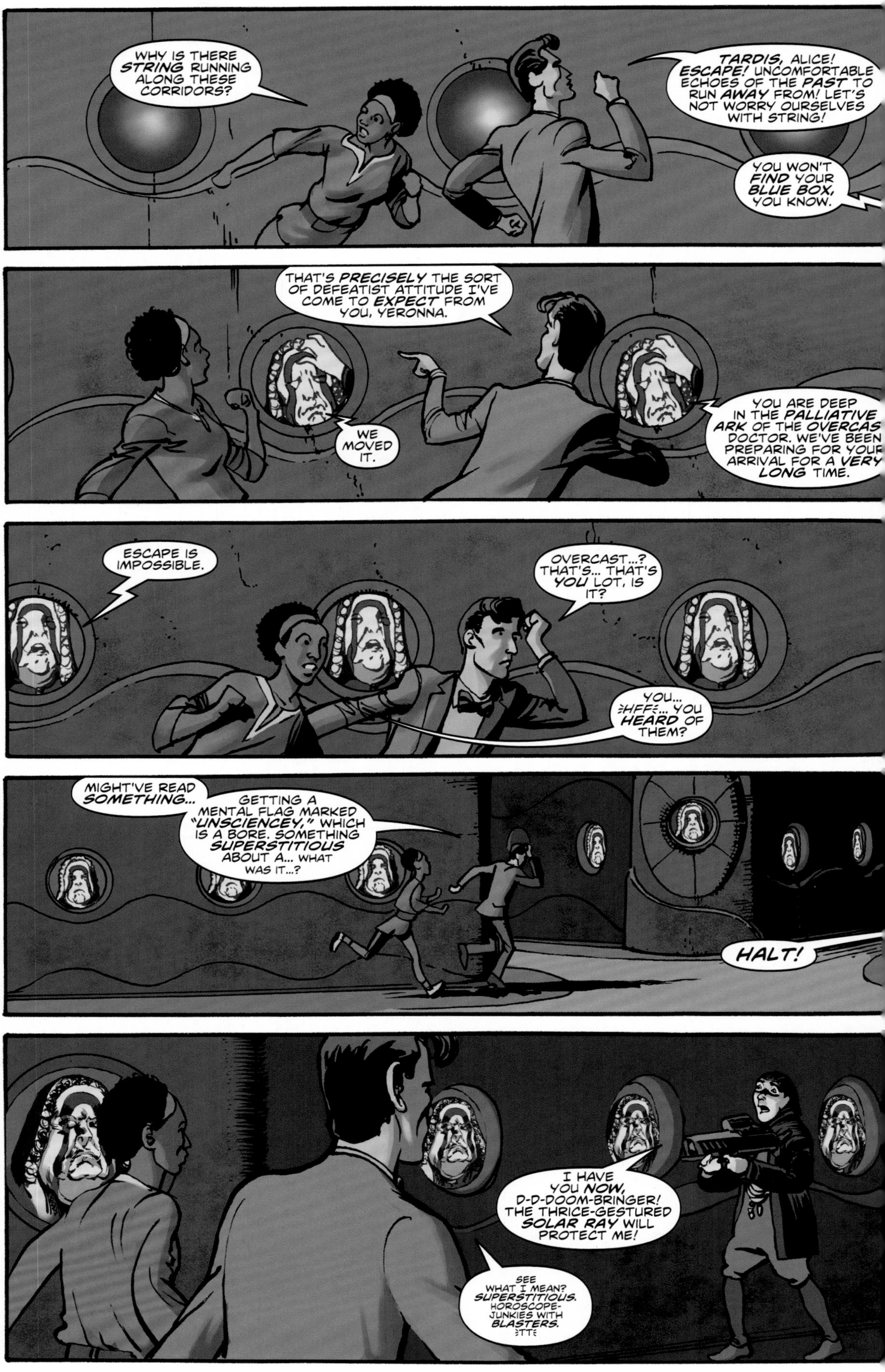

WHY IS THERE STRING RUNNING ALONG THESE CORRIDORS?
TARDIS, ALICE! ESCAPE! UNCOMFORTABLE ECHOES OF THE PAST TO RUN AWAY FROM! LET'S NOT WORRY OURSELVES WITH STRING!
YOU WON'T FIND YOUR BLUE BOX, YOU KNOW.
THAT'S PRECISELY THE SORT OF DEFEATIST ATTITUDE I'VE COME TO EXPECT FROM YOU, YERONNA.
WE MOVED IT.
YOU ARE DEEP IN THE PALLIATIVE ARK OF THE OVERCAST DOCTOR. WE'VE BEEN PREPARING FOR YOUR ARRIVAL FOR A VERY LONG TIME.
ESCAPE IS IMPOSSIBLE.
OVERCAST...? THAT'S... THAT'S YOU LOT, IS IT?
YOU... HFF... YOU HEARD OF THEM?
MIGHT'VE READ SOMETHING...
GETTING A MENTAL FLAG MARKED "UNSCIENCEY," WHICH IS A BORE. SOMETHING SUPERSTITIOUS ABOUT A... WHAT WAS IT...?
HALT!
I HAVE YOU NOW, D-D-DOOM-BRINGER! THE THRICE-GESTURED SOLAR RAY WILL PROTECT ME!
SEE WHAT I MEAN? SUPERSTITIOUS. HOROSCOPE-JUNKIES WITH BLASTERS. TTT

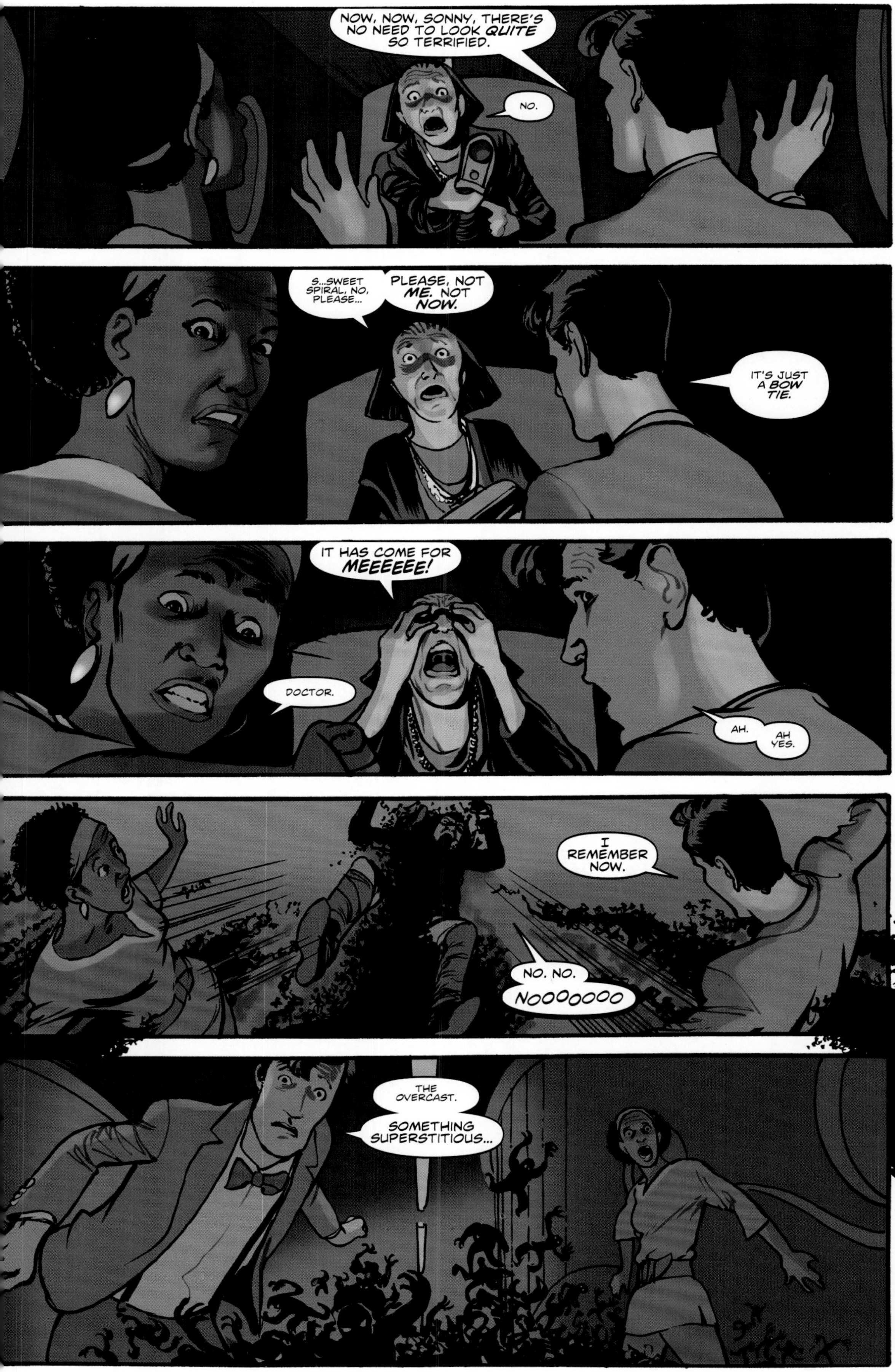
NOW, NOW, SONNY, THERE'S NO NEED TO LOOK QUITE SO TERRIFIED.
NO.
S...SWEET SPIRAL, NO, PLEASE...
PLEASE, NOT ME. NOT NOW.
IT'S JUST A BOW TIE.
IT HAS COME FOR MEEEEEE!
DOCTOR.
AH.
AH YES.
I REMEMBER NOW.
NO. NO.
NOOOOOOO
THE OVERCAST.
SOMETHING SUPERSTITIOUS...

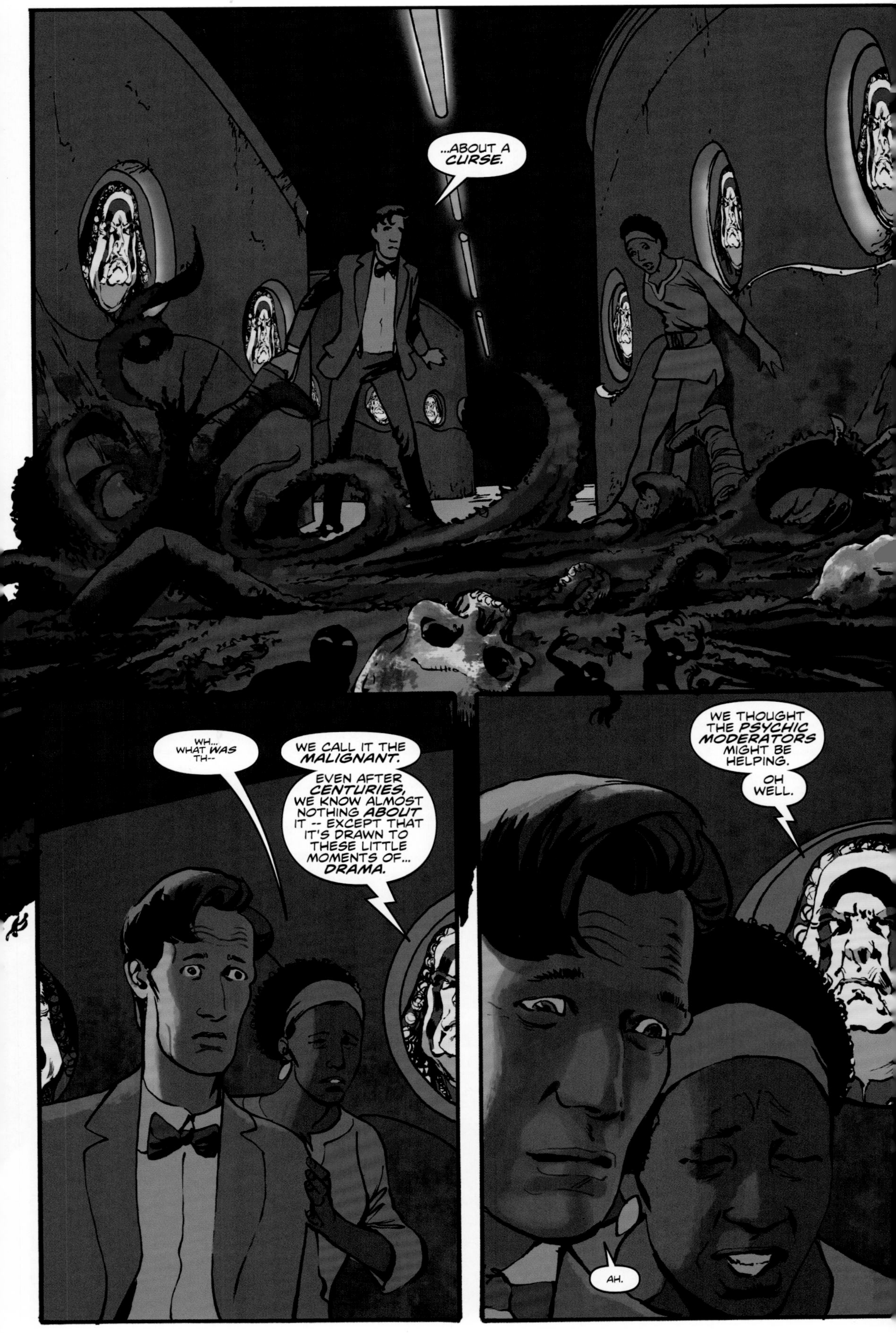
...ABOUT A *CURSE.*
WH... WHAT *WAS* TH--
WE CALL IT THE *MALIGNANT.*
EVEN AFTER *CENTURIES,* WE KNOW ALMOST NOTHING *ABOUT* IT -- EXCEPT THAT IT'S DRAWN TO THESE LITTLE MOMENTS OF... *DRAMA.*
WE THOUGHT THE *PSYCHIC MODERATORS* MIGHT BE HELPING.
OH WELL.
AH.

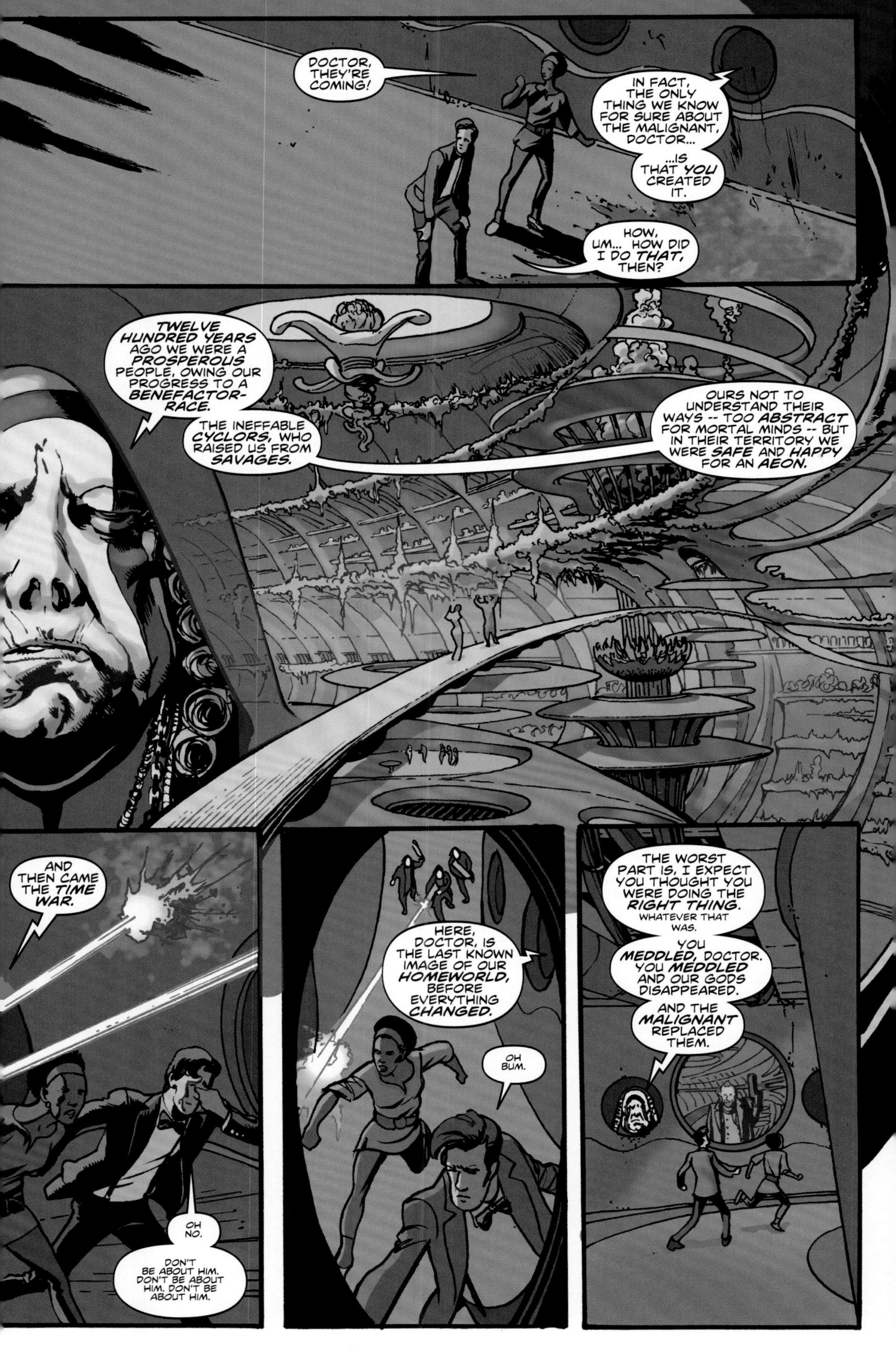
DOCTOR, THEY'RE COMING!
IN FACT, THE ONLY THING WE KNOW FOR SURE ABOUT THE MALIGNANT, DOCTOR...
...IS THAT YOU CREATED IT.
HOW, UM... HOW DID I DO THAT, THEN?
TWELVE HUNDRED YEARS AGO WE WERE A PROSPEROUS PEOPLE, OWING OUR PROGRESS TO A BENEFACTOR-RACE.
THE INEFFABLE CYCLORS, WHO RAISED US FROM SAVAGES.
OURS NOT TO UNDERSTAND THEIR WAYS -- TOO ABSTRACT FOR MORTAL MINDS -- BUT IN THEIR TERRITORY WE WERE SAFE AND HAPPY FOR AN AEON.
AND THEN CAME THE TIME WAR.
OH NO.
DON'T BE ABOUT HIM. DON'T BE ABOUT HIM. DON'T BE ABOUT HIM.
HERE, DOCTOR, IS THE LAST KNOWN IMAGE OF OUR HOMEWORLD, BEFORE EVERYTHING CHANGED.
OH BUM.
THE WORST PART IS, I EXPECT YOU THOUGHT YOU WERE DOING THE RIGHT THING. WHATEVER THAT WAS.
YOU MEDDLED, DOCTOR. YOU MEDDLED AND OUR GODS DISAPPEARED.
AND THE MALIGNANT REPLACED THEM.

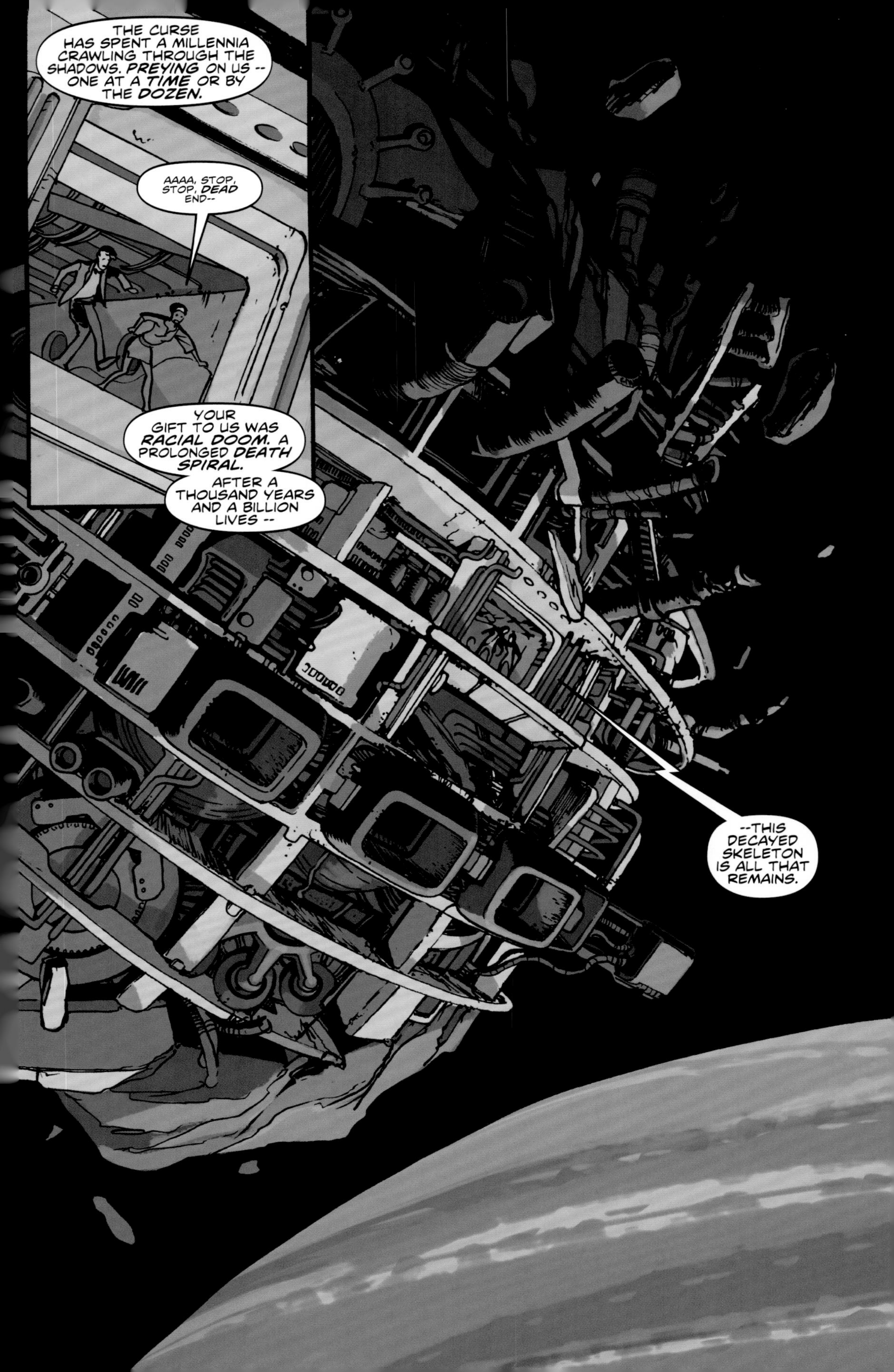
THE CURSE HAS SPENT A MILLENNIA CRAWLING THROUGH THE SHADOWS. PREYING ON US -- ONE AT A TIME OR BY THE DOZEN.
AAAA, STOP, STOP, DEAD END--
YOUR GIFT TO US WAS RACIAL DOOM. A PROLONGED DEATH SPIRAL.
AFTER A THOUSAND YEARS AND A BILLION LIVES --
--THIS DECAYED SKELETON IS ALL THAT REMAINS.

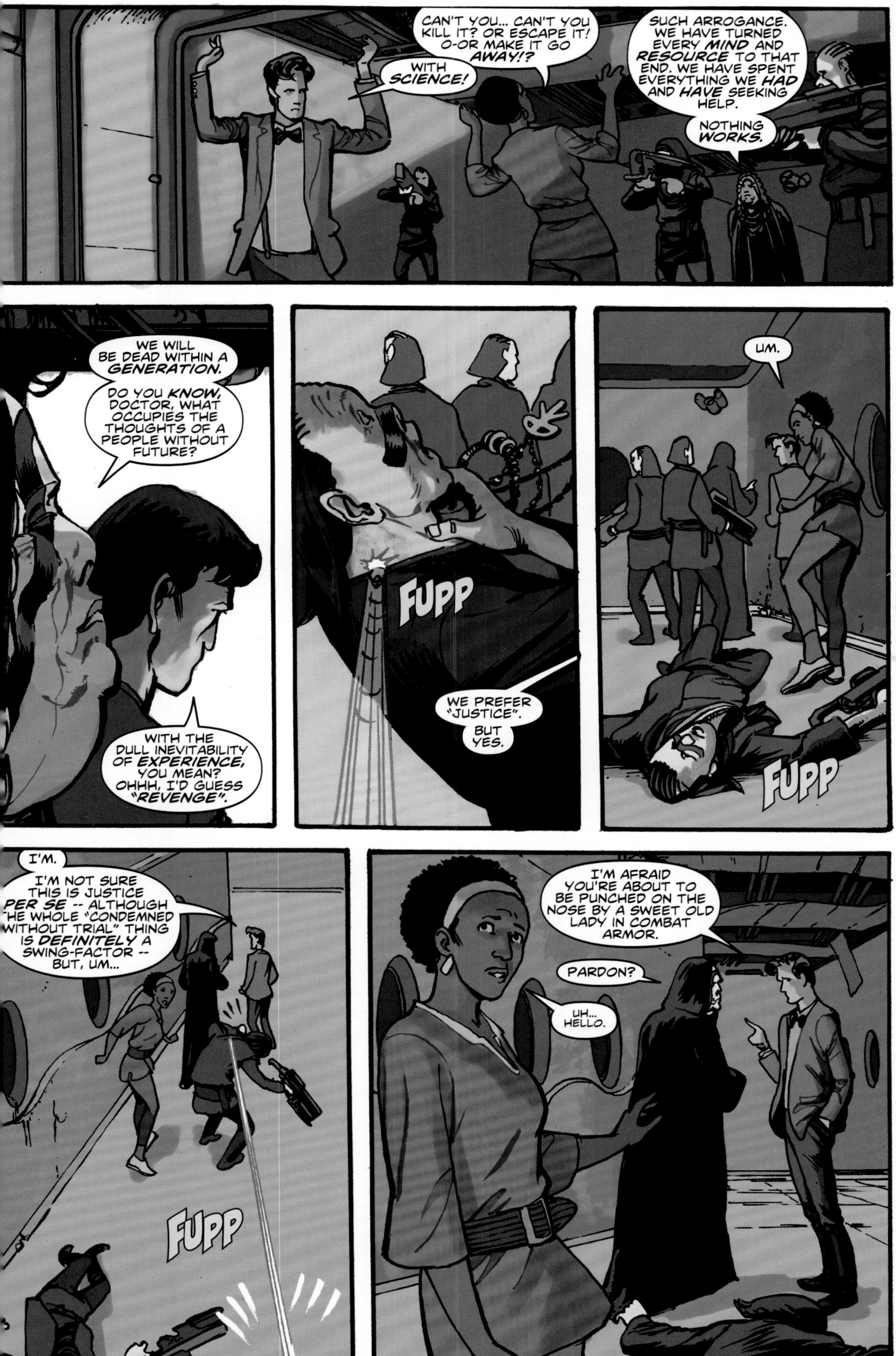
CAN'T YOU... CAN'T YOU KILL IT? OR ESCAPE IT! O-OR MAKE IT GO AWAY!?
WITH SCIENCE!
SUCH ARROGANCE. WE HAVE TURNED EVERY MIND AND RESOURCE TO THAT END. WE HAVE SPENT EVERYTHING WE HAD AND HAVE SEEKING HELP.
NOTHING WORKS.
WE WILL BE DEAD WITHIN A GENERATION.
DO YOU KNOW, DOCTOR, WHAT OCCUPIES THE THOUGHTS OF A PEOPLE WITHOUT FUTURE?
WITH THE DULL INEVITABILITY OF EXPERIENCE, YOU MEAN? OHHH, I'D GUESS "REVENGE".
FUPP
WE PREFER "JUSTICE".
BUT YES.
UM.
FUPP
I'M.
I'M NOT SURE THIS IS JUSTICE PER SE -- ALTHOUGH THE WHOLE "CONDEMNED WITHOUT TRIAL" THING IS DEFINITELY A SWING-FACTOR -- BUT, UM...
FUPP
I'M AFRAID YOU'RE ABOUT TO BE PUNCHED ON THE NOSE BY A SWEET OLD LADY IN COMBAT ARMOR.
PARDON?
UH... HELLO.

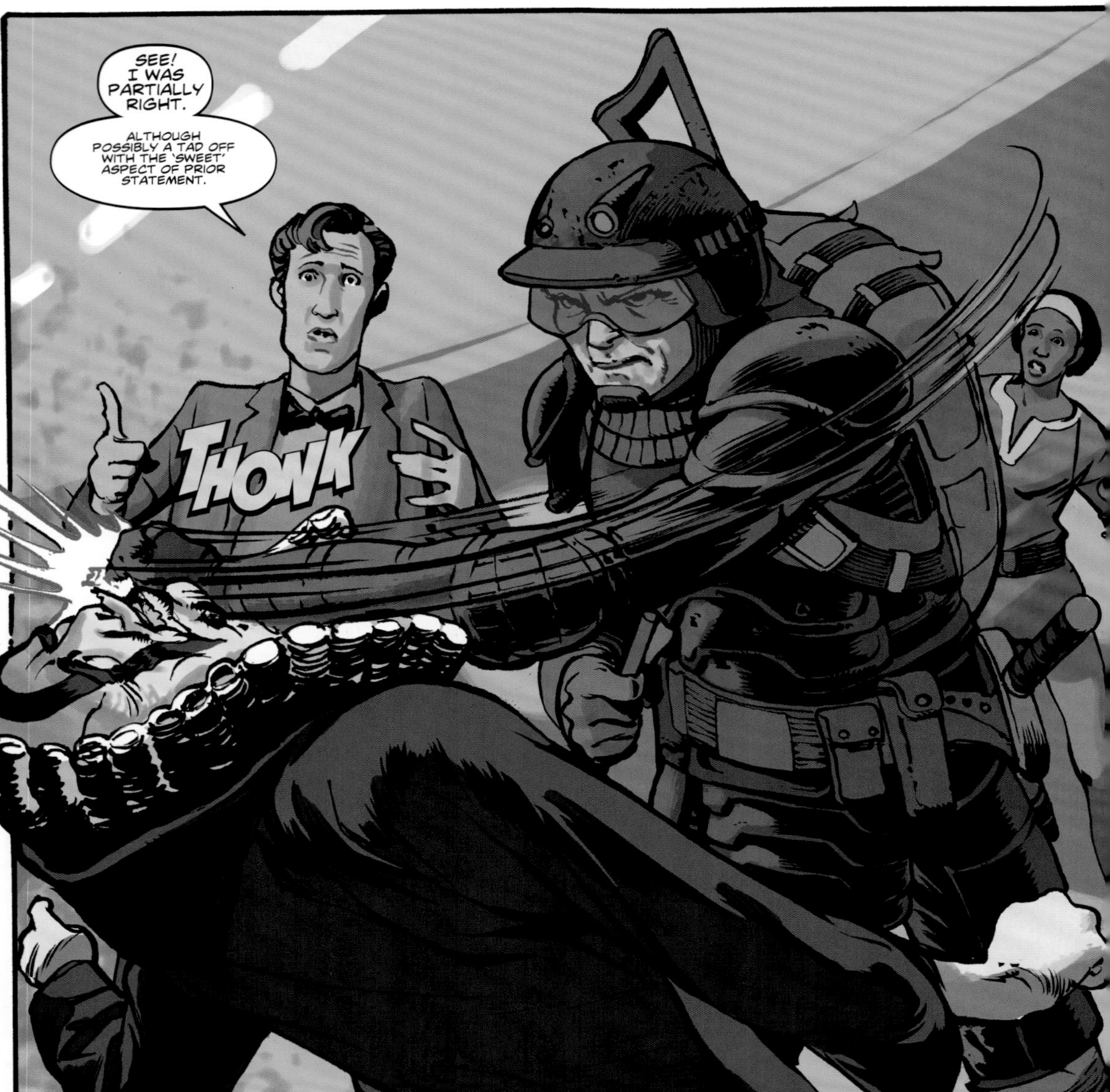
SEE! I WAS PARTIALLY RIGHT.
ALTHOUGH POSSIBLY A TAD OFF WITH THE 'SWEET' ASPECT OF PRIOR STATEMENT.
THONK

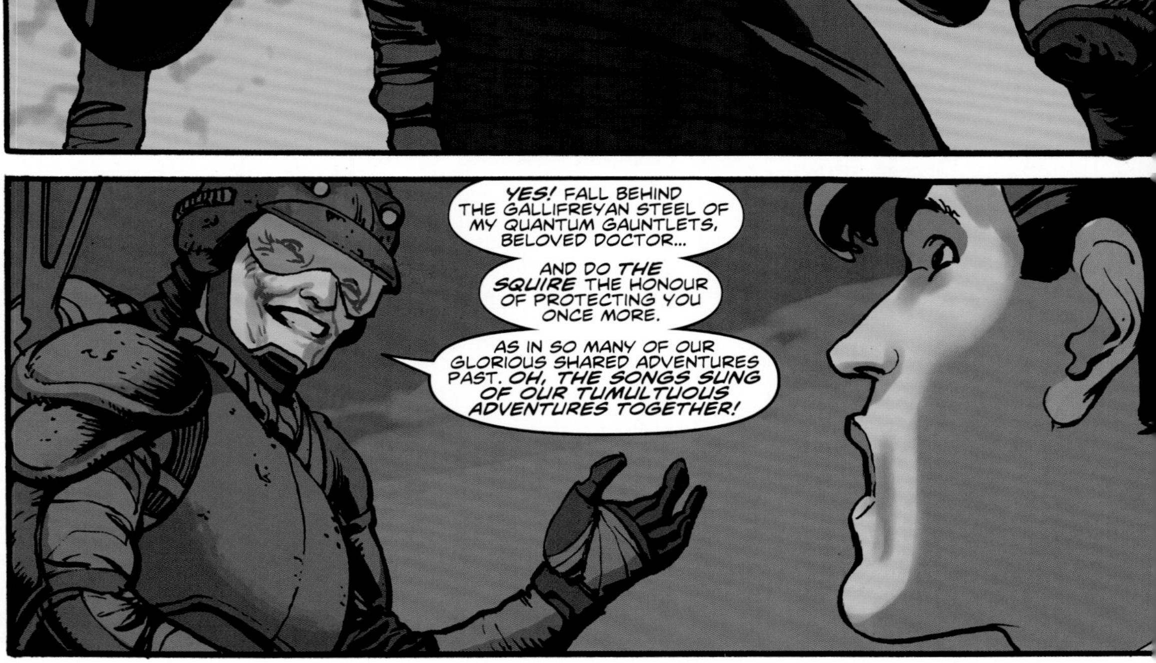
YES! FALL BEHIND THE GALLIFREYAN STEEL OF MY QUANTUM GAUNTLETS, BELOVED DOCTOR...
AND DO THE SQUIRE THE HONOUR OF PROTECTING YOU ONCE MORE.
AS IN SO MANY OF OUR GLORIOUS SHARED ADVENTURES PAST. OH, THE SONGS SUNG OF OUR TUMULTUOUS ADVENTURES TOGETHER!

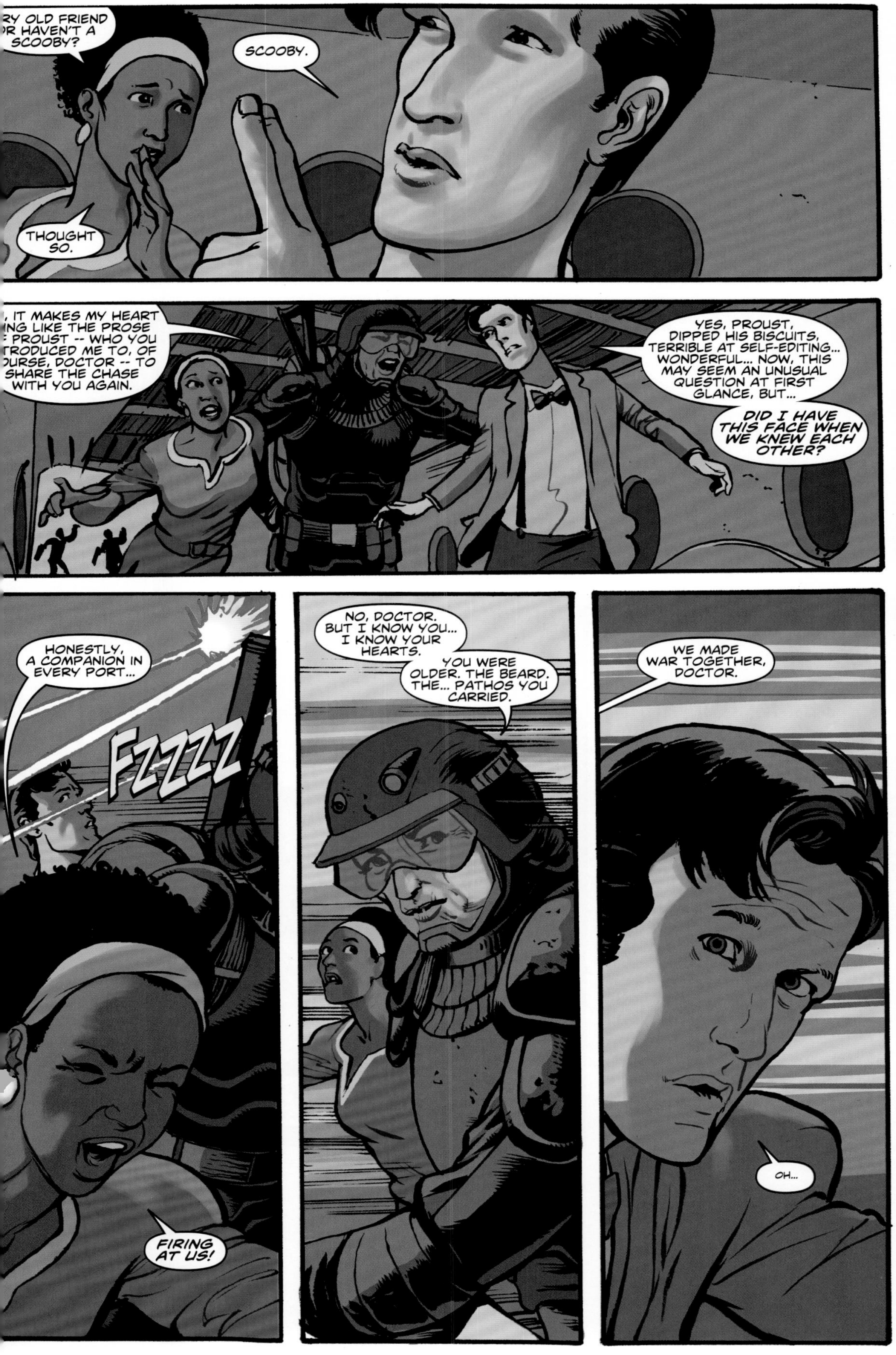
RY OLD FRIEND
OR HAVEN'T A
SCOOBY?
SCOOBY.
THOUGHT
SO.
, IT MAKES MY HEART
ING LIKE THE PROSE
F PROUST -- WHO YOU
TRODUCED ME TO, OF
OURSE, DOCTOR -- TO
SHARE THE CHASE
WITH YOU AGAIN.
YES, PROUST,
DIPPED HIS BISCUITS,
TERRIBLE AT SELF-EDITING...
WONDERFUL... NOW, THIS
MAY SEEM AN UNUSUAL
QUESTION AT FIRST
GLANCE, BUT...
DID I HAVE
THIS FACE WHEN
WE KNEW EACH
OTHER?
HONESTLY,
A COMPANION IN
EVERY PORT...
FZZZZ
FIRING
AT US!
NO, DOCTOR.
BUT I KNOW YOU...
I KNOW YOUR
HEARTS.
YOU WERE
OLDER. THE BEARD.
THE... PATHOS YOU
CARRIED.
WE MADE
WAR TOGETHER,
DOCTOR.
OH...

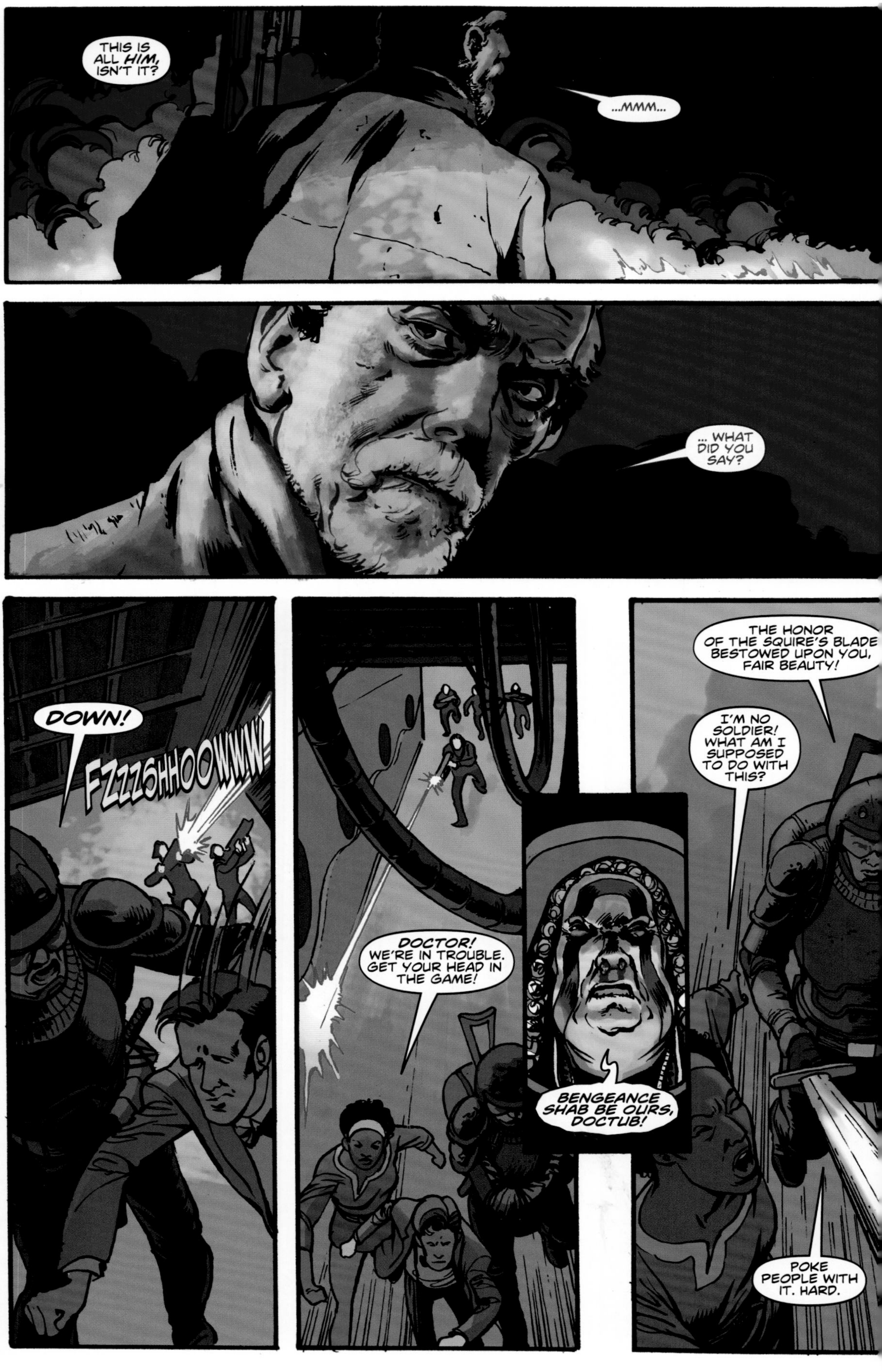
THIS IS ALL *HIM*, ISN'T IT?
...MMM...
... WHAT DID YOU SAY?
DOWN!
FZZZSHHOOWWW
DOCTOR! WE'RE IN TROUBLE. GET YOUR HEAD IN THE GAME!
BENGEANCE SHAB BE OURS, DOCTUB!
THE HONOR OF THE SQUIRE'S BLADE BESTOWED UPON YOU, FAIR BEAUTY!
I'M NO SOLDIER! WHAT AM I SUPPOSED TO DO WITH THIS?
POKE PEOPLE WITH IT. HARD.

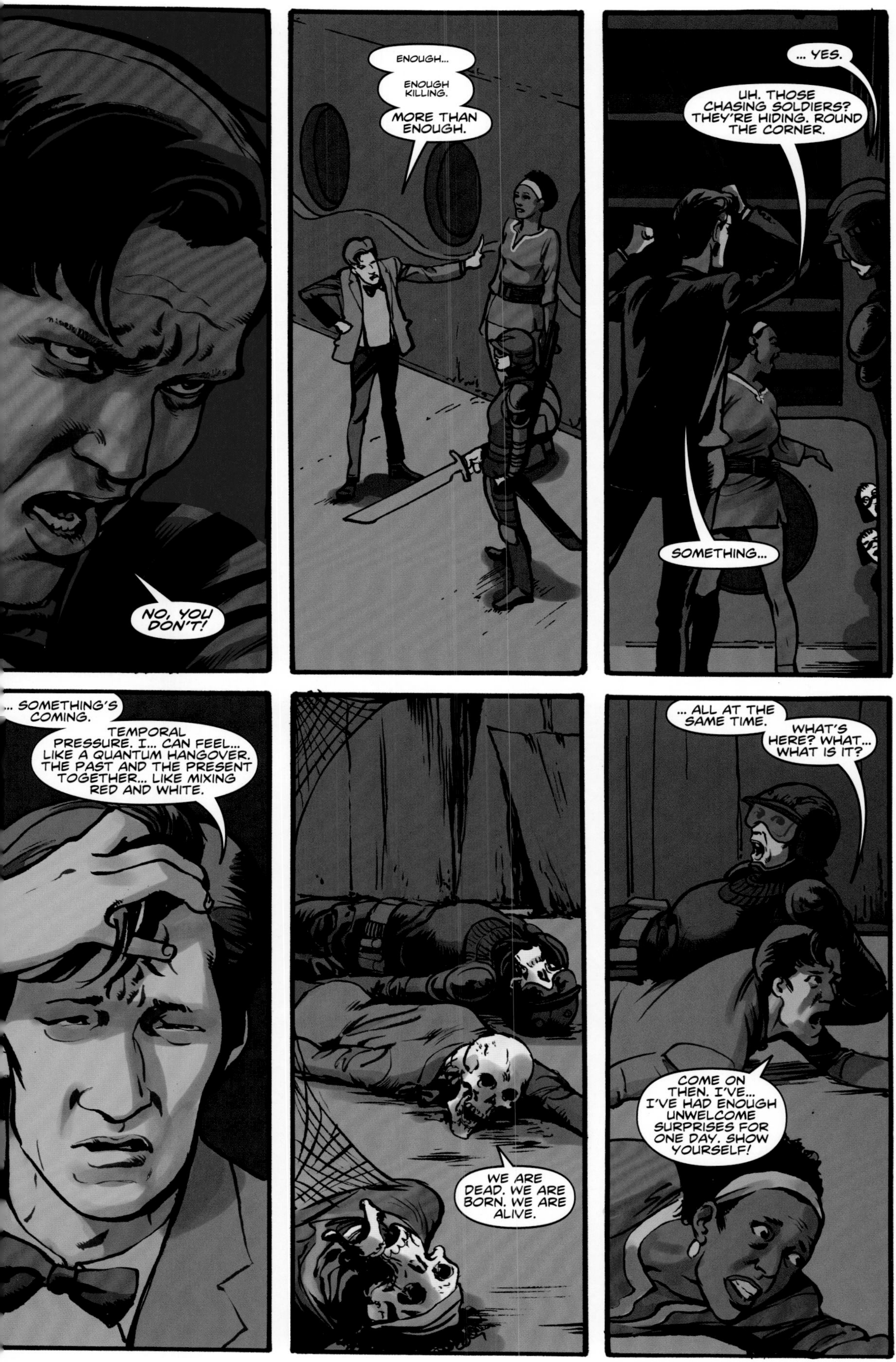
NO, YOU DON'T!
ENOUGH...
ENOUGH KILLING.
MORE THAN ENOUGH.
... YES.
UH. THOSE CHASING SOLDIERS? THEY'RE HIDING. ROUND THE CORNER.
SOMETHING...
... SOMETHING'S COMING.
TEMPORAL PRESSURE. I... CAN FEEL... LIKE A QUANTUM HANGOVER. THE PAST AND THE PRESENT TOGETHER... LIKE MIXING RED AND WHITE.
WE ARE DEAD. WE ARE BORN. WE ARE ALIVE.
... ALL AT THE SAME TIME.
WHAT'S HERE? WHAT... WHAT IS IT?
COME ON THEN. I'VE... I'VE HAD ENOUGH UNWELCOME SURPRISES FOR ONE DAY. SHOW YOURSELF!

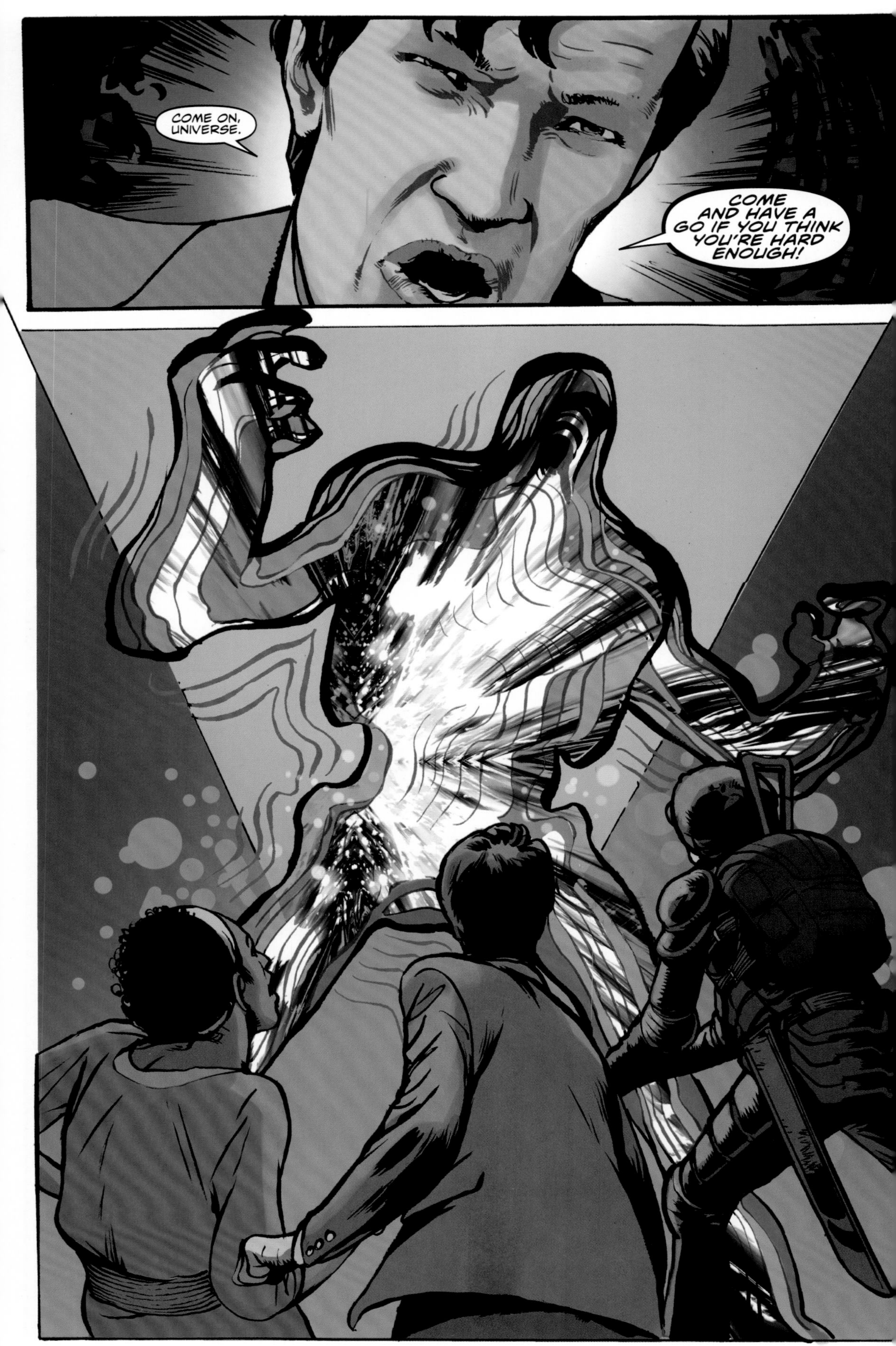
COME ON, UNIVERSE.
COME AND HAVE A GO IF YOU THINK YOU'RE HARD ENOUGH!

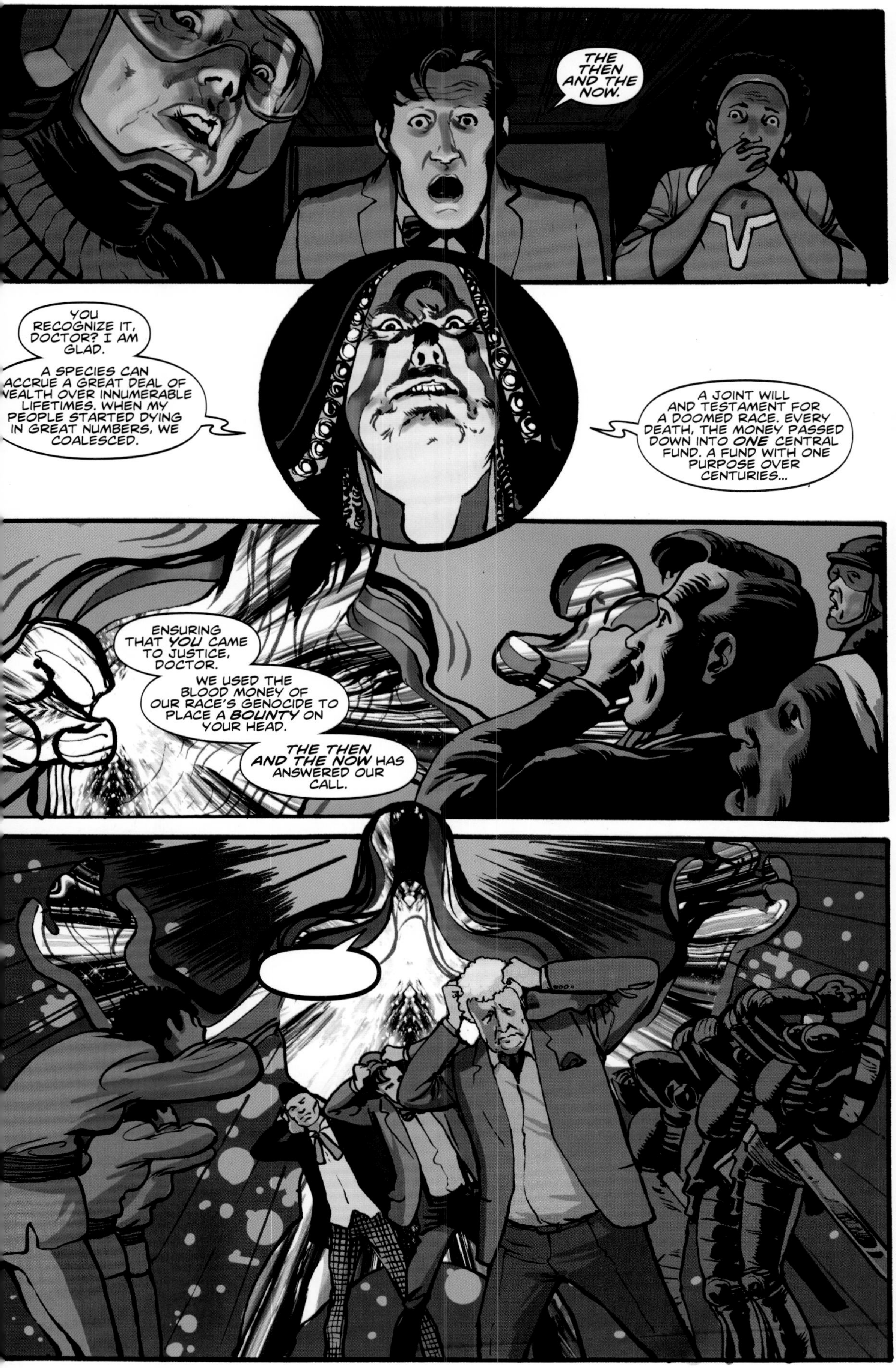
THE THEN AND THE NOW.
YOU RECOGNIZE IT, DOCTOR? I AM GLAD.
A SPECIES CAN ACCRUE A GREAT DEAL OF WEALTH OVER INNUMERABLE LIFETIMES. WHEN MY PEOPLE STARTED DYING IN GREAT NUMBERS, WE COALESCED.
A JOINT WILL AND TESTAMENT FOR A DOOMED RACE. EVERY DEATH, THE MONEY PASSED DOWN INTO ONE CENTRAL FUND. A FUND WITH ONE PURPOSE OVER CENTURIES...
ENSURING THAT YOU CAME TO JUSTICE, DOCTOR.
WE USED THE BLOOD MONEY OF OUR RACE'S GENOCIDE TO PLACE A BOUNTY ON YOUR HEAD.
THE THEN AND THE NOW HAS ANSWERED OUR CALL.

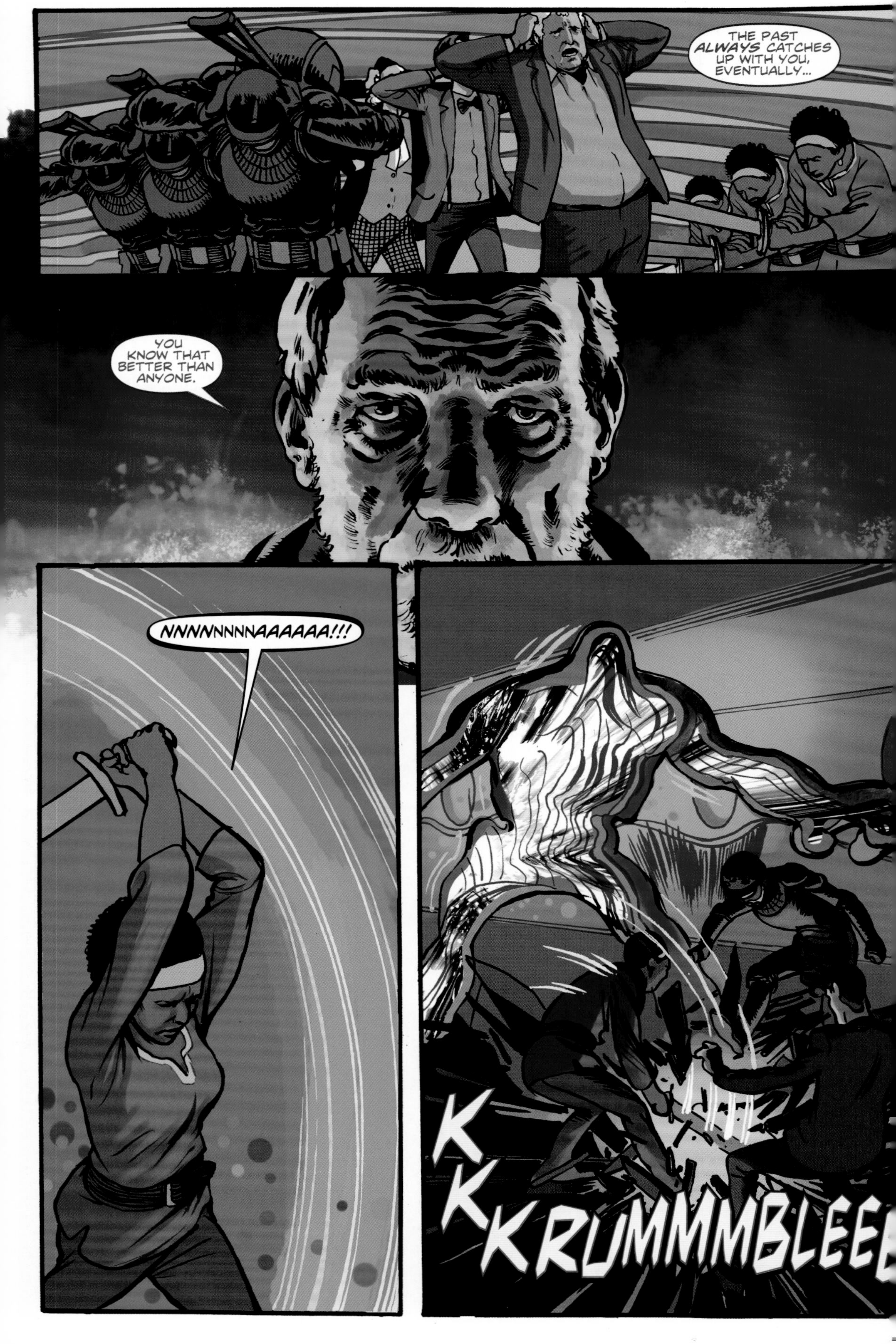
THE PAST ALWAYS CATCHES UP WITH YOU, EVENTUALLY...
YOU KNOW THAT BETTER THAN ANYONE.
NNNNNNNNAAAAAA!!!
KKRUMMMBLEE

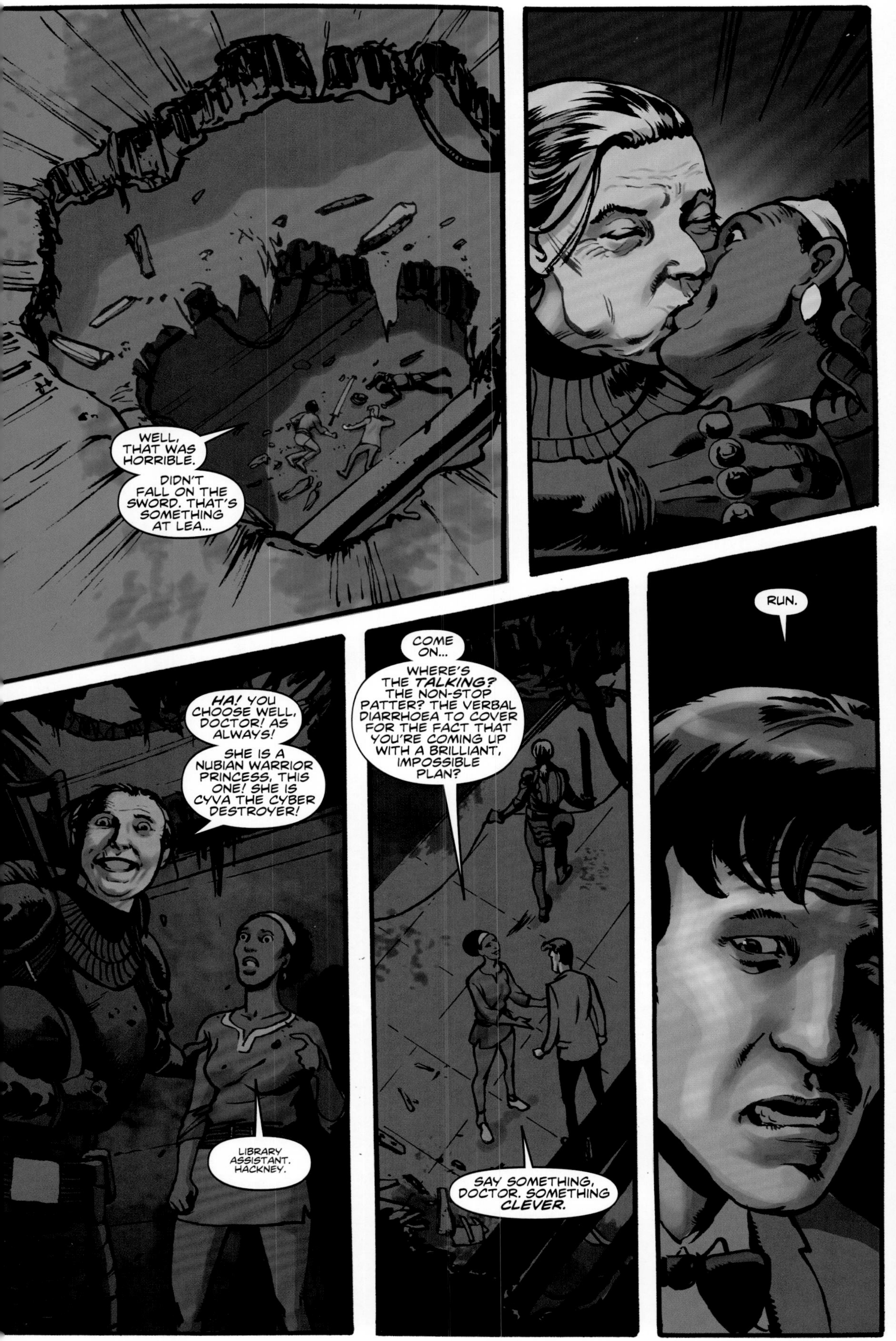
WELL, THAT WAS HORRIBLE.
DIDN'T FALL ON THE SWORD. THAT'S SOMETHING AT LEA...
HA! YOU CHOOSE WELL, DOCTOR! AS ALWAYS!
SHE IS A NUBIAN WARRIOR PRINCESS, THIS ONE! SHE IS CYVA THE CYBER DESTROYER!
LIBRARY ASSISTANT. HACKNEY.
COME ON...
WHERE'S THE TALKING? THE NON-STOP PATTER? THE VERBAL DIARRHOEA TO COVER FOR THE FACT THAT YOU'RE COMING UP WITH A BRILLIANT, IMPOSSIBLE PLAN?
SAY SOMETHING, DOCTOR. SOMETHING CLEVER.
RUN.

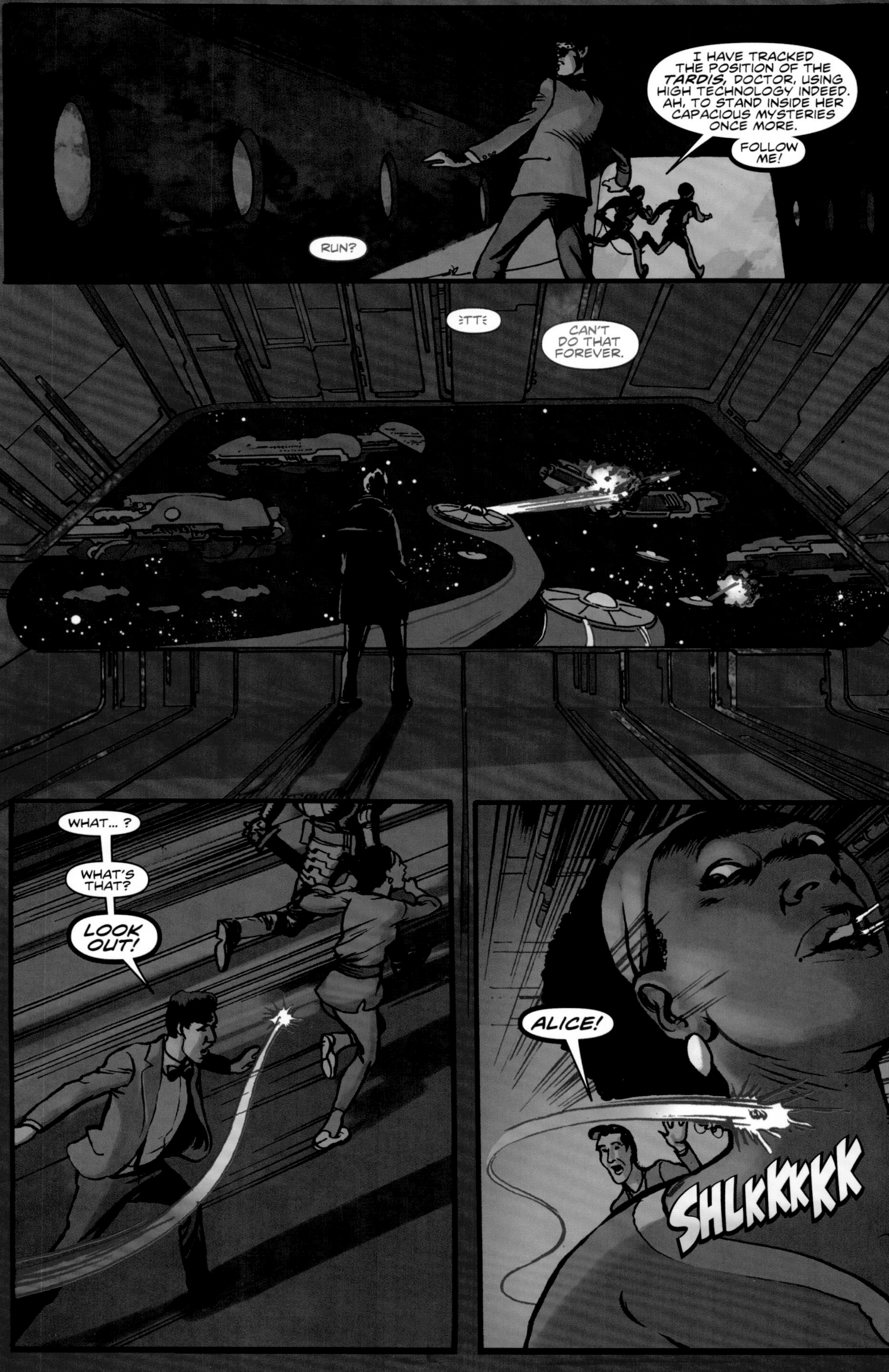

I HAVE TRACKED THE POSITION OF THE *TARDIS,* DOCTOR, USING HIGH TECHNOLOGY INDEED. AH, TO STAND INSIDE HER CAPACIOUS MYSTERIES ONCE MORE.
FOLLOW ME!
RUN?
TT
CAN'T DO THAT FOREVER.
WHAT... ?
WHAT'S THAT?
LOOK OUT!
ALICE!
SHLKKKKK

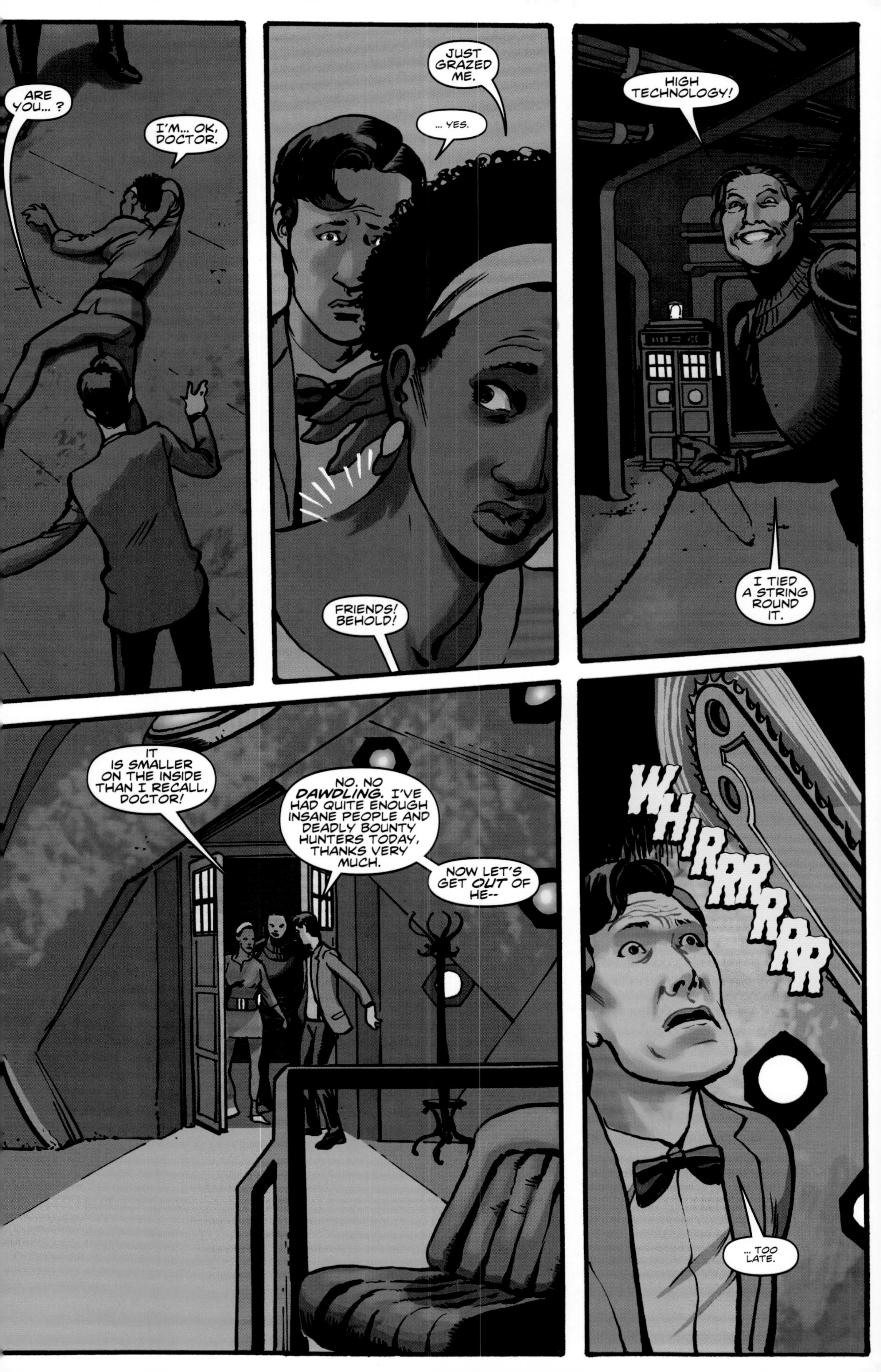

ARE YOU... ?
I'M... OK, DOCTOR.
JUST GRAZED ME.
... YES.
FRIENDS! BEHOLD!
HIGH TECHNOLOGY!
I TIED A STRING ROUND IT.
IT IS SMALLER ON THE INSIDE THAN I RECALL, DOCTOR!
NO. NO DAWDLING. I'VE HAD QUITE ENOUGH INSANE PEOPLE AND DEADLY BOUNTY HUNTERS TODAY, THANKS VERY MUCH.
NOW LET'S GET OUT OF HE--
WHIRRRRRRR
... TOO LATE.

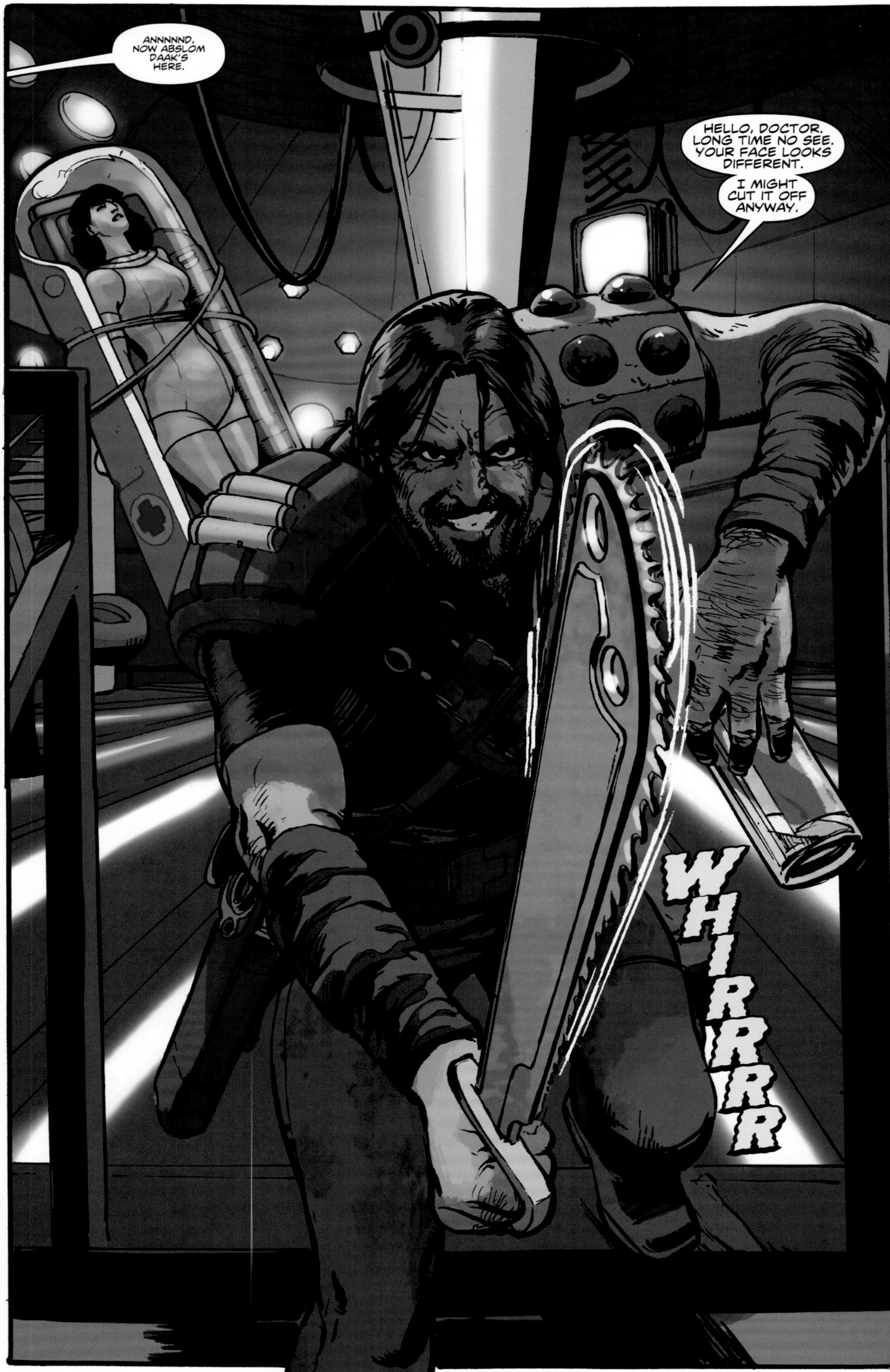
ANNNNND, NOW ABSLOM DAAK'S HERE.
HELLO, DOCTOR. LONG TIME NO SEE. YOUR FACE LOOKS DIFFERENT.
I MIGHT CUT IT OFF ANYWAY.
WHIRRRR

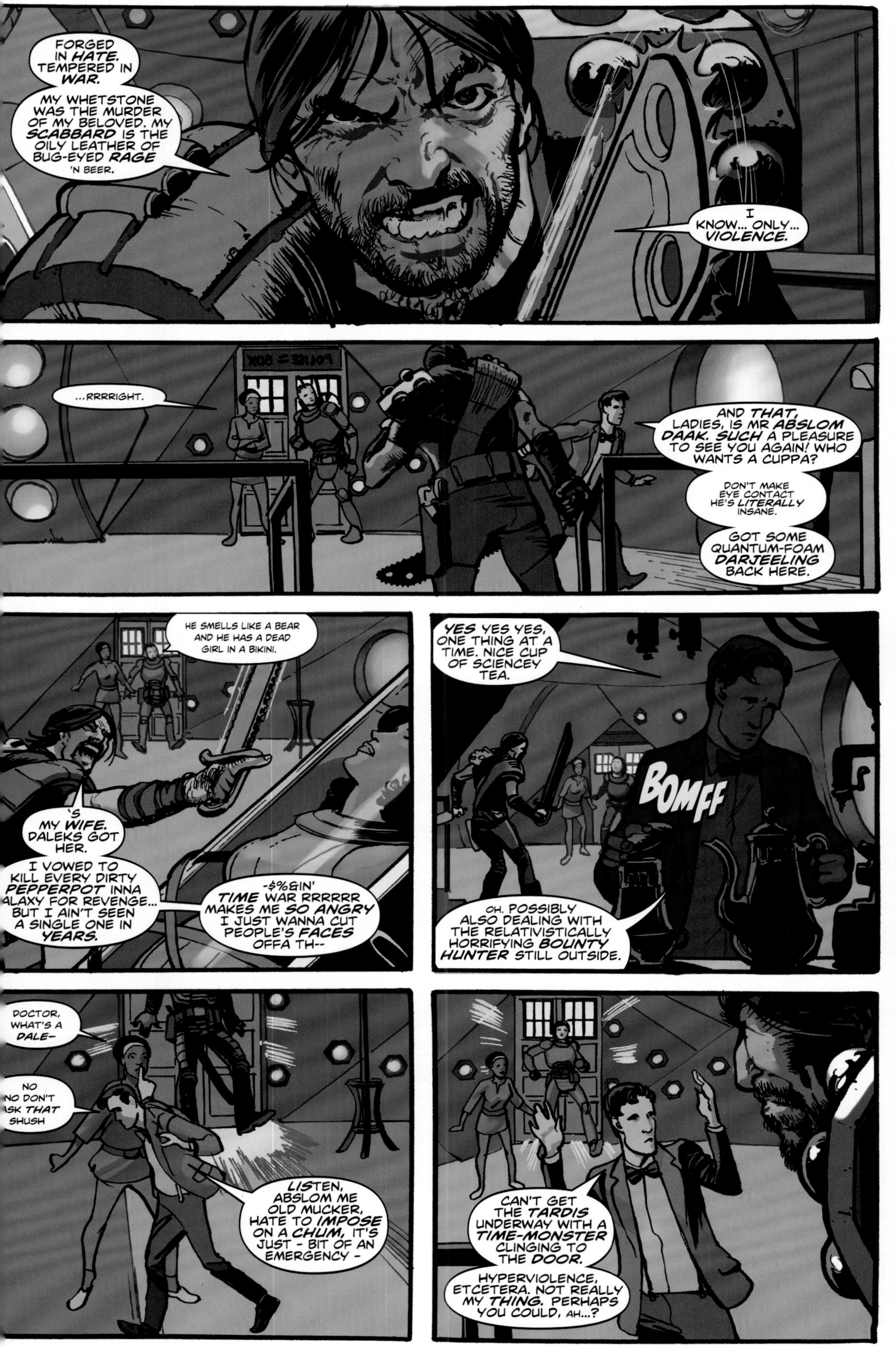
FORGED IN HATE. TEMPERED IN WAR.
MY WHETSTONE WAS THE MURDER OF MY BELOVED. MY SCABBARD IS THE OILY LEATHER OF BUG-EYED RAGE 'N BEER.
I KNOW... ONLY... VIOLENCE.
...RRRRIGHT.
AND THAT, LADIES, IS MR ABSLOM DAAK. SUCH A PLEASURE TO SEE YOU AGAIN! WHO WANTS A CUPPA?
DON'T MAKE EYE CONTACT HE'S LITERALLY INSANE.
GOT SOME QUANTUM-FOAM DARJEELING BACK HERE.
HE SMELLS LIKE A BEAR AND HE HAS A DEAD GIRL IN A BIKINI.
'S MY WIFE. DALEKS GOT HER.
I VOWED TO KILL EVERY DIRTY PEPPERPOT INNA ALAXY FOR REVENGE... BUT I AIN'T SEEN A SINGLE ONE IN YEARS.
-$%&IN' TIME WAR RRRRRR MAKES ME SO ANGRY I JUST WANNA CUT PEOPLE'S FACES OFFA TH--
YES YES YES, ONE THING AT A TIME. NICE CUP OF SCIENCEY TEA.
BOMFF
OH. POSSIBLY ALSO DEALING WITH THE RELATIVISTICALLY HORRIFYING BOUNTY HUNTER STILL OUTSIDE.
DOCTOR, WHAT'S A DALE-
NO NO DON'T ASK THAT SHUSH
LISTEN, ABSLOM ME OLD MUCKER, HATE TO IMPOSE ON A CHUM, IT'S JUST - BIT OF AN EMERGENCY -
CAN'T GET THE TARDIS UNDERWAY WITH A TIME-MONSTER CLINGING TO THE DOOR.
HYPERVIOLENCE, ETCETERA. NOT REALLY MY THING. PERHAPS YOU COULD, AH...?

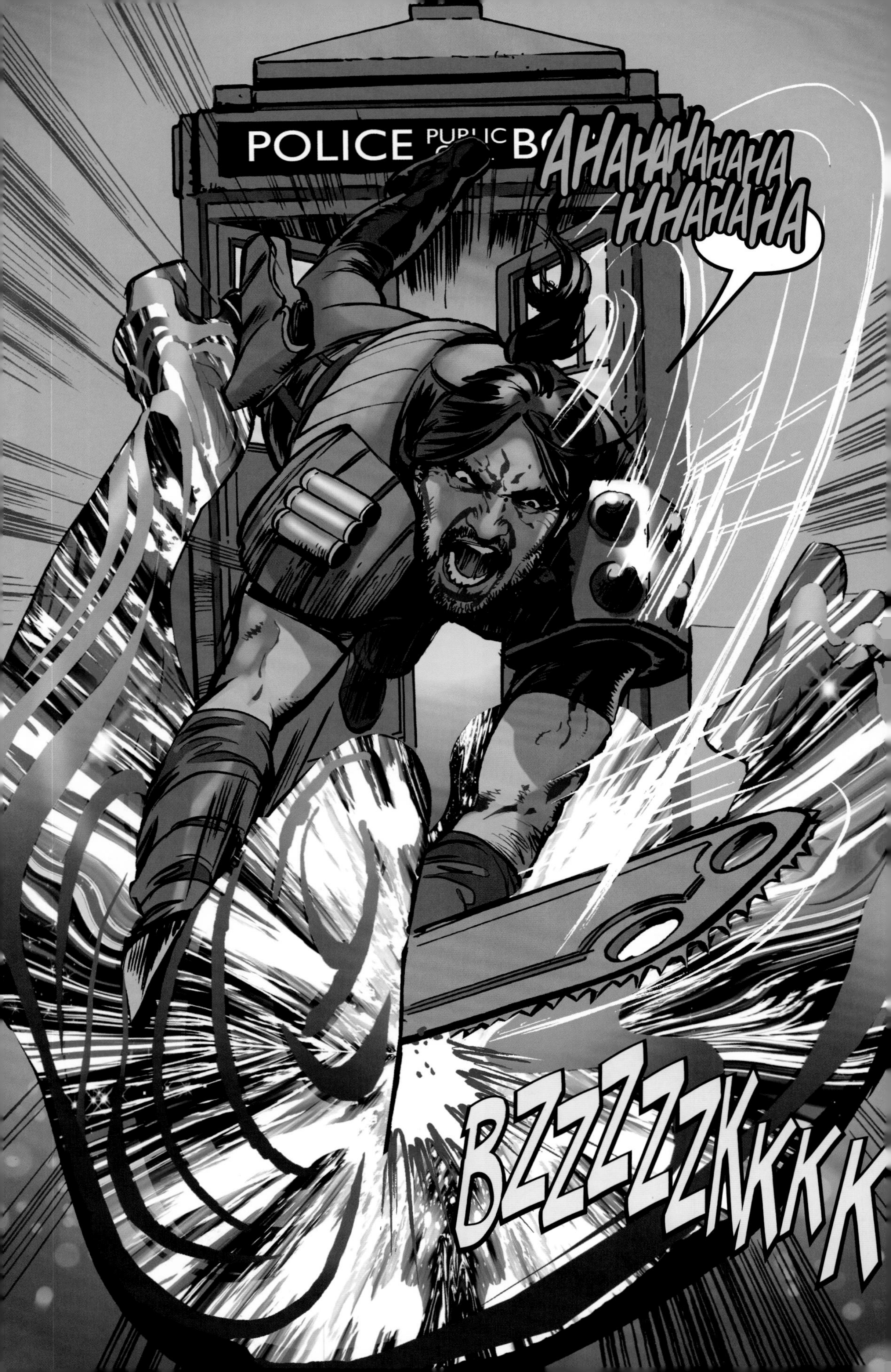
POLICE PUBLIC BO
AHAHAHAHAHA
HHAHAHA
BZZZZZKKKK

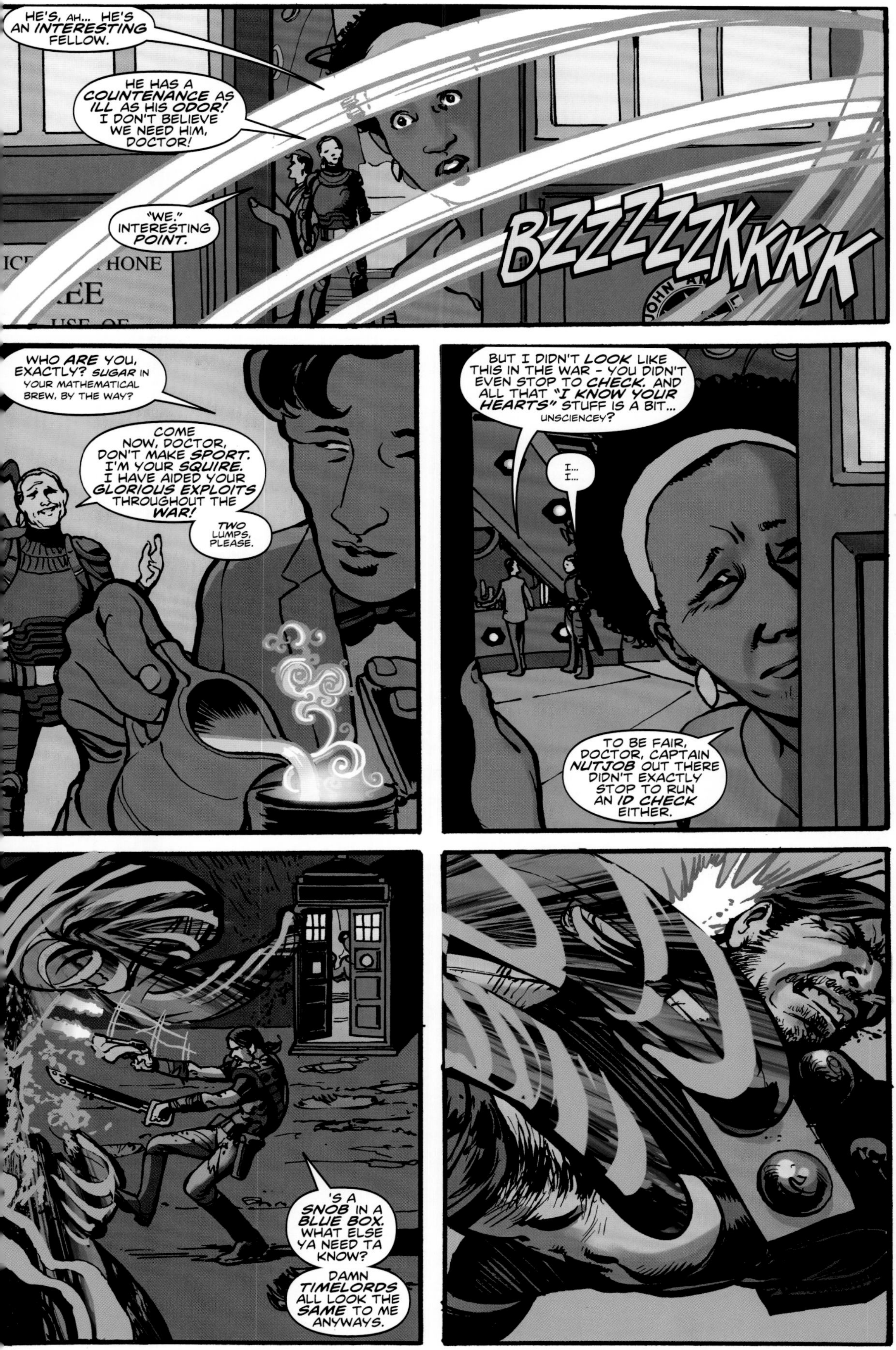
HE'S, AH... HE'S AN INTERESTING FELLOW.
HE HAS A COUNTENANCE AS ILL AS HIS ODOR! I DON'T BELIEVE WE NEED HIM, DOCTOR!
"WE." INTERESTING POINT.
BZZZZZZKKKKK
WHO ARE YOU, EXACTLY? SUGAR IN YOUR MATHEMATICAL BREW, BY THE WAY?
COME NOW, DOCTOR, DON'T MAKE SPORT. I'M YOUR SQUIRE. I HAVE AIDED YOUR GLORIOUS EXPLOITS THROUGHOUT THE WAR!
TWO LUMPS, PLEASE.
BUT I DIDN'T LOOK LIKE THIS IN THE WAR - YOU DIDN'T EVEN STOP TO CHECK. AND ALL THAT "I KNOW YOUR HEARTS" STUFF IS A BIT... UNSCIENCEY?
I... I...
TO BE FAIR, DOCTOR, CAPTAIN NUTJOB OUT THERE DIDN'T EXACTLY STOP TO RUN AN ID CHECK EITHER.
'S A SNOB IN A BLUE BOX. WHAT ELSE YA NEED TA KNOW?
DAMN TIMELORDS ALL LOOK THE SAME TO ME ANYWAYS.

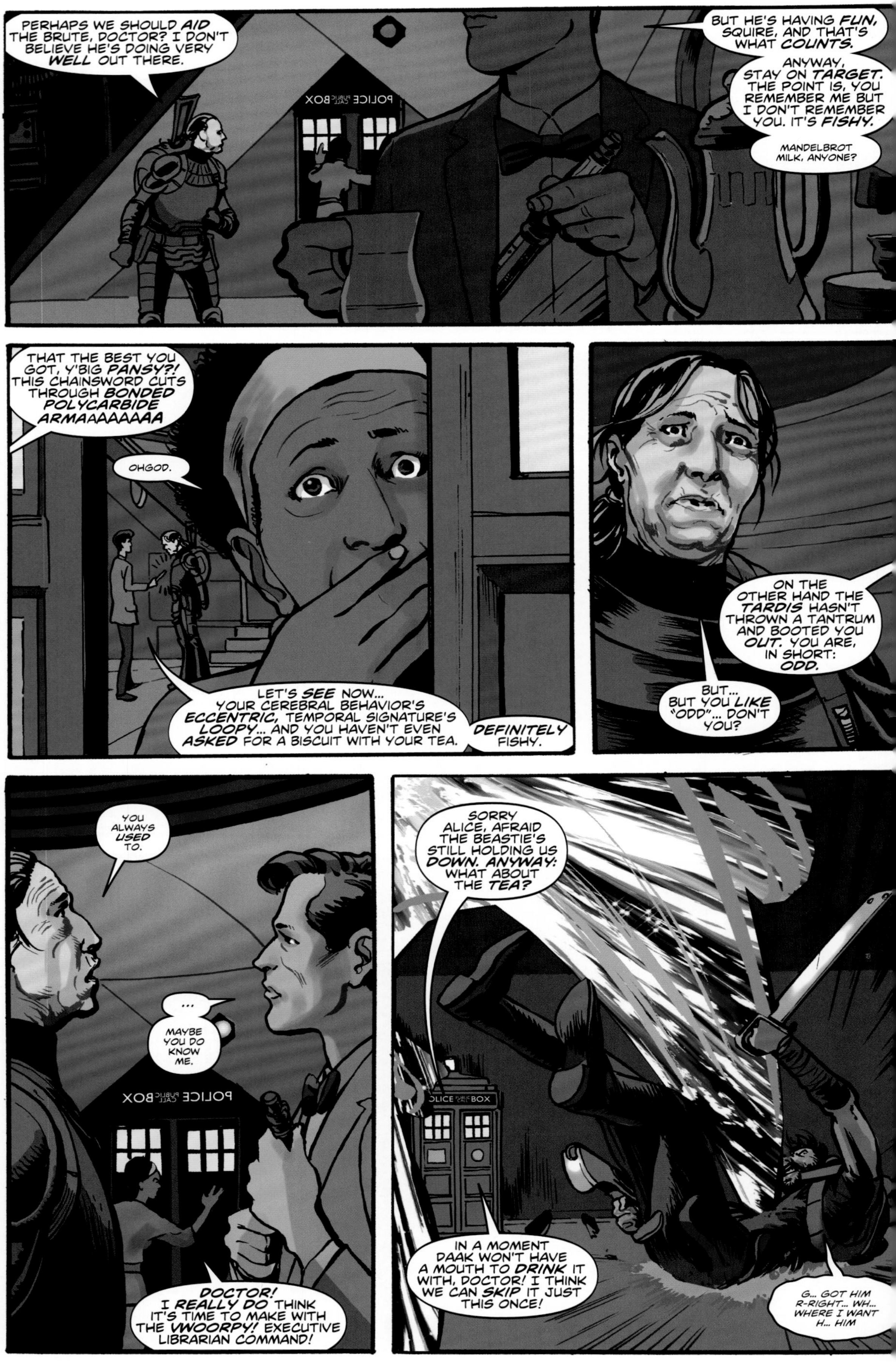
PERHAPS WE SHOULD AID THE BRUTE, DOCTOR? I DON'T BELIEVE HE'S DOING VERY WELL OUT THERE.
BUT HE'S HAVING FUN, SQUIRE, AND THAT'S WHAT COUNTS.
ANYWAY, STAY ON TARGET. THE POINT IS, YOU REMEMBER ME BUT I DON'T REMEMBER YOU. IT'S FISHY.
MANDELBROT MILK, ANYONE?
POLICE PUBLIC CALL BOX
THAT THE BEST YOU GOT, Y'BIG PANSY?! THIS CHAINSWORD CUTS THROUGH BONDED POLYCARBIDE ARMAAAAAAAA
OHGOD.
LET'S SEE NOW... YOUR CEREBRAL BEHAVIOR'S ECCENTRIC, TEMPORAL SIGNATURE'S LOOPY... AND YOU HAVEN'T EVEN ASKED FOR A BISCUIT WITH YOUR TEA.
DEFINITELY FISHY.
ON THE OTHER HAND THE TARDIS HASN'T THROWN A TANTRUM AND BOOTED YOU OUT. YOU ARE, IN SHORT: ODD.
BUT... BUT YOU LIKE "ODD"... DON'T YOU?
YOU ALWAYS USED TO.
...
MAYBE YOU DO KNOW ME.
POLICE PUBLIC CALL BOX
DOCTOR! I REALLY DO THINK IT'S TIME TO MAKE WITH THE VWOORPY! EXECUTIVE LIBRARIAN COMMAND!
SORRY ALICE, AFRAID THE BEASTIE'S STILL HOLDING US DOWN. ANYWAY: WHAT ABOUT THE TEA?
IN A MOMENT DAAK WON'T HAVE A MOUTH TO DRINK IT WITH, DOCTOR! I THINK WE CAN SKIP IT JUST THIS ONCE!
G... GOT HIM R-RIGHT... WH... WHERE I WANT H... HIM

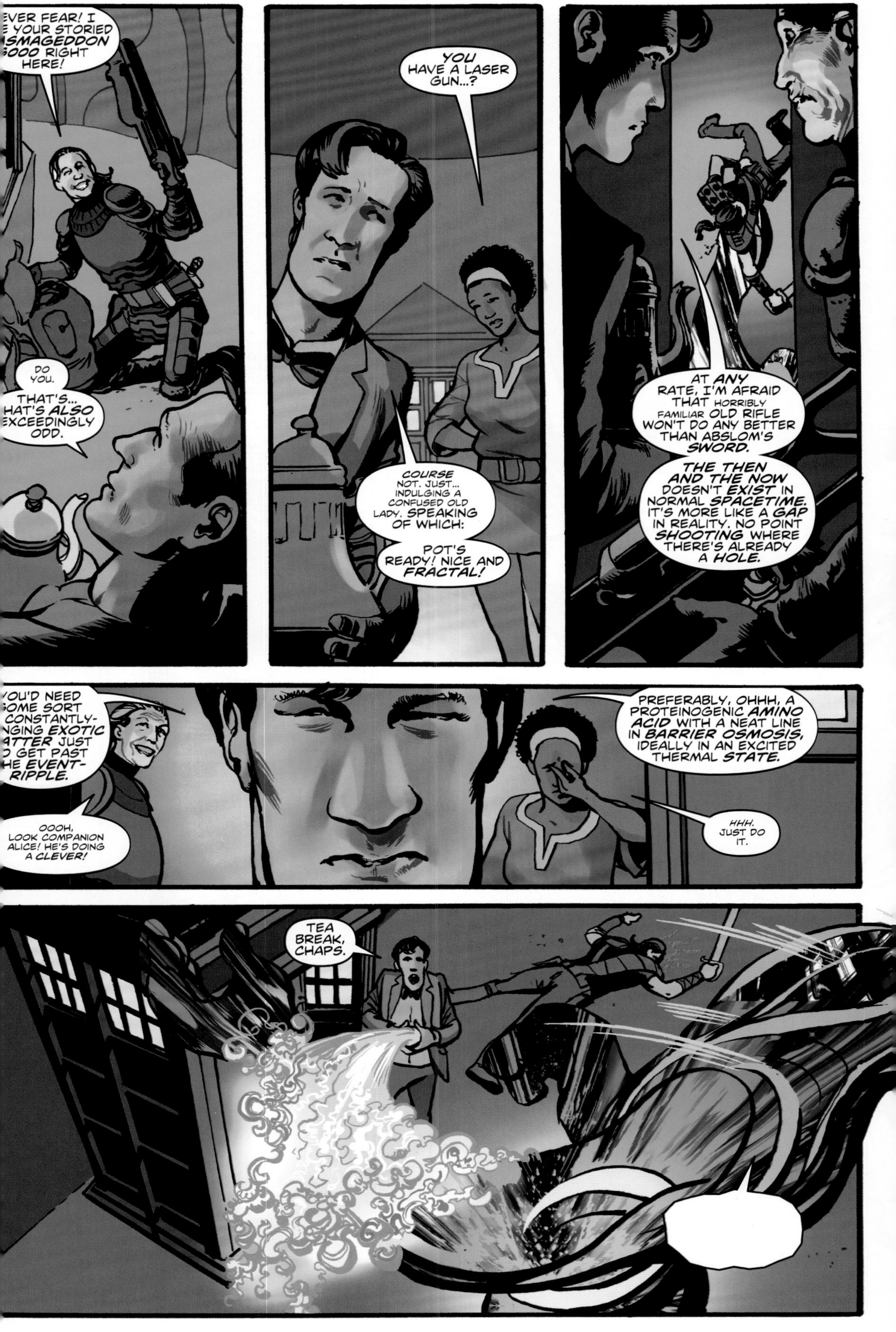

EVER FEAR! I E YOUR STORIED SMAGEDDON 6000 RIGHT HERE!
DO YOU.
THAT'S... HAT'S ALSO EXCEEDINGLY ODD.
YOU HAVE A LASER GUN...?
COURSE NOT. JUST... INDULGING A CONFUSED OLD LADY. SPEAKING OF WHICH:
POT'S READY! NICE AND FRACTAL!
AT ANY RATE, I'M AFRAID THAT HORRIBLY FAMILIAR OLD RIFLE WON'T DO ANY BETTER THAN ABSLOM'S SWORD.
THE THEN AND THE NOW DOESN'T EXIST IN NORMAL SPACETIME. IT'S MORE LIKE A GAP IN REALITY. NO POINT SHOOTING WHERE THERE'S ALREADY A HOLE.
YOU'D NEED SOME SORT CONSTANTLY- NGING EXOTIC ATTER JUST O GET PAST HE EVENT- RIPPLE.
PREFERABLY, OHHH, A PROTEINOGENIC AMINO ACID WITH A NEAT LINE IN BARRIER OSMOSIS, IDEALLY IN AN EXCITED THERMAL STATE.
OOOH, LOOK COMPANION ALICE! HE'S DOING A CLEVER!
HHH. JUST DO IT.
TEA BREAK, CHAPS.

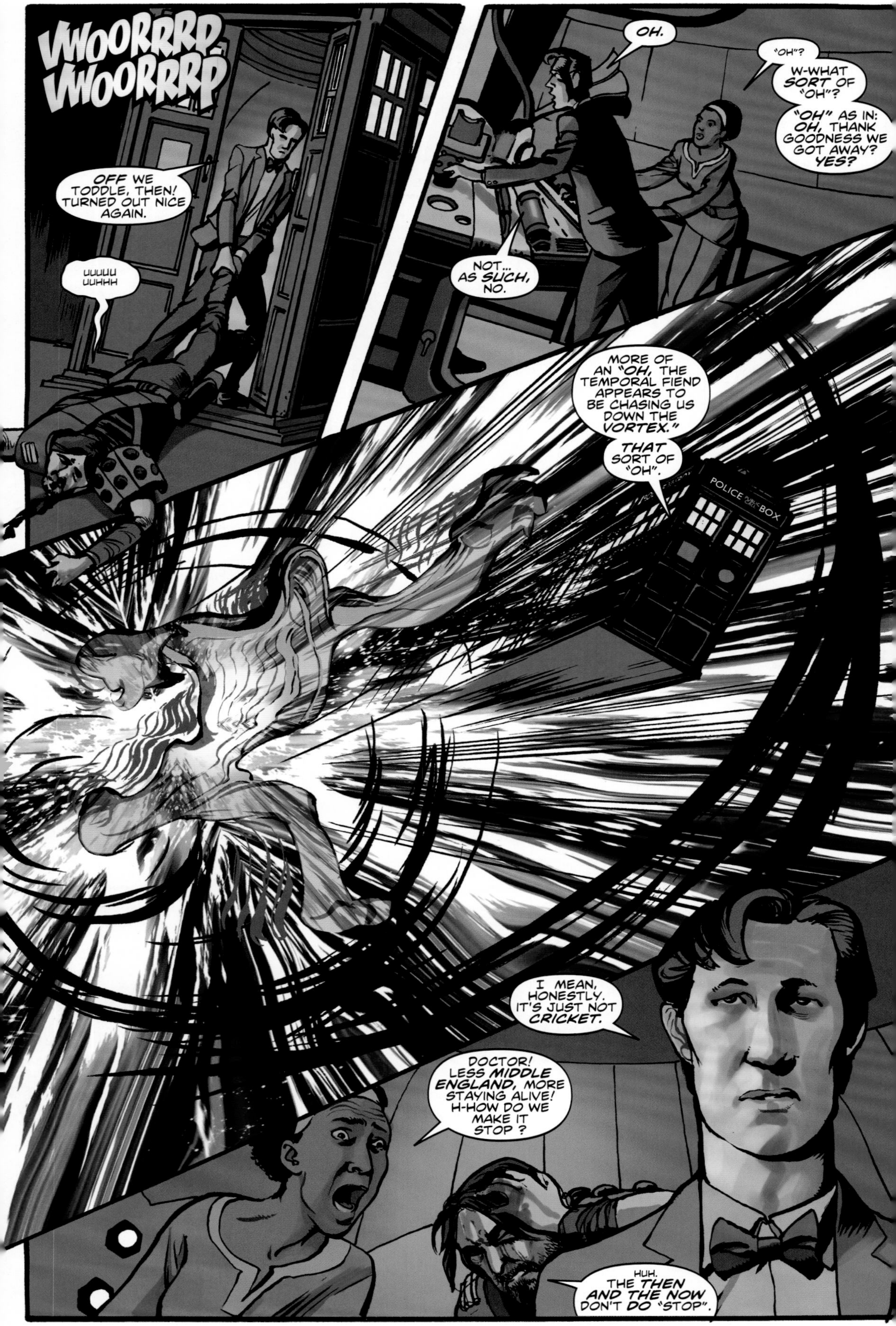

VWOORRRP VWOORRRP
OFF WE TODDLE, THEN! TURNED OUT NICE AGAIN.
UUUUU UUHHH
OH.
NOT... AS SUCH, NO.
"OH"? W-WHAT SORT OF "OH"?
"OH" AS IN: OH, THANK GOODNESS WE GOT AWAY? YES?
MORE OF AN "OH, THE TEMPORAL FIEND APPEARS TO BE CHASING US DOWN THE VORTEX."
THAT SORT OF "OH".
POLICE BOX
I MEAN, HONESTLY. IT'S JUST NOT CRICKET.
DOCTOR! LESS MIDDLE ENGLAND, MORE STAYING ALIVE! H-HOW DO WE MAKE IT STOP ?
HUH. THE THEN AND THE NOW DON'T DO "STOP".

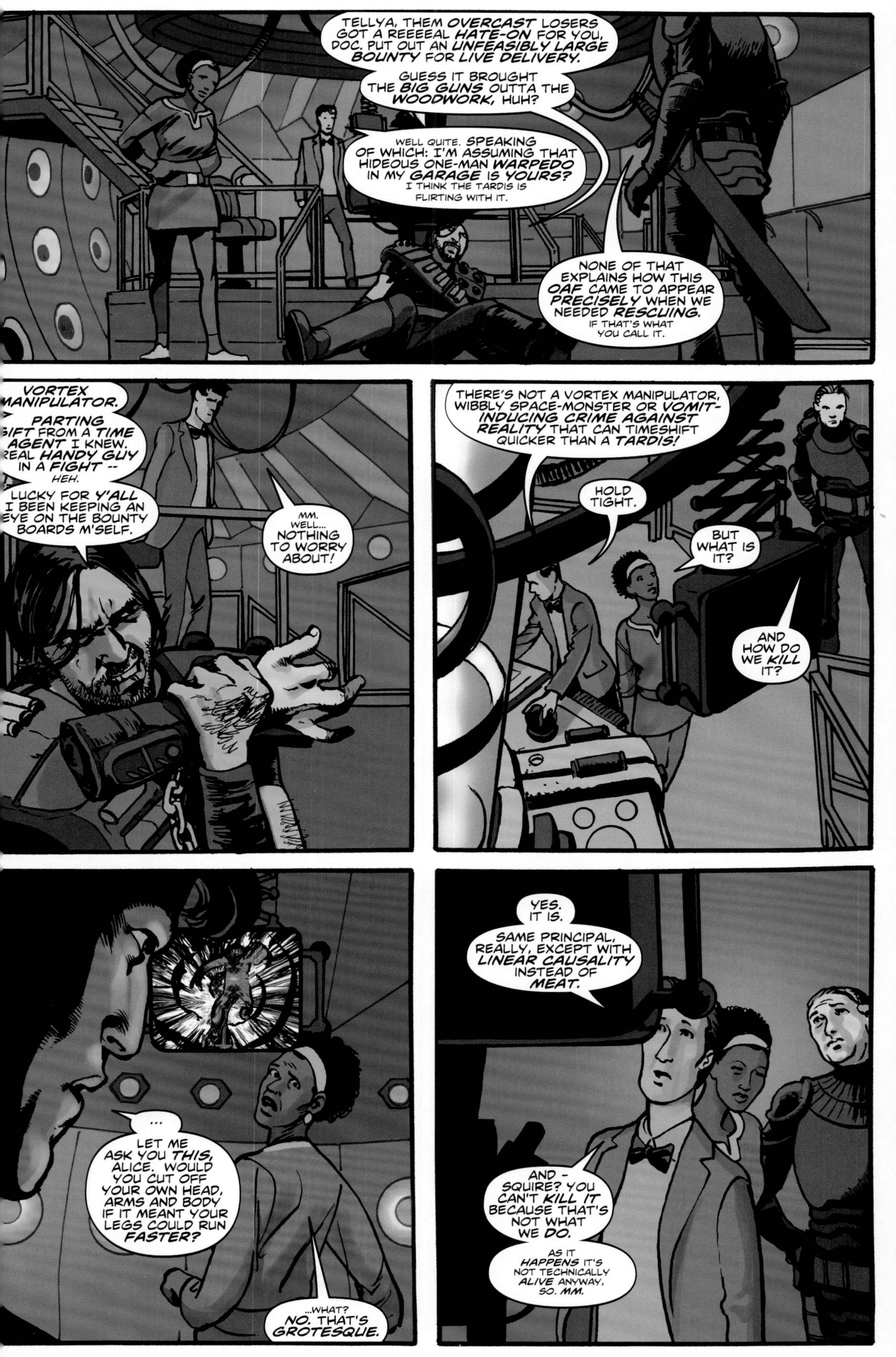
TELLYA, THEM OVERCAST LOSERS GOT A REEEEAL HATE-ON FOR YOU, DOC. PUT OUT AN UNFEASIBLY LARGE BOUNTY FOR LIVE DELIVERY.
GUESS IT BROUGHT THE BIG GUNS OUTTA THE WOODWORK, HUH?
WELL QUITE. SPEAKING OF WHICH: I'M ASSUMING THAT HIDEOUS ONE-MAN WARPEDO IN MY GARAGE IS YOURS?
I THINK THE TARDIS IS FLIRTING WITH IT.
NONE OF THAT EXPLAINS HOW THIS OAF CAME TO APPEAR PRECISELY WHEN WE NEEDED RESCUING.
IF THAT'S WHAT YOU CALL IT.
VORTEX MANIPULATOR.
PARTING GIFT FROM A TIME AGENT I KNEW. REAL HANDY GUY IN A FIGHT --
HEH.
LUCKY FOR Y'ALL I BEEN KEEPING AN EYE ON THE BOUNTY BOARDS M'SELF.
MM. WELL... NOTHING TO WORRY ABOUT!
THERE'S NOT A VORTEX MANIPULATOR, WIBBLY SPACE-MONSTER OR VOMIT-INDUCING CRIME AGAINST REALITY THAT CAN TIMESHIFT QUICKER THAN A TARDIS!
HOLD TIGHT.
BUT WHAT IS IT?
AND HOW DO WE KILL IT?
...
LET ME ASK YOU THIS, ALICE. WOULD YOU CUT OFF YOUR OWN HEAD, ARMS AND BODY IF IT MEANT YOUR LEGS COULD RUN FASTER?
...WHAT? NO. THAT'S GROTESQUE.
YES. IT IS.
SAME PRINCIPAL, REALLY, EXCEPT WITH LINEAR CAUSALITY INSTEAD OF MEAT.
AND - SQUIRE? YOU CAN'T KILL IT BECAUSE THAT'S NOT WHAT WE DO.
AS IT HAPPENS IT'S NOT TECHNICALLY ALIVE ANYWAY, SO. MM.

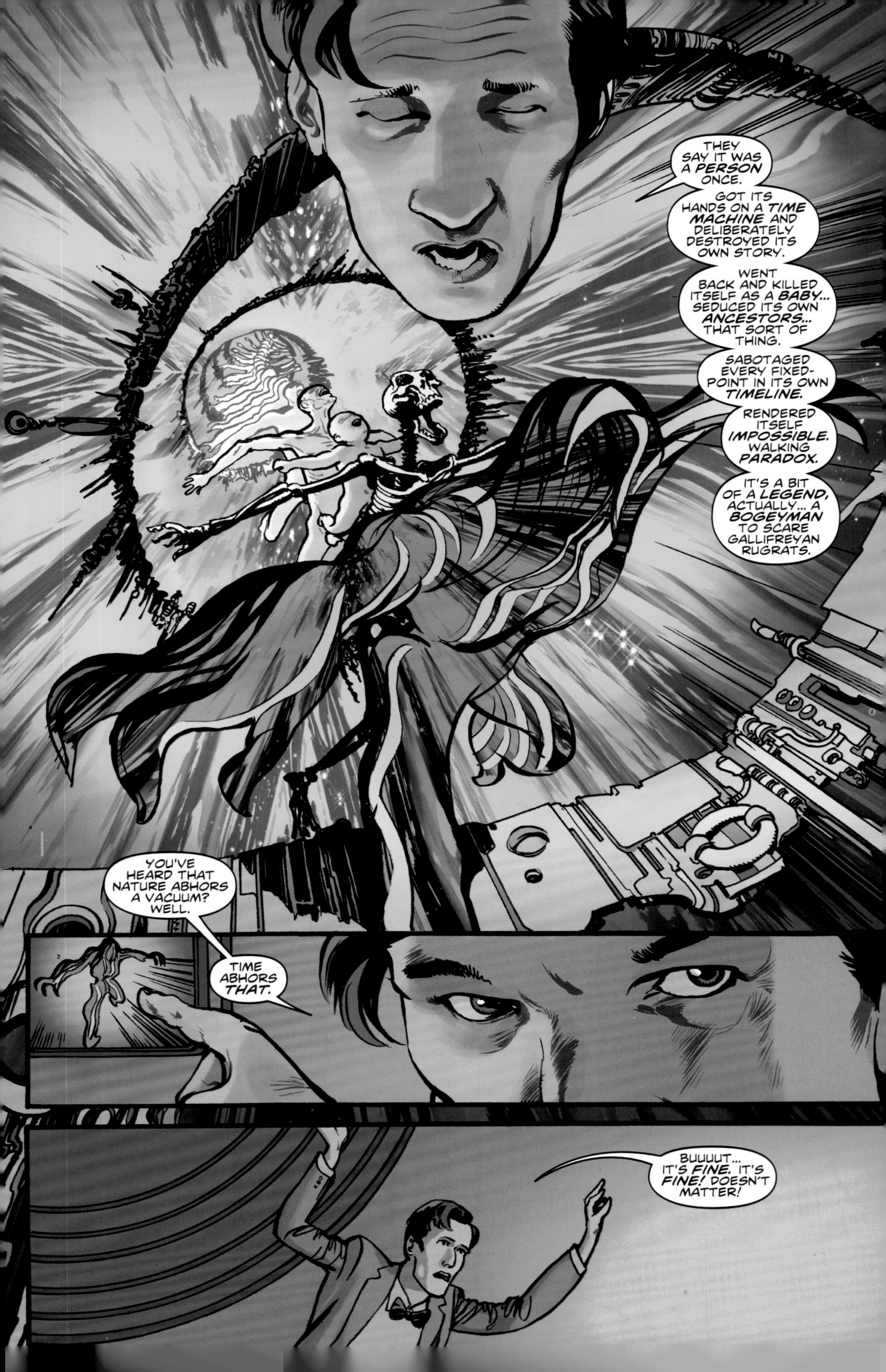
THEY SAY IT WAS A PERSON ONCE.
GOT ITS HANDS ON A TIME MACHINE AND DELIBERATELY DESTROYED ITS OWN STORY.
WENT BACK AND KILLED ITSELF AS A BABY... SEDUCED ITS OWN ANCESTORS... THAT SORT OF THING.
SABOTAGED EVERY FIXED-POINT IN ITS OWN TIMELINE.
RENDERED ITSELF IMPOSSIBLE. WALKING PARADOX.
IT'S A BIT OF A LEGEND, ACTUALLY... A BOGEYMAN TO SCARE GALLIFREYAN RUGRATS.
YOU'VE HEARD THAT NATURE ABHORS A VACUUM? WELL.
TIME ABHORS THAT.
BUUUUT... IT'S FINE. IT'S FINE! DOESN'T MATTER!

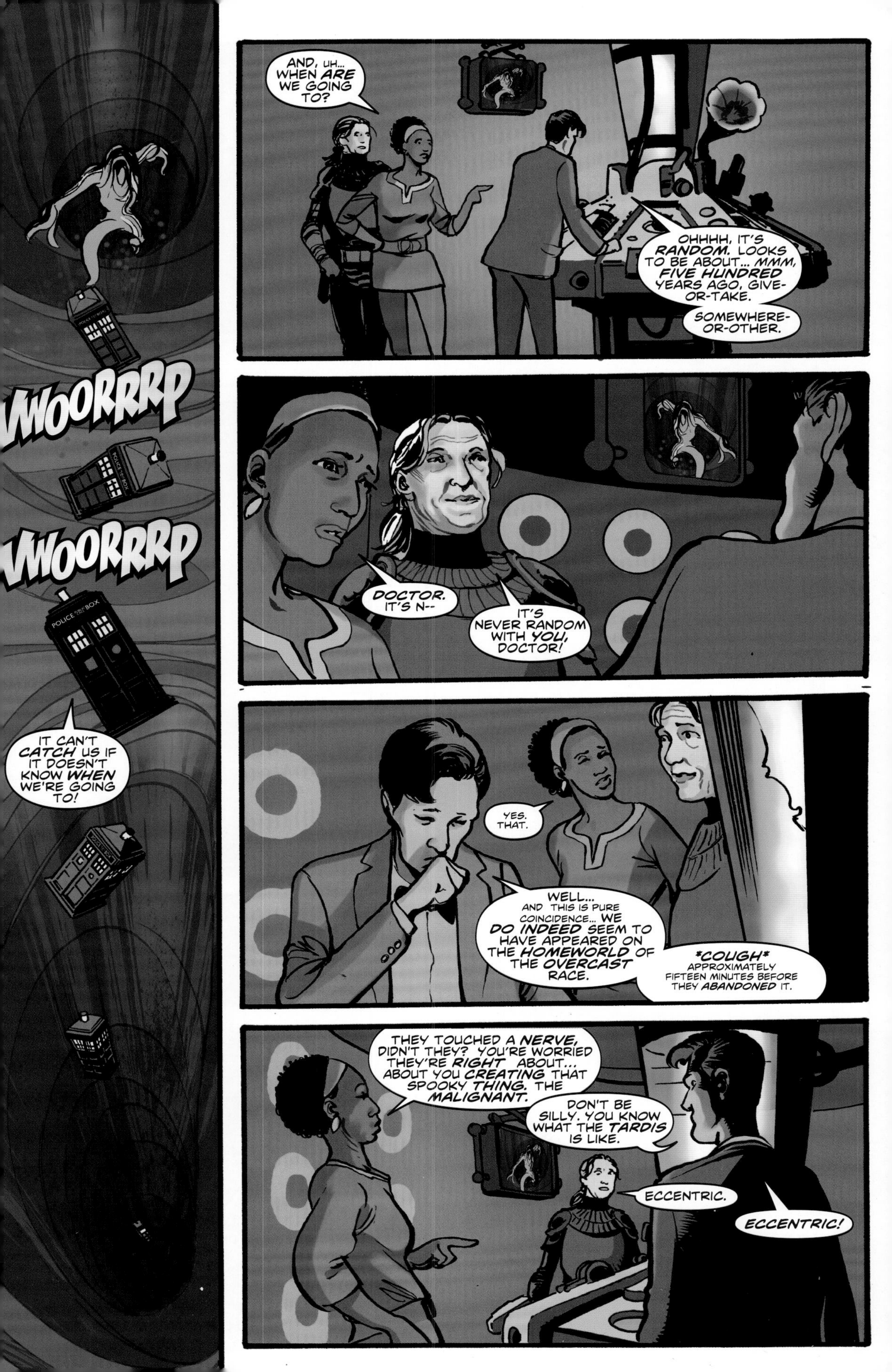
VWOORRRP
VWOORRRP
IT CAN'T CATCH US IF IT DOESN'T KNOW WHEN WE'RE GOING TO!
AND, UH... WHEN ARE WE GOING TO?
OHHHH, IT'S RANDOM. LOOKS TO BE ABOUT... MMM, FIVE HUNDRED YEARS AGO, GIVE-OR-TAKE.
SOMEWHERE-OR-OTHER.
DOCTOR. IT'S N--
IT'S NEVER RANDOM WITH YOU, DOCTOR!
YES. THAT.
WELL... AND THIS IS PURE COINCIDENCE... WE DO INDEED SEEM TO HAVE APPEARED ON THE HOMEWORLD OF THE OVERCAST RACE.
COUGH APPROXIMATELY FIFTEEN MINUTES BEFORE THEY ABANDONED IT.
THEY TOUCHED A NERVE, DIDN'T THEY? YOU'RE WORRIED THEY'RE RIGHT ABOUT... ABOUT YOU CREATING THAT SPOOKY THING. THE MALIGNANT.
DON'T BE SILLY. YOU KNOW WHAT THE TARDIS IS LIKE.
ECCENTRIC.
ECCENTRIC!

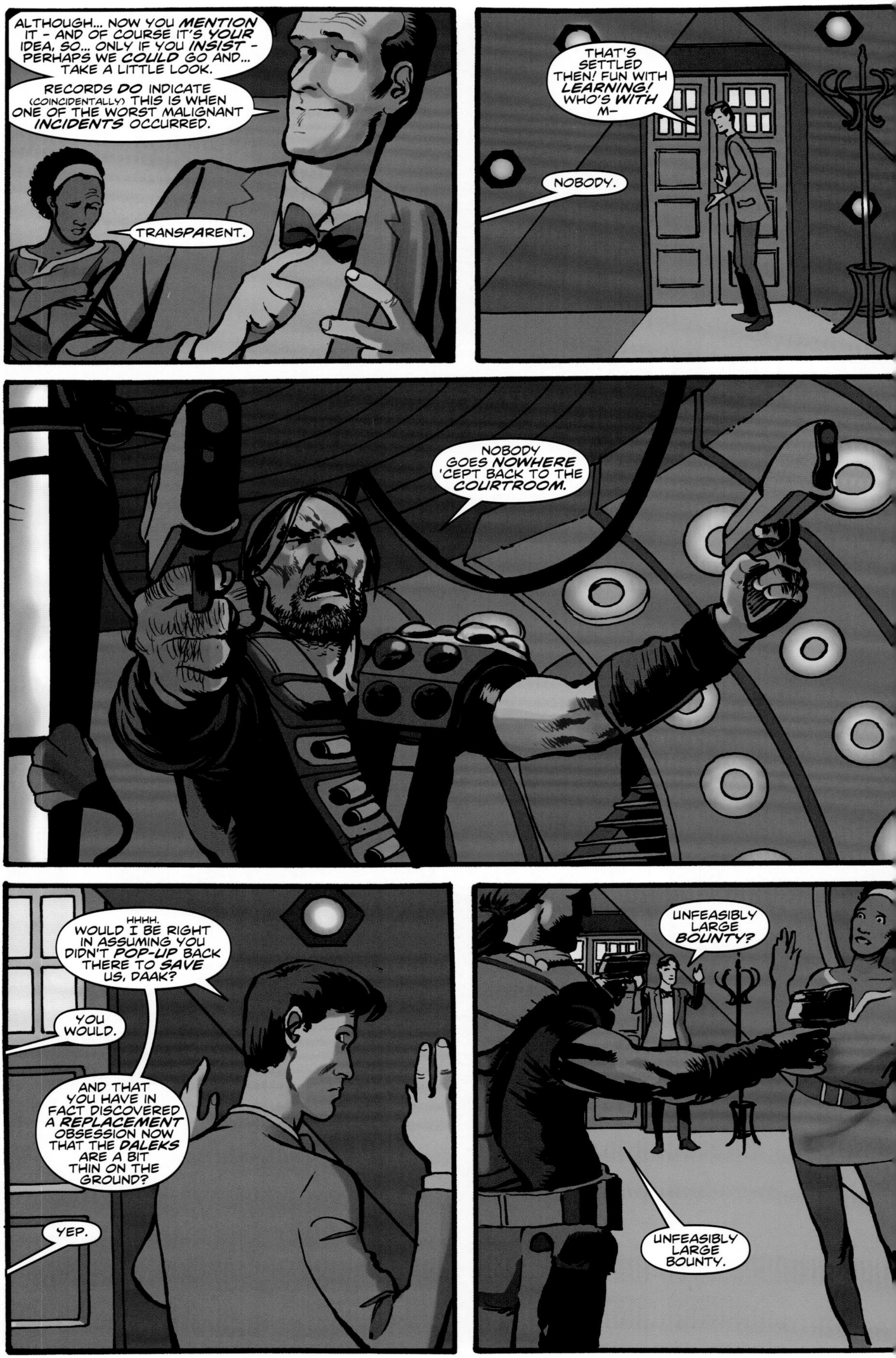
ALTHOUGH... NOW YOU MENTION IT - AND OF COURSE IT'S YOUR IDEA, SO... ONLY IF YOU INSIST - PERHAPS WE COULD GO AND... TAKE A LITTLE LOOK.
RECORDS DO INDICATE (COINCIDENTALLY) THIS IS WHEN ONE OF THE WORST MALIGNANT INCIDENTS OCCURRED.
TRANSPARENT.
THAT'S SETTLED THEN! FUN WITH LEARNING! WHO'S WITH M—
NOBODY.
NOBODY GOES NOWHERE 'CEPT BACK TO THE COURTROOM.
HHHH. WOULD I BE RIGHT IN ASSUMING YOU DIDN'T POP-UP BACK THERE TO SAVE US, DAAK?
YOU WOULD.
AND THAT YOU HAVE IN FACT DISCOVERED A REPLACEMENT OBSESSION NOW THAT THE DALEKS ARE A BIT THIN ON THE GROUND?
YEP.
UNFEASIBLY LARGE BOUNTY?
UNFEASIBLY LARGE BOUNTY.

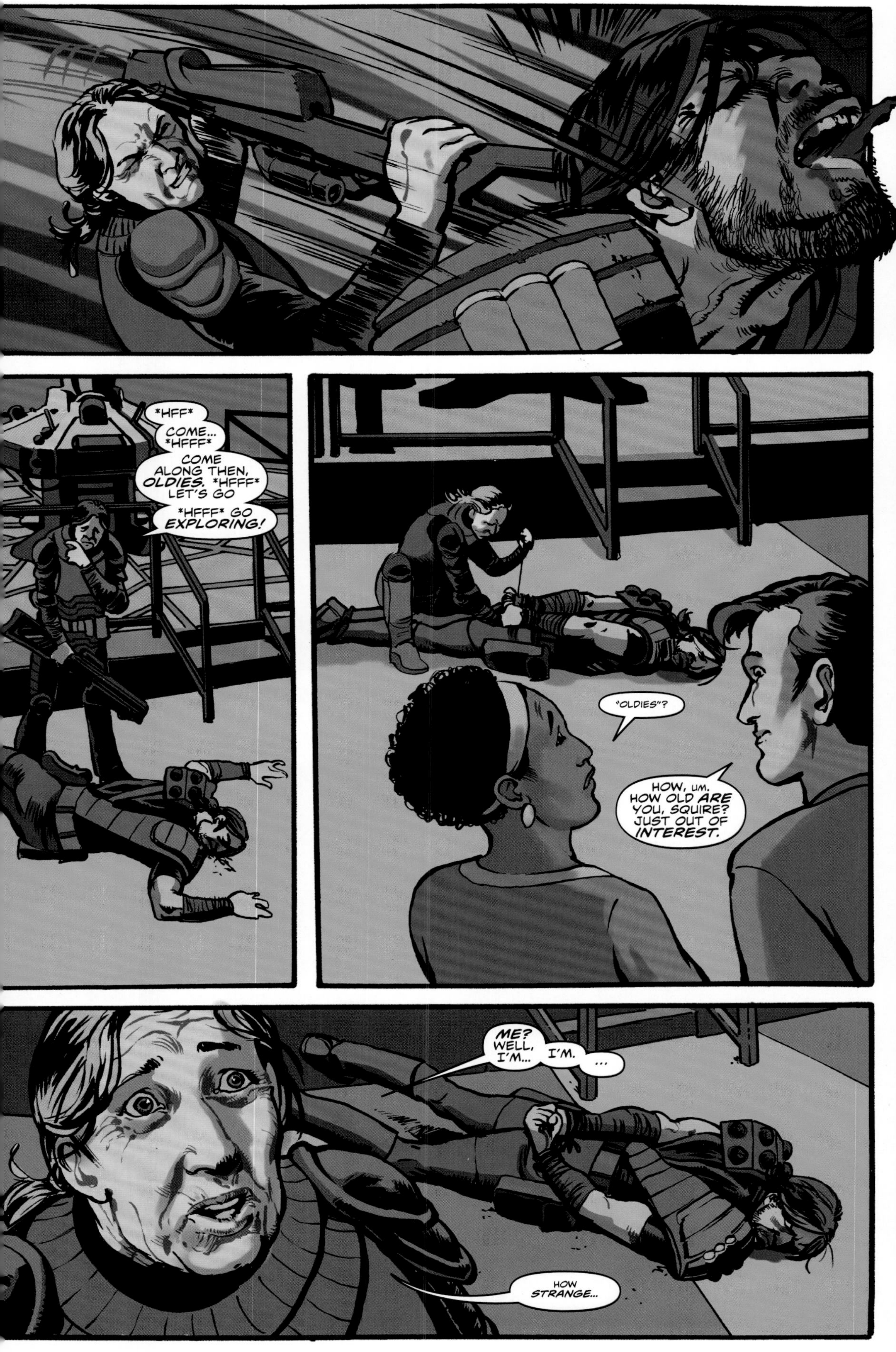
HFF
COME... *HFFF*
COME ALONG THEN, OLDIES. *HFFF* LET'S GO
HFFF GO EXPLORING!
"OLDIES"?
HOW, UM. HOW OLD ARE YOU, SQUIRE? JUST OUT OF INTEREST.
ME? WELL, I'M...
I'M.
...
HOW STRANGE...

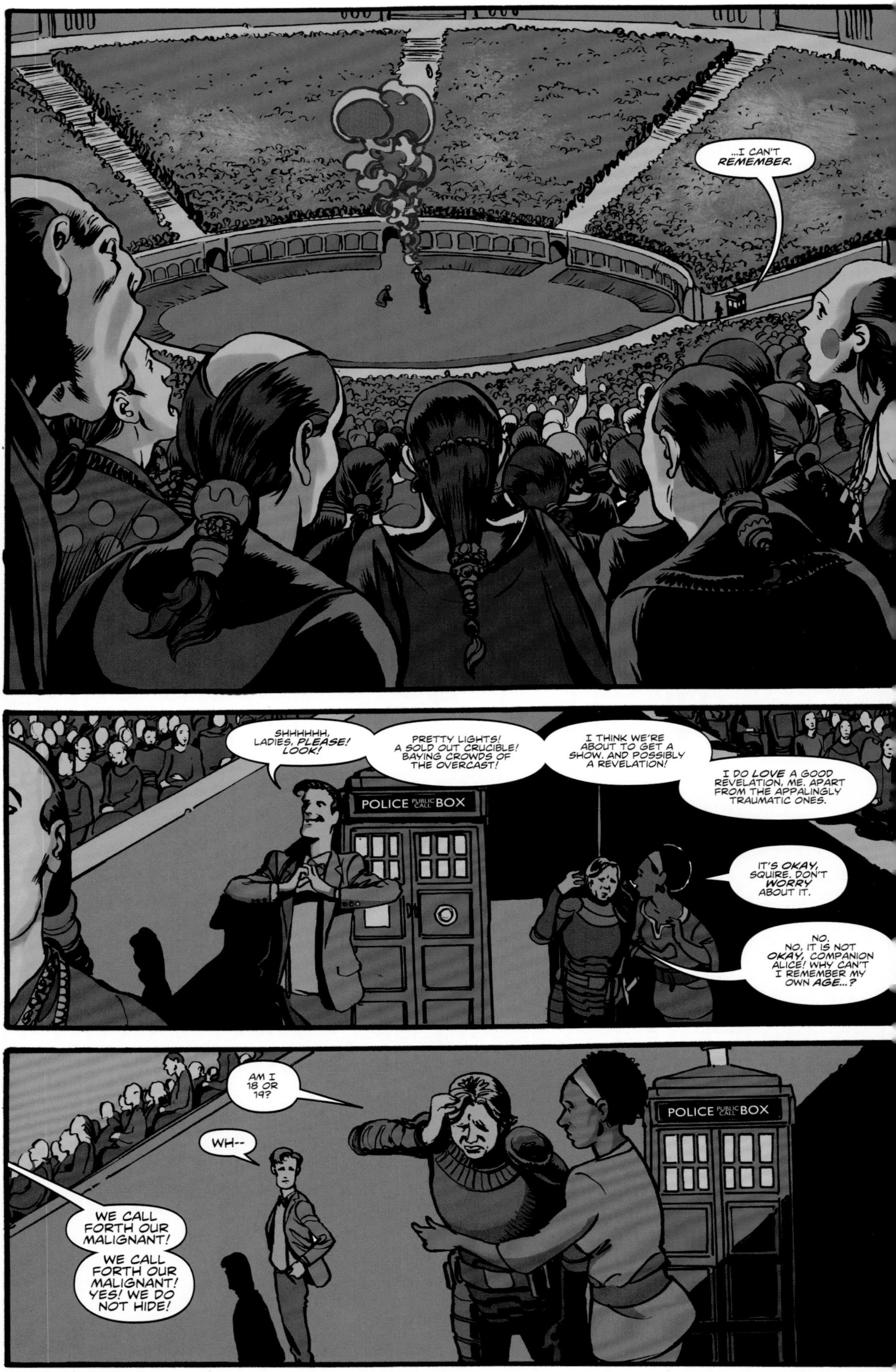

...I CAN'T REMEMBER.
SHHHHHH, LADIES, PLEASE! LOOK!
PRETTY LIGHTS! A SOLD OUT CRUCIBLE! BAYING CROWDS OF THE OVERCAST!
I THINK WE'RE ABOUT TO GET A SHOW. AND POSSIBLY A REVELATION!
I DO LOVE A GOOD REVELATION, ME. APART FROM THE APPALINGLY TRAUMATIC ONES.
POLICE PUBLIC CALL BOX
IT'S OKAY, SQUIRE. DON'T WORRY ABOUT IT.
NO. NO, IT IS NOT OKAY, COMPANION ALICE! WHY CAN'T I REMEMBER MY OWN AGE...?
AM I 18 OR 19?
WH--
POLICE PUBLIC CALL BOX
WE CALL FORTH OUR MALIGNANT!
WE CALL FORTH OUR MALIGNANT! YES! WE DO NOT HIDE!

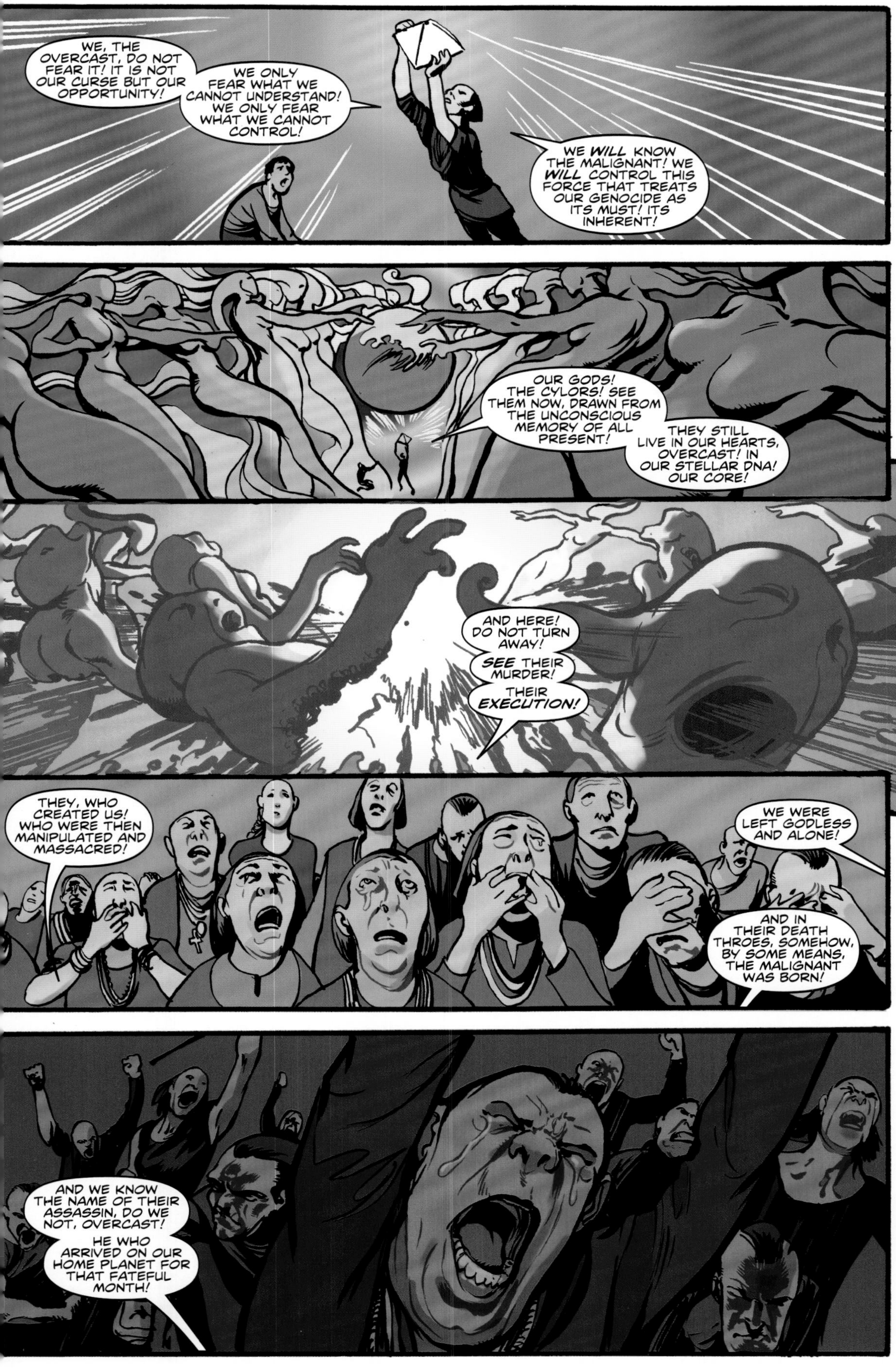
WE, THE OVERCAST, DO NOT FEAR IT! IT IS NOT OUR CURSE BUT OUR OPPORTUNITY!
WE ONLY FEAR WHAT WE CANNOT UNDERSTAND! WE ONLY FEAR WHAT WE CANNOT CONTROL!
WE WILL KNOW THE MALIGNANT! WE WILL CONTROL THIS FORCE THAT TREATS OUR GENOCIDE AS ITS MUST! ITS INHERENT!
OUR GODS! THE CYLORS! SEE THEM NOW, DRAWN FROM THE UNCONSCIOUS MEMORY OF ALL PRESENT!
THEY STILL LIVE IN OUR HEARTS, OVERCAST! IN OUR STELLAR DNA! OUR CORE!
AND HERE! DO NOT TURN AWAY!
SEE THEIR MURDER!
THEIR EXECUTION!
THEY, WHO CREATED US! WHO WERE THEN MANIPULATED AND MASSACRED!
WE WERE LEFT GODLESS AND ALONE!
AND IN THEIR DEATH THROES, SOMEHOW, BY SOME MEANS, THE MALIGNANT WAS BORN!
AND WE KNOW THE NAME OF THEIR ASSASSIN, DO WE NOT, OVERCAST!
HE WHO ARRIVED ON OUR HOME PLANET FOR THAT FATEFUL MONTH!

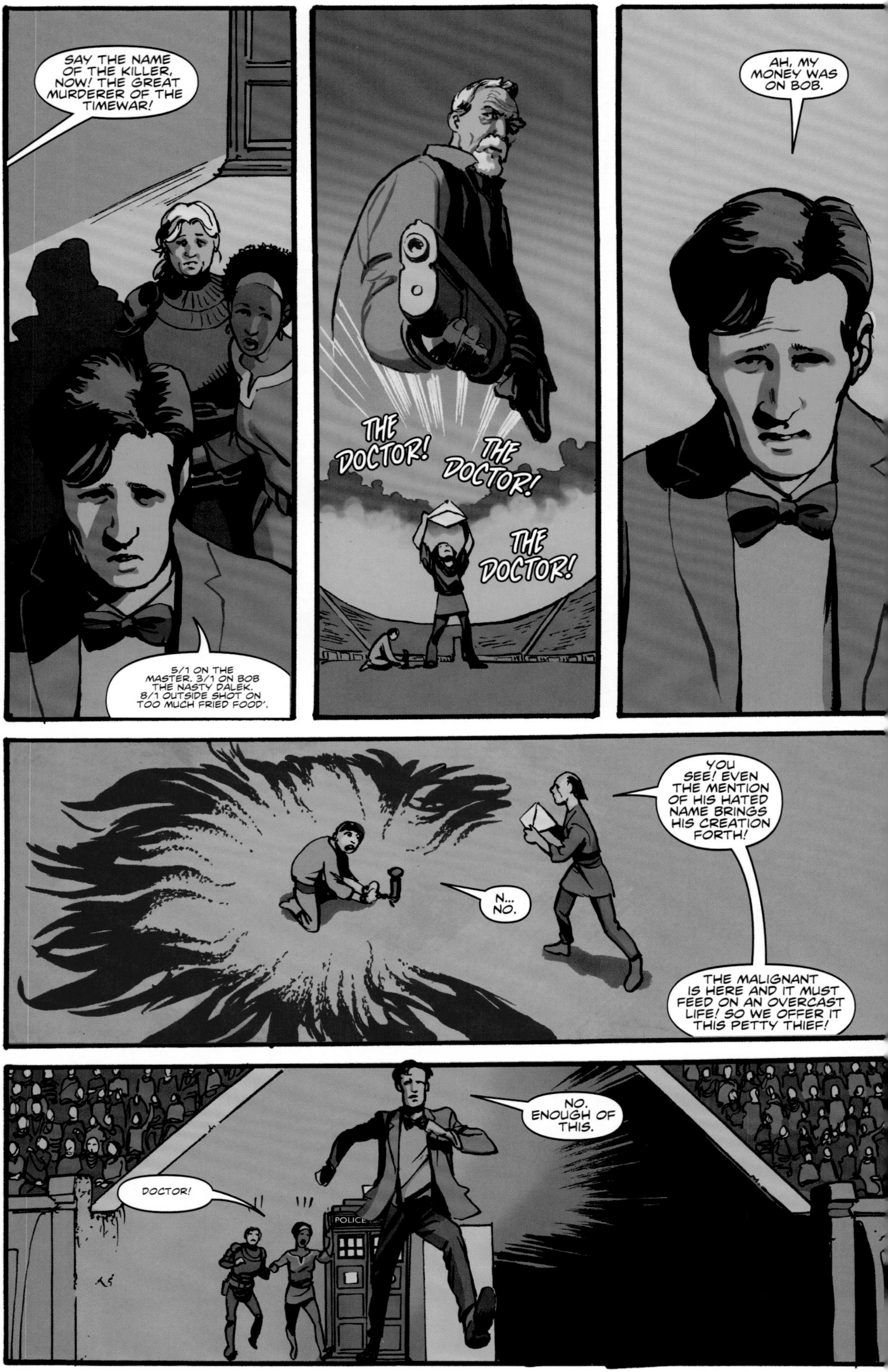
SAY THE NAME OF THE KILLER, NOW! THE GREAT MURDERER OF THE TIMEWAR!
5/1 ON THE MASTER. 3/1 ON BOB THE NASTY DALEK. 8/1 OUTSIDE SHOT ON 'TOO MUCH FRIED FOOD'.
THE DOCTOR!
THE DOCTOR!
THE DOCTOR!
AH, MY MONEY WAS ON BOB.
YOU SEE! EVEN THE MENTION OF HIS HATED NAME BRINGS HIS CREATION FORTH!
N... NO.
THE MALIGNANT IS HERE AND IT MUST FEED ON AN OVERCAST LIFE! SO WE OFFER IT THIS PETTY THIEF!
NO. ENOUGH OF THIS.
DOCTOR!
POLICE

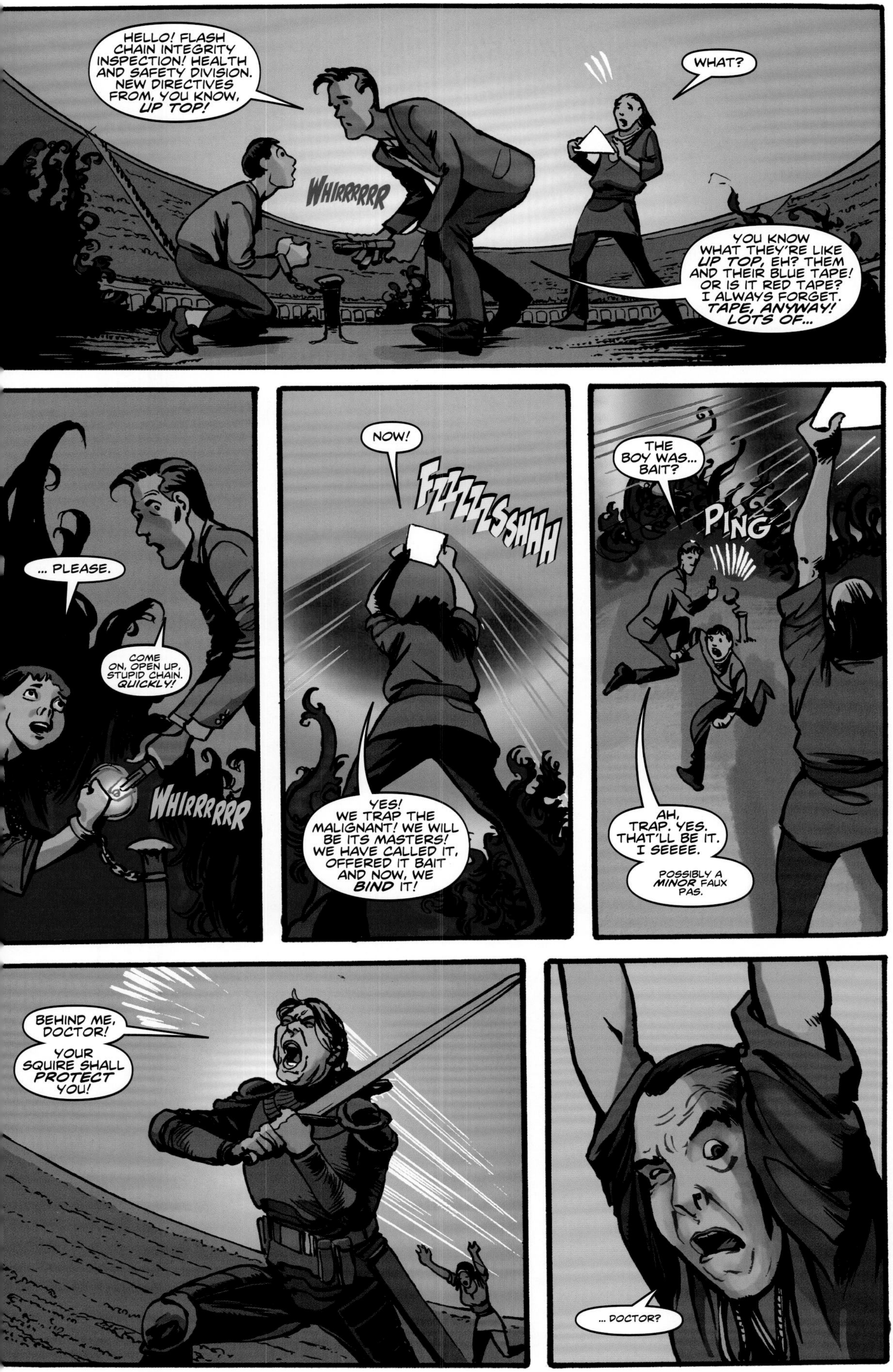

HELLO! FLASH CHAIN INTEGRITY INSPECTION! HEALTH AND SAFETY DIVISION. NEW DIRECTIVES FROM, YOU KNOW, UP TOP!
WHAT?
WHIRRRRRR
YOU KNOW WHAT THEY'RE LIKE UP TOP, EH? THEM AND THEIR BLUE TAPE! OR IS IT RED TAPE? I ALWAYS FORGET. TAPE, ANYWAY! LOTS OF...
... PLEASE.
COME ON, OPEN UP, STUPID CHAIN. QUICKLY!
WHIRRRRRR
NOW!
FZZZZZSHHH
YES! WE TRAP THE MALIGNANT! WE WILL BE ITS MASTERS! WE HAVE CALLED IT, OFFERED IT BAIT AND NOW, WE BIND IT!
THE BOY WAS... BAIT?
PING
AH, TRAP. YES. THAT'LL BE IT. I SEEEE.
POSSIBLY A MINOR FAUX PAS.
BEHIND ME, DOCTOR!
YOUR SQUIRE SHALL PROTECT YOU!
... DOCTOR?

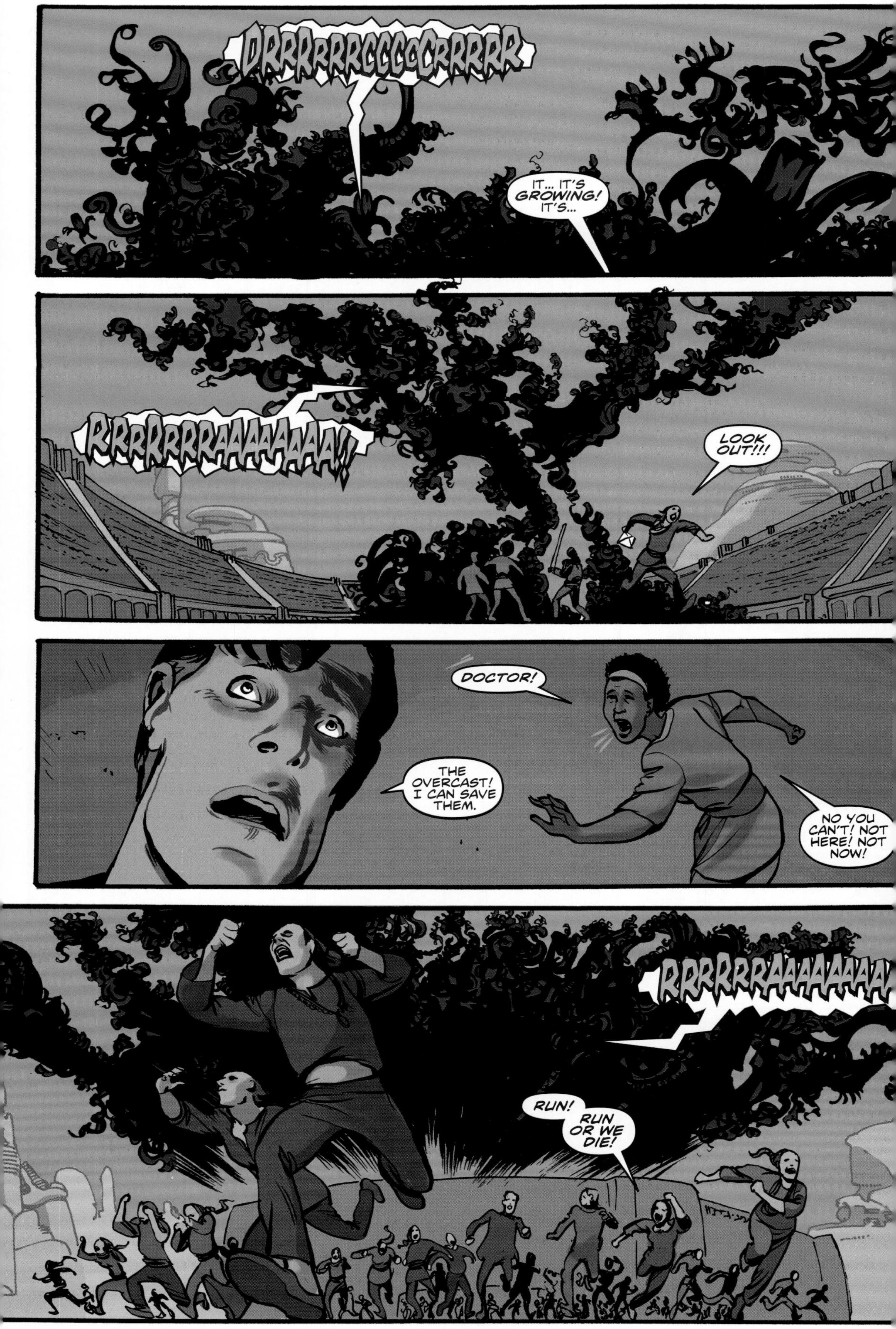
DRRRRRRCCCCCRRRRR
IT... IT'S GROWING! IT'S...
RRRRRRRAAAAAAAA!!
LOOK OUT!!!
DOCTOR!
THE OVERCAST! I CAN SAVE THEM.
NO YOU CAN'T! NOT HERE! NOT NOW!
RRRRRRAAAAAAAA
RUN!
RUN OR WE DIE!

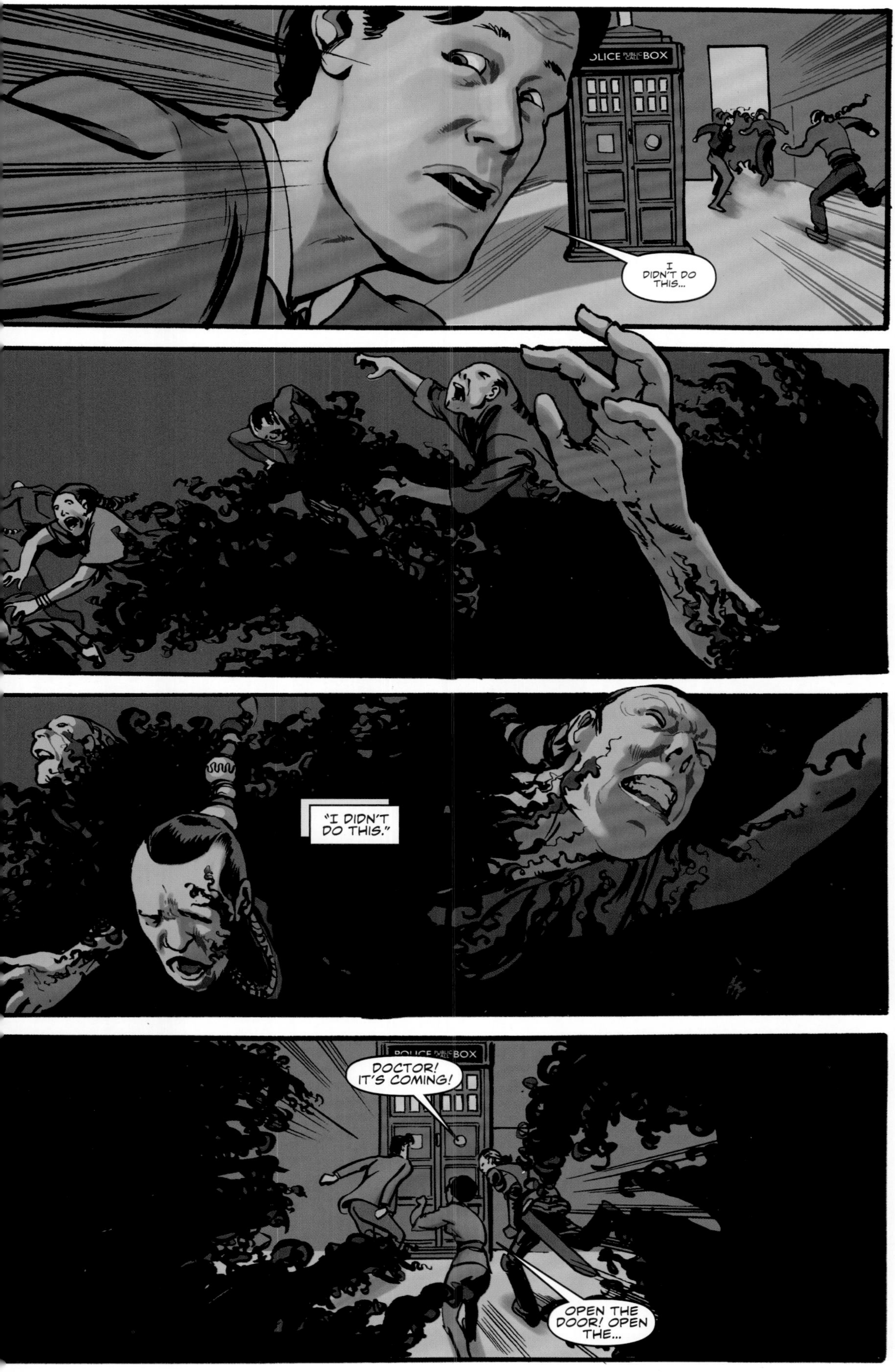
OLICE PUBLIC CALL BOX
I DIDN'T DO THIS...
"I DIDN'T DO THIS."
POLICE PUBLIC CALL BOX
DOCTOR! IT'S COMING!
OPEN THE DOOR! OPEN THE...

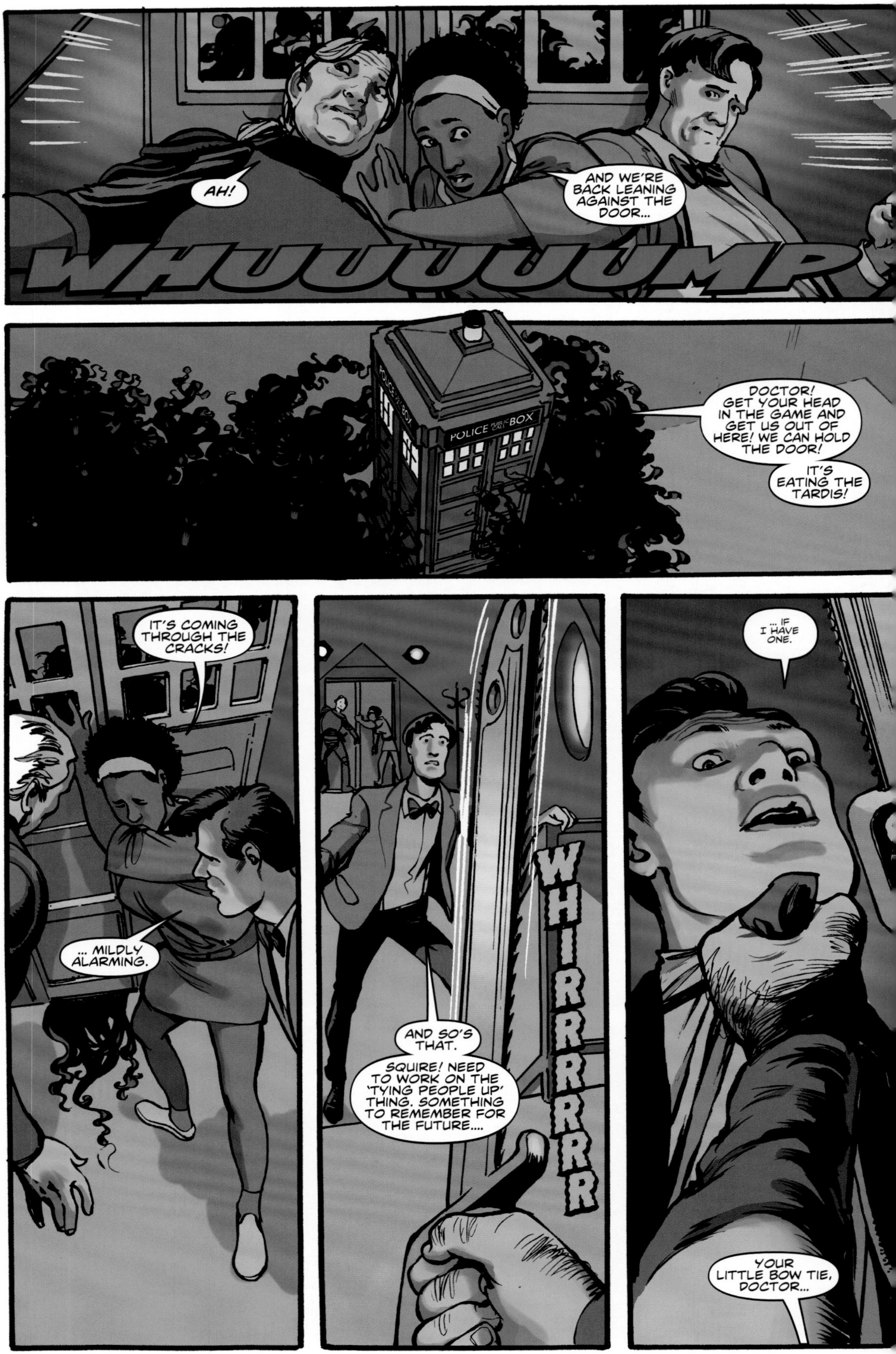
AH!
AND WE'RE BACK LEANING AGAINST THE DOOR...
WHUUUUUUMP
POLICE PUBLIC CALL BOX
DOCTOR! GET YOUR HEAD IN THE GAME AND GET US OUT OF HERE! WE CAN HOLD THE DOOR!
IT'S EATING THE TARDIS!
IT'S COMING THROUGH THE CRACKS!
... MILDLY ALARMING.
AND SO'S THAT.
SQUIRE! NEED TO WORK ON THE 'TYING PEOPLE UP' THING. SOMETHING TO REMEMBER FOR THE FUTURE....
WHIRRRRRR
... IF I HAVE ONE.
YOUR LITTLE BOW TIE, DOCTOR...

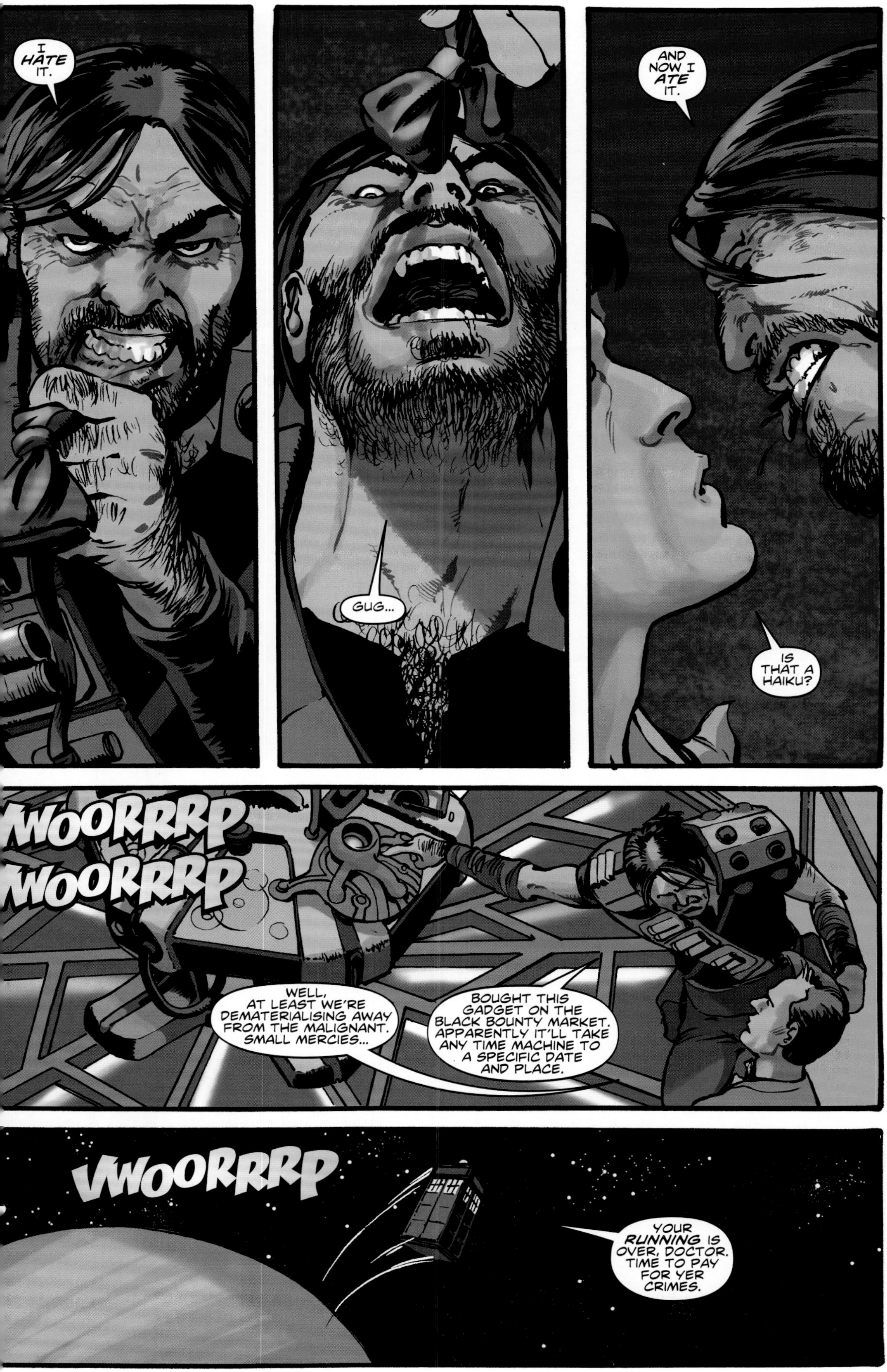
I HATE IT.
GUG...
AND NOW I ATE IT.
IS THAT A HAIKU?
VWOORRRP
VWOORRRP
WELL, AT LEAST WE'RE DEMATERIALISING AWAY FROM THE MALIGNANT. SMALL MERCIES...
BOUGHT THIS GADGET ON THE BLACK BOUNTY MARKET. APPARENTLY IT'LL TAKE ANY TIME MACHINE TO A SPECIFIC DATE AND PLACE.
VWOORRRP
YOUR RUNNING IS OVER, DOCTOR. TIME TO PAY FOR YER CRIMES.

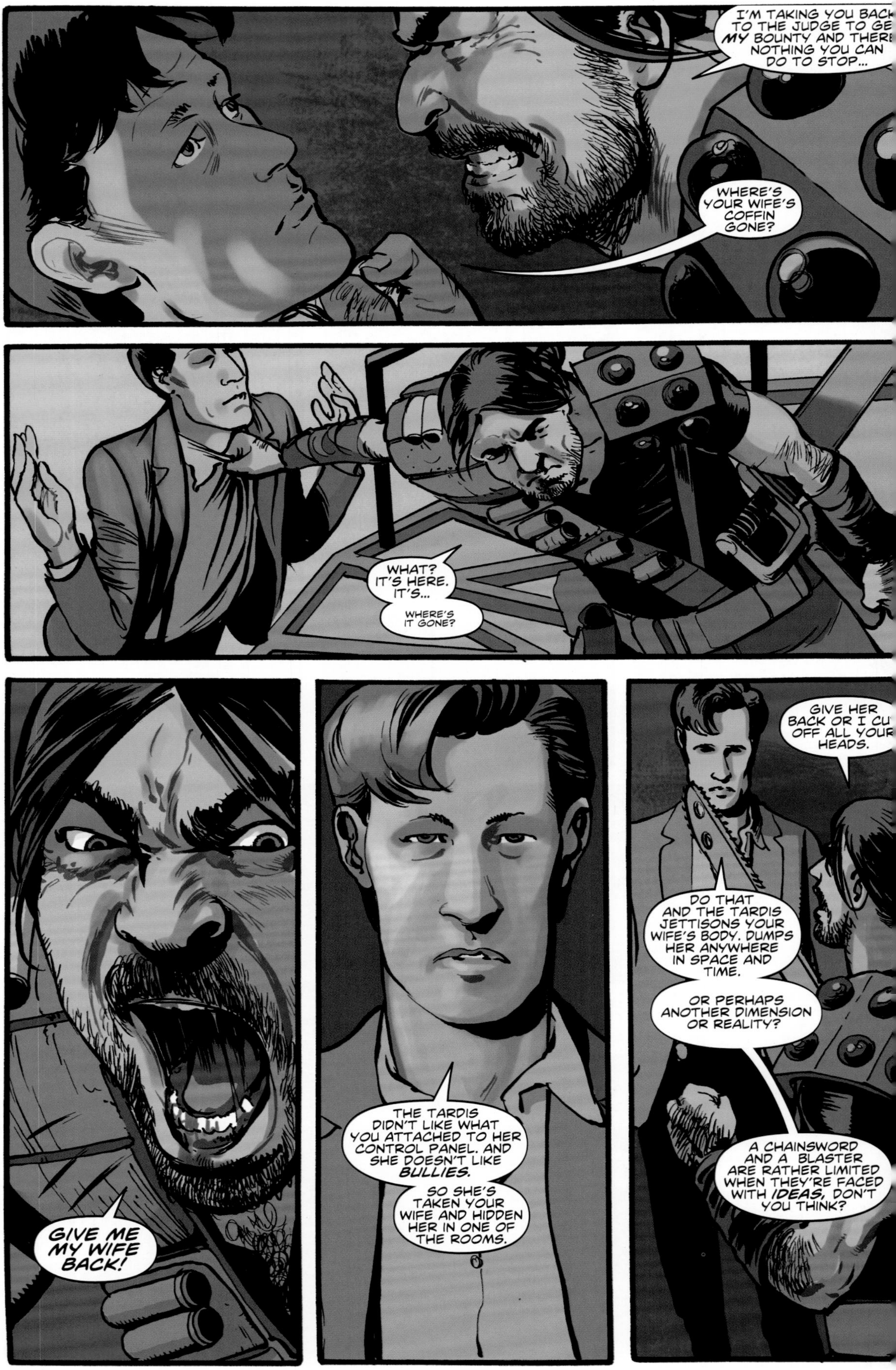

I'M TAKING YOU BACK TO THE JUDGE TO GET MY BOUNTY AND THERE'S NOTHING YOU CAN DO TO STOP...
WHERE'S YOUR WIFE'S COFFIN GONE?
WHAT? IT'S HERE. IT'S...
WHERE'S IT GONE?
GIVE ME MY WIFE BACK!
THE TARDIS DIDN'T LIKE WHAT YOU ATTACHED TO HER CONTROL PANEL. AND SHE DOESN'T LIKE BULLIES.
SO SHE'S TAKEN YOUR WIFE AND HIDDEN HER IN ONE OF THE ROOMS.
GIVE HER BACK OR I CUT OFF ALL YOUR HEADS.
DO THAT AND THE TARDIS JETTISONS YOUR WIFE'S BODY. DUMPS HER ANYWHERE IN SPACE AND TIME.
OR PERHAPS ANOTHER DIMENSION OR REALITY?
A CHAINSWORD AND A BLASTER ARE RATHER LIMITED WHEN THEY'RE FACED WITH IDEAS, DON'T YOU THINK?

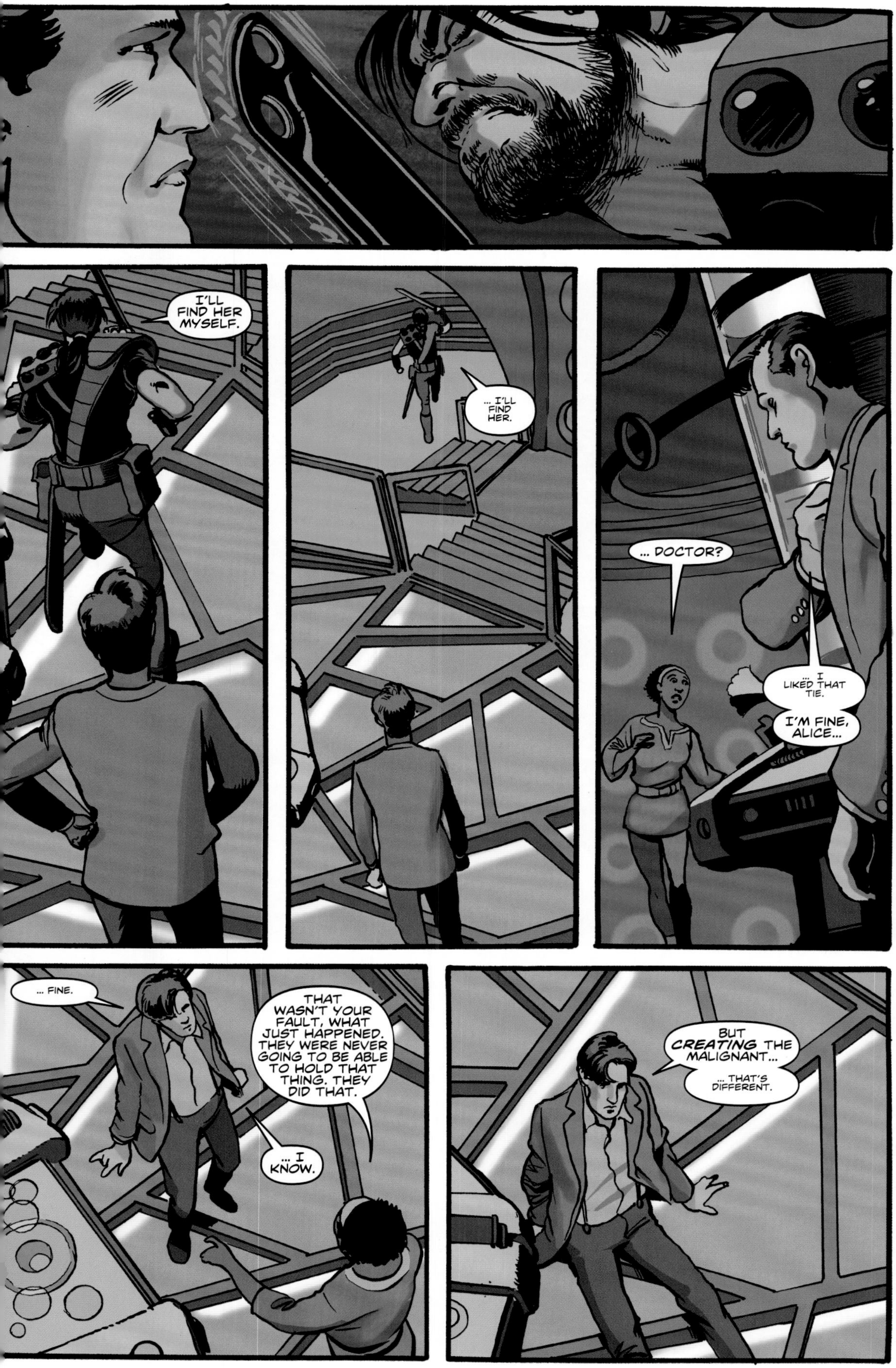
I'LL FIND HER MYSELF.
... I'LL FIND HER.
... DOCTOR?
... I LIKED THAT TIE.
I'M FINE, ALICE...
... FINE.
THAT WASN'T YOUR FAULT, WHAT JUST HAPPENED. THEY WERE NEVER GOING TO BE ABLE TO HOLD THAT THING. THEY DID THAT.
... I KNOW.
BUT CREATING THE MALIGNANT...
... THAT'S DIFFERENT.

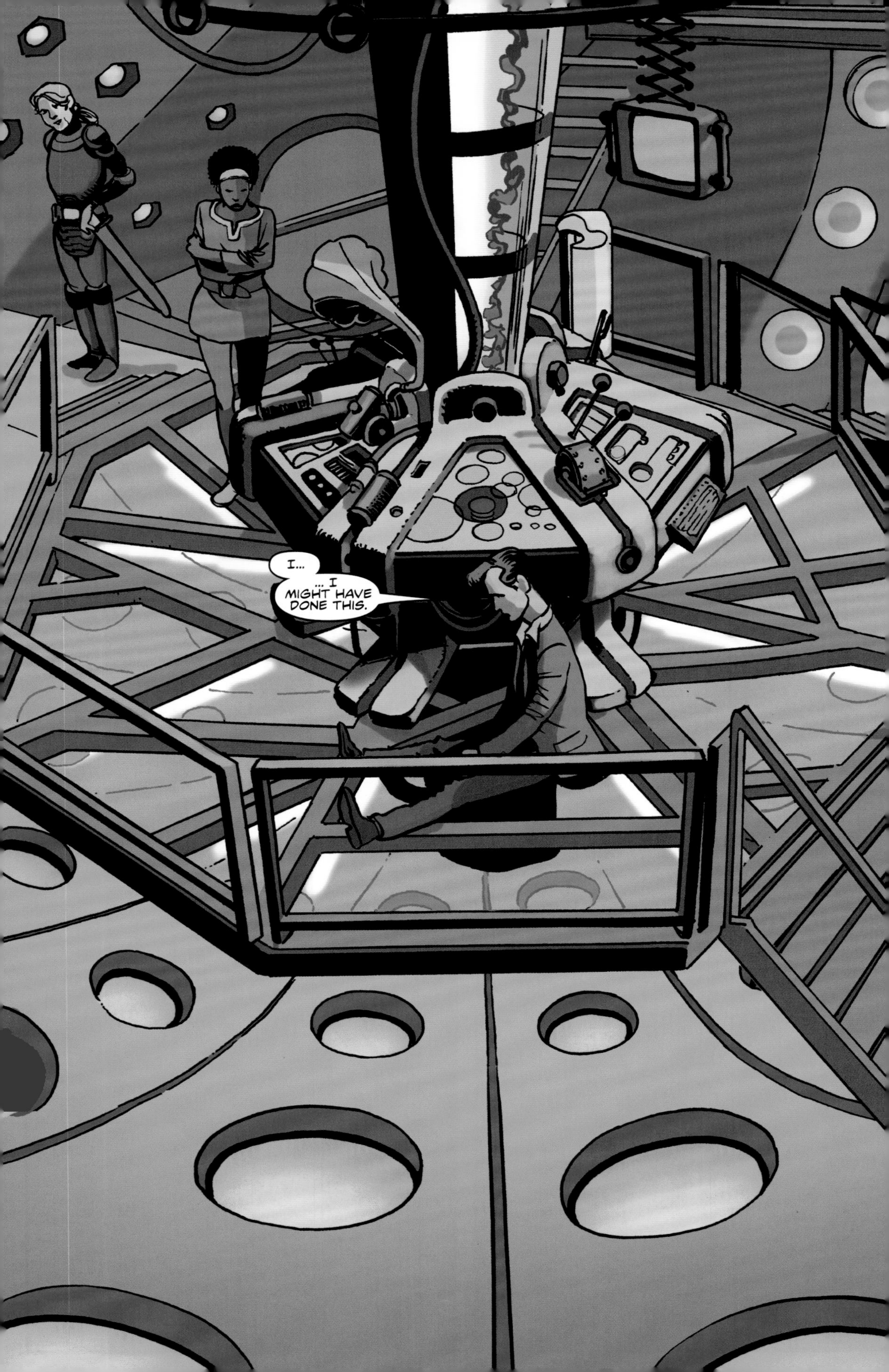
I...
... I MIGHT HAVE DONE THIS.

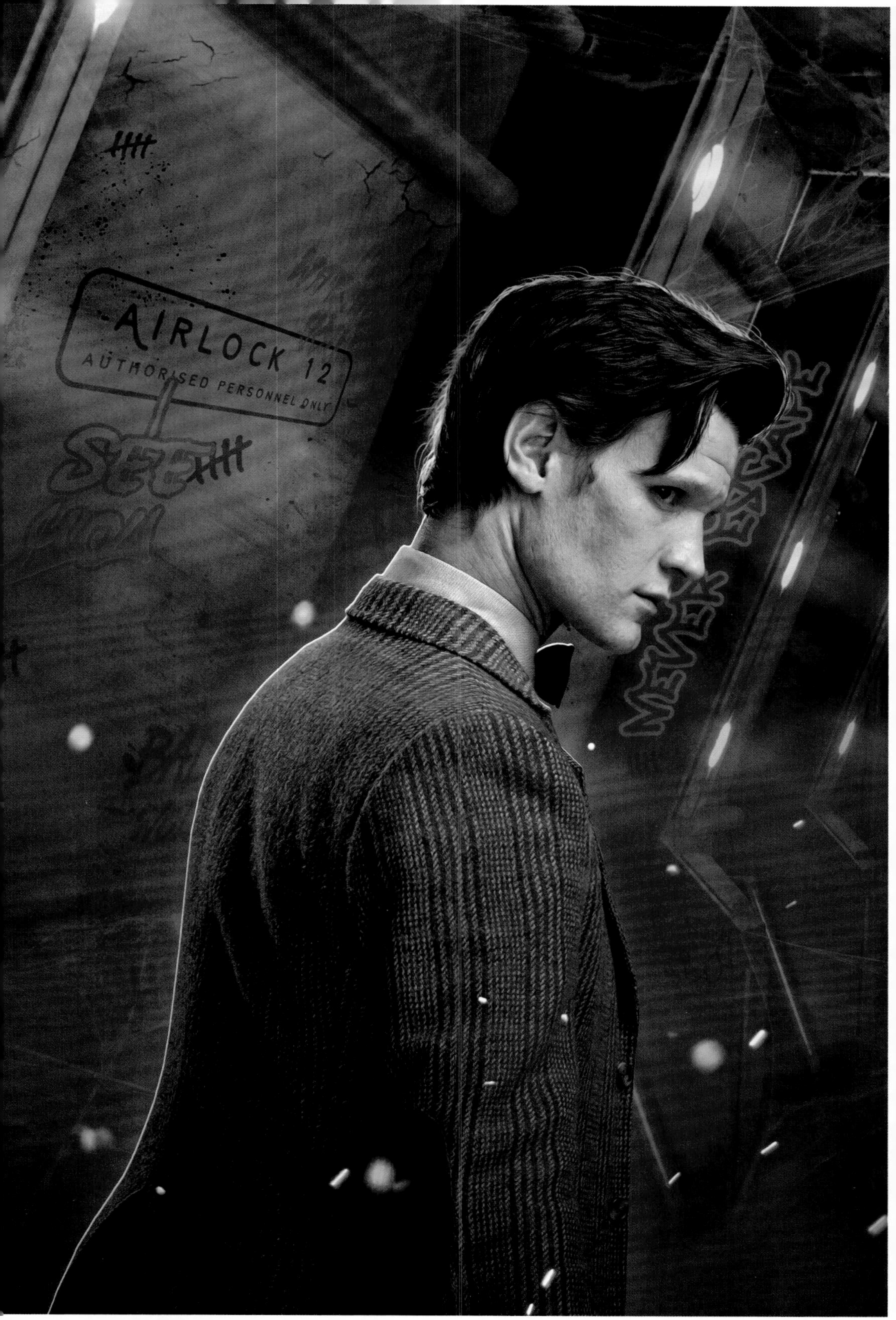
AIRLOCK 12
AUTHORISED PERSONNEL ONLY

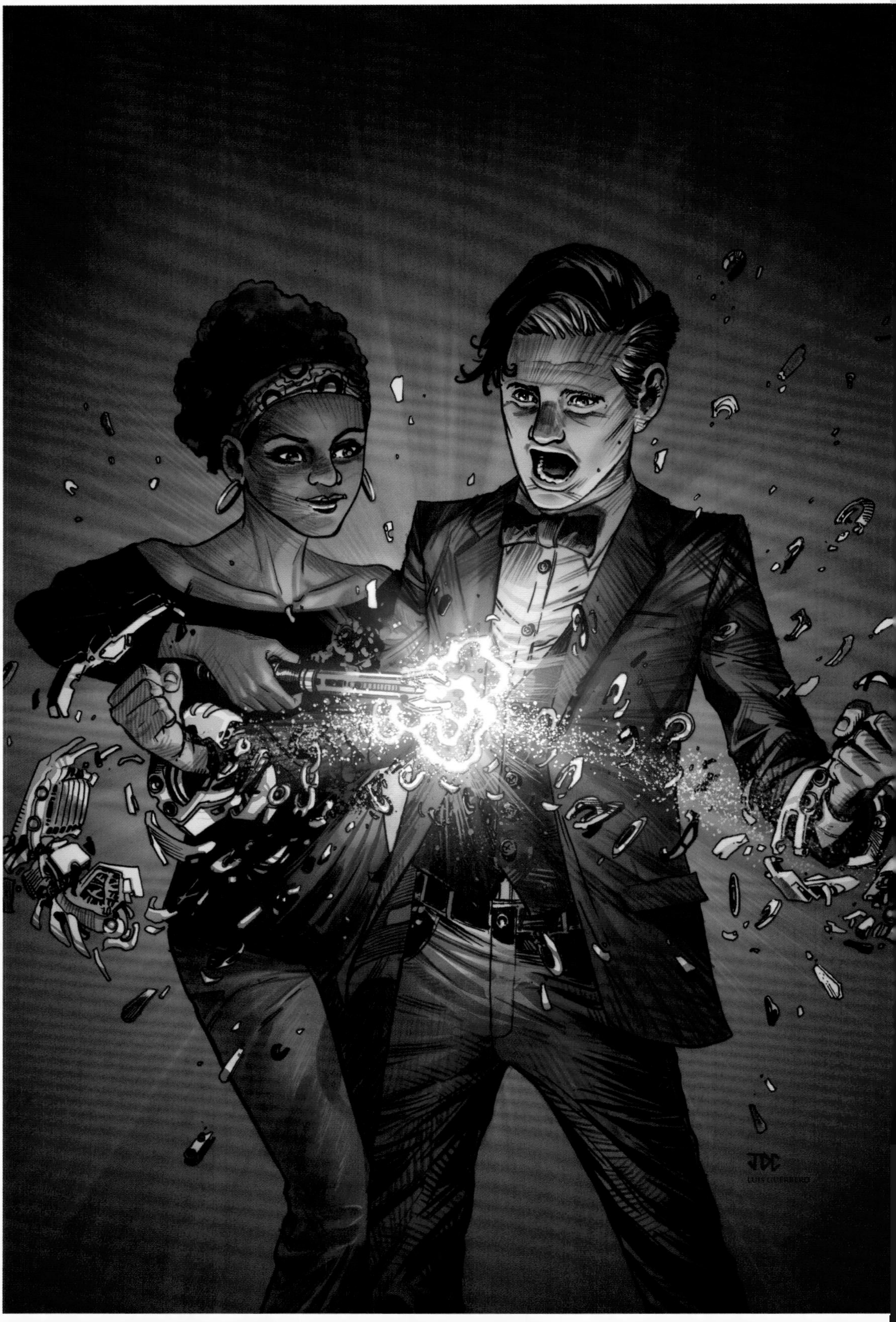

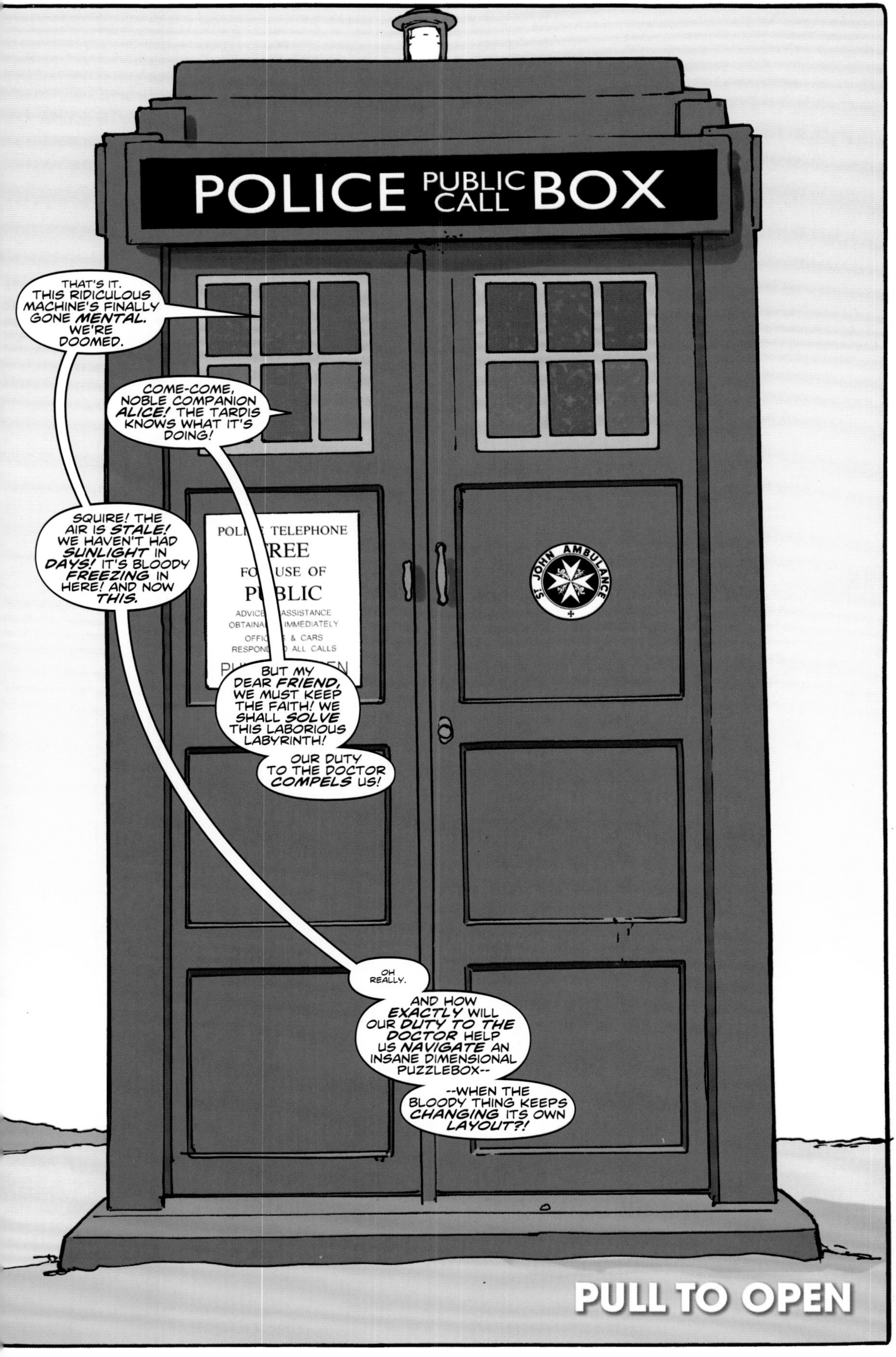
POLICE PUBLIC CALL BOX
THAT'S IT. THIS RIDICULOUS MACHINE'S FINALLY GONE MENTAL. WE'RE DOOMED.
COME-COME, NOBLE COMPANION ALICE! THE TARDIS KNOWS WHAT IT'S DOING!
SQUIRE! THE AIR IS STALE! WE HAVEN'T HAD SUNLIGHT IN DAYS! IT'S BLOODY FREEZING IN HERE! AND NOW THIS.
BUT MY DEAR FRIEND, WE MUST KEEP THE FAITH! WE SHALL SOLVE THIS LABORIOUS LABYRINTH!
OUR DUTY TO THE DOCTOR COMPELS US!
OH REALLY.
AND HOW EXACTLY WILL OUR DUTY TO THE DOCTOR HELP US NAVIGATE AN INSANE DIMENSIONAL PUZZLEBOX--
--WHEN THE BLOODY THING KEEPS CHANGING ITS OWN LAYOUT?!
ST. JOHN AMBULANCE
PULL TO OPEN

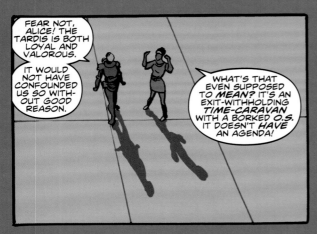

FEAR NOT, ALICE! THE TARDIS IS BOTH LOYAL AND VALOROUS.

IT WOULD NOT HAVE CONFOUNDED US SO WITHOUT GOOD REASON.

WHAT'S THAT EVEN SUPPOSED TO *MEAN*? IT'S AN EXIT-WITHHOLDING *TIME-CARAVAN* WITH A BORKED *O.S.* IT DOESN'T *HAVE* AN AGENDA!

I FEAR YOU'RE *WRONG.* WHY, SHORTLY AFTER I ENTERED HIS *SERVICE* I ASKED THE DOCTOR ABOUT THIS VERY THING.

WHAT IS THE *TARDIS?* SAID I.

YOU KNOW WHAT HE *SAID?*

HE CALLED IT "A MACHINE OF SUCH

INCONCEIVABLE COMPLEXITY

IT CAN BE PERCEIVED ONLY AS AN EXPRESSION OF

SIMPLICITY."

HE SAID, "THE ONE AND ONLY THING IT CANNOT DO

IS STOP."

EVENTUALLY I REALIZED HE WAS PROBABLY TALKING ABOUT *HIMSELF.*

LOOK! LOOK!

WE'VE ALREADY BEEN *PAST* THIS BLOODY... *THING*--

--IT'S A QUANTUM *PERCEPTION* DIODE, OLD CHUM, FOR TH--

WHATEVER! IT'S NOT A *WAY OUT* AND WE'VE WALKED PAST IT *TWICE* ALREADY!

CALM YOURSELF! WE ALREADY *KNOW* THE MACHINE IS ALTERING ITS INTERIOR DIMENSIONS FOR SOME REASON, SO--

THAT'S NOT THE *POINT!* IT'S NOT *MOVING!* NO BLINKY *LIGHTS...* NO UNSETTLINGLY ORGANIC *NOISES!*

YOU'VE SPENT *HOURS* HARPING-ON ABOUT BEING *BEST FRIENDS FOREVER* WITH THE DOCTOR -- HAVE YOU *EVER* KNOWN THIS THING TO BE SO STILL?

UH.

"THE *TARDIS* CAN'T STOP", YOU SAY?

FEELS PRETTY BLOODY STOPPED TO *ME.*

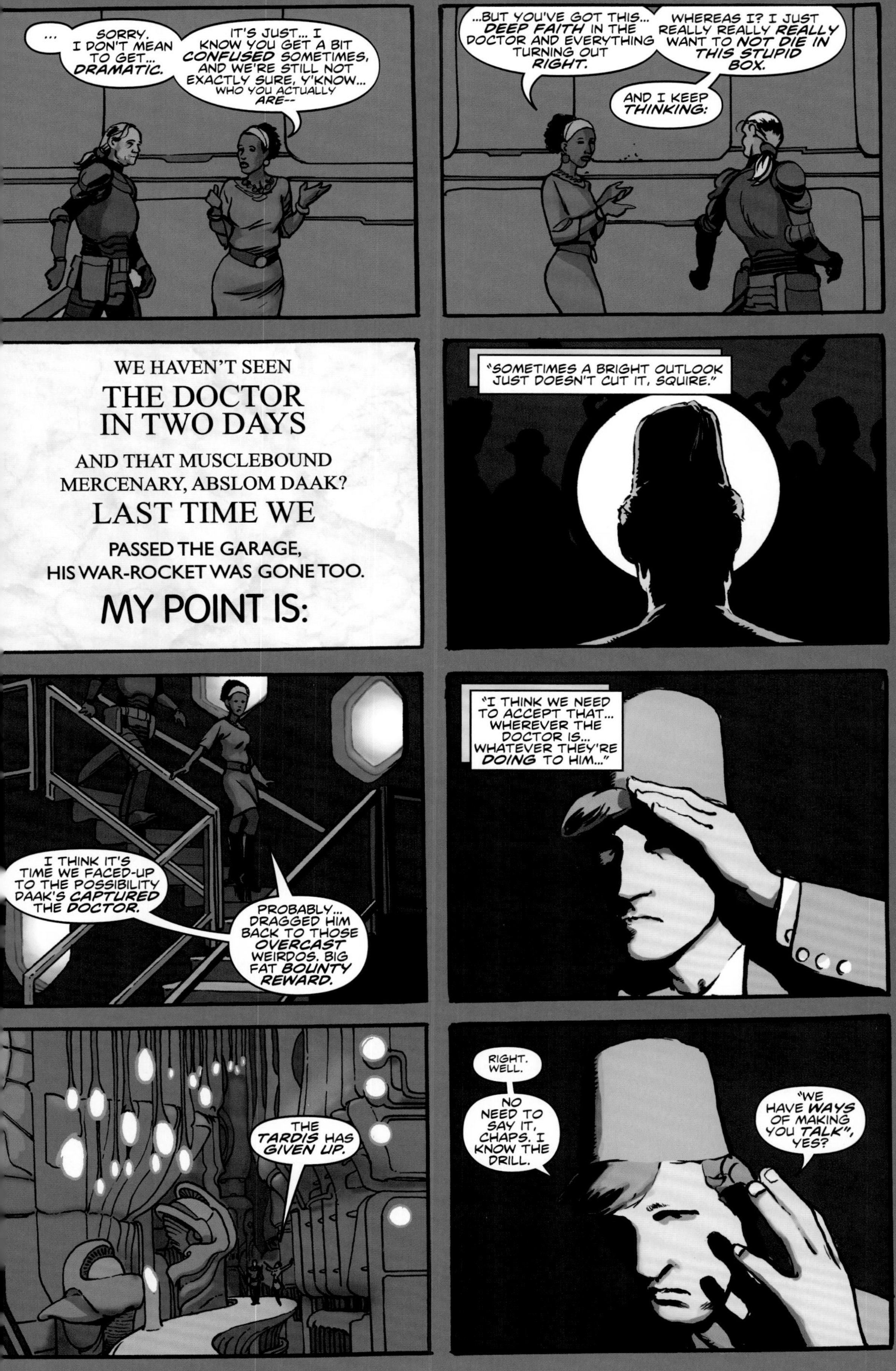
...
SORRY. I DON'T MEAN TO GET... DRAMATIC.
IT'S JUST... I KNOW YOU GET A BIT CONFUSED SOMETIMES, AND WE'RE STILL NOT EXACTLY SURE, Y'KNOW... WHO YOU ACTUALLY ARE--
...BUT YOU'VE GOT THIS... DEEP FAITH IN THE DOCTOR AND EVERYTHING TURNING OUT RIGHT.
WHEREAS I? I JUST REALLY REALLY REALLY WANT TO NOT DIE IN THIS STUPID BOX.
AND I KEEP THINKING:
WE HAVEN'T SEEN
THE DOCTOR IN TWO DAYS
AND THAT MUSCLEBOUND MERCENARY, ABSLOM DAAK?
LAST TIME WE
PASSED THE GARAGE, HIS WAR-ROCKET WAS GONE TOO.
MY POINT IS:
"SOMETIMES A BRIGHT OUTLOOK JUST DOESN'T CUT IT, SQUIRE."
I THINK IT'S TIME WE FACED-UP TO THE POSSIBILITY DAAK'S CAPTURED THE DOCTOR.
PROBABLY... DRAGGED HIM BACK TO THOSE OVERCAST WEIRDOS. BIG FAT BOUNTY REWARD.
"I THINK WE NEED TO ACCEPT THAT... WHEREVER THE DOCTOR IS... WHATEVER THEY'RE DOING TO HIM..."
THE TARDIS HAS GIVEN UP.
RIGHT. WELL.
NO NEED TO SAY IT, CHAPS. I KNOW THE DRILL.
"WE HAVE WAYS OF MAKING YOU TALK", YES?

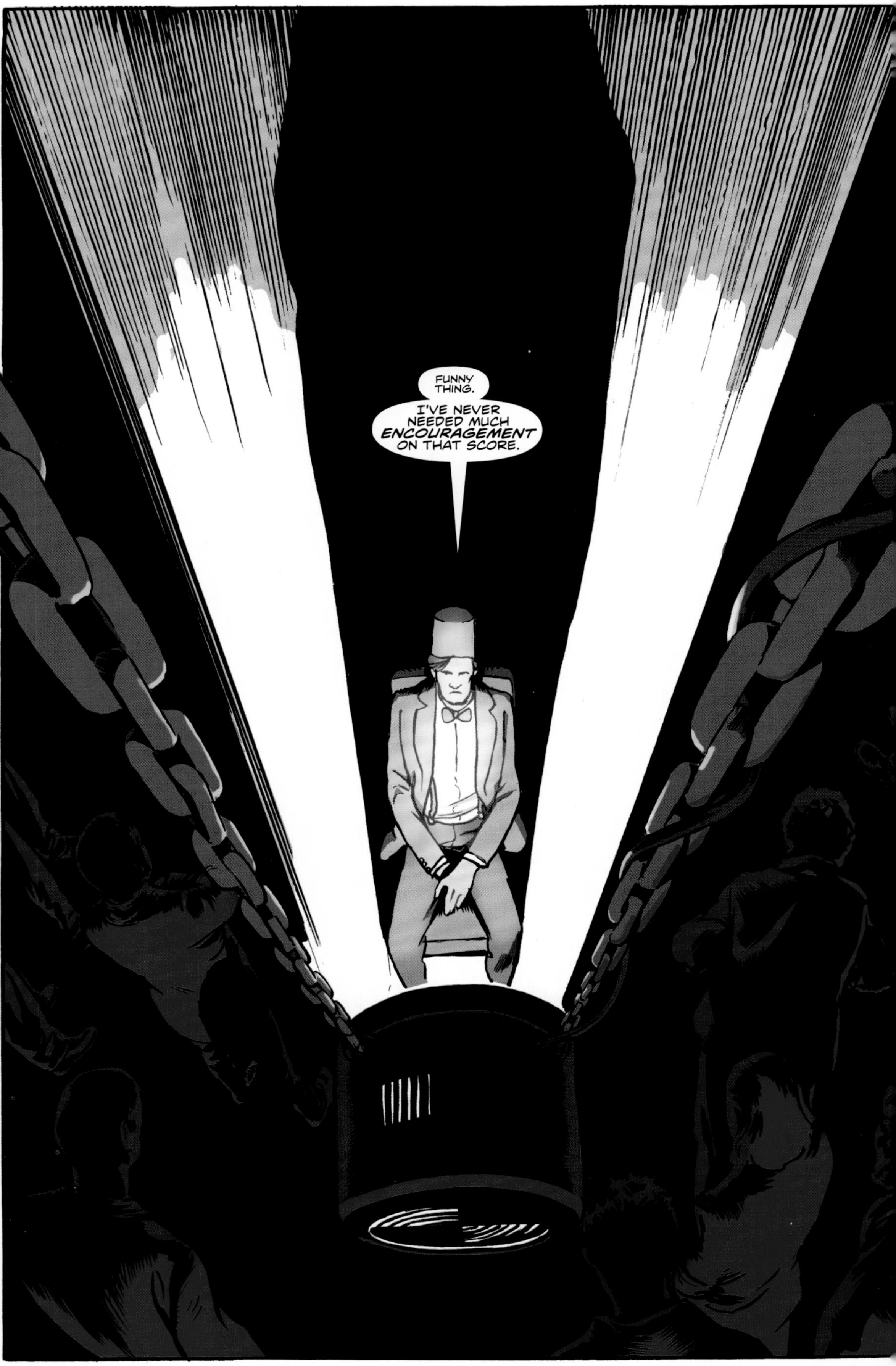
FUNNY THING.
I'VE NEVER NEEDED MUCH ENCOURAGEMENT ON THAT SCORE.

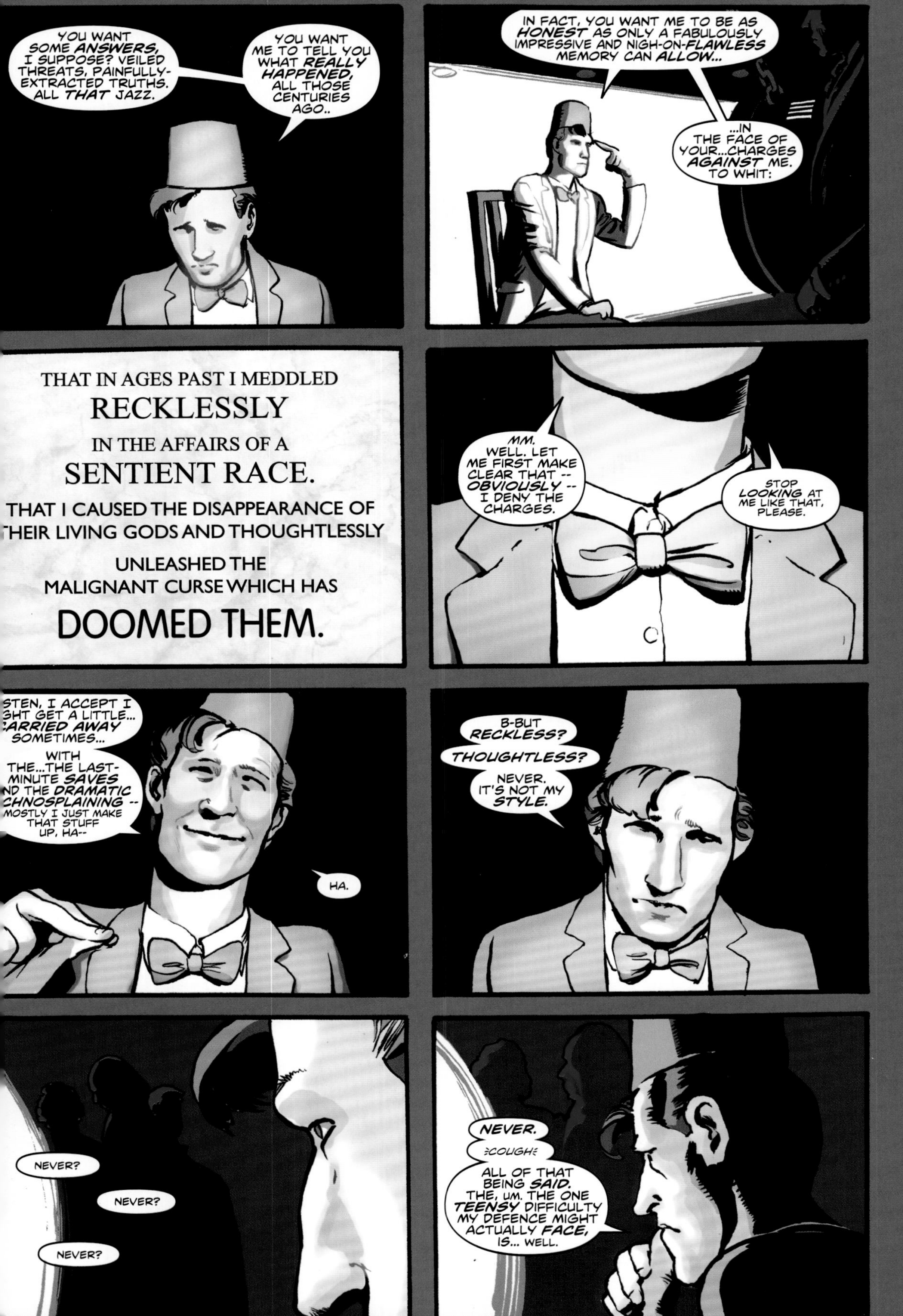

YOU WANT SOME ANSWERS, I SUPPOSE? VEILED THREATS, PAINFULLY-EXTRACTED TRUTHS. ALL THAT JAZZ.
YOU WANT ME TO TELL YOU WHAT REALLY HAPPENED, ALL THOSE CENTURIES AGO..
IN FACT, YOU WANT ME TO BE AS HONEST AS ONLY A FABULOUSLY IMPRESSIVE AND NIGH-ON-FLAWLESS MEMORY CAN ALLOW...
...IN THE FACE OF YOUR...CHARGES AGAINST ME. TO WHIT:
THAT IN AGES PAST I MEDDLED RECKLESSLY IN THE AFFAIRS OF A SENTIENT RACE.
THAT I CAUSED THE DISAPPEARANCE OF THEIR LIVING GODS AND THOUGHTLESSLY UNLEASHED THE MALIGNANT CURSE WHICH HAS DOOMED THEM.
MM. WELL. LET ME FIRST MAKE CLEAR THAT -- OBVIOUSLY -- I DENY THE CHARGES.
STOP LOOKING AT ME LIKE THAT, PLEASE.
STEN, I ACCEPT I GHT GET A LITTLE... CARRIED AWAY SOMETIMES...
WITH THE...THE LAST-MINUTE SAVES ND THE DRAMATIC CHNOSPLAINING -- MOSTLY I JUST MAKE THAT STUFF UP, HA--
HA.
B-BUT RECKLESS?
THOUGHTLESS?
NEVER. IT'S NOT MY STYLE.
NEVER?
NEVER?
NEVER?
NEVER.
COUGH
ALL OF THAT BEING SAID. THE, UM. THE ONE TEENSY DIFFICULTY MY DEFENCE MIGHT ACTUALLY FACE, IS... WELL.

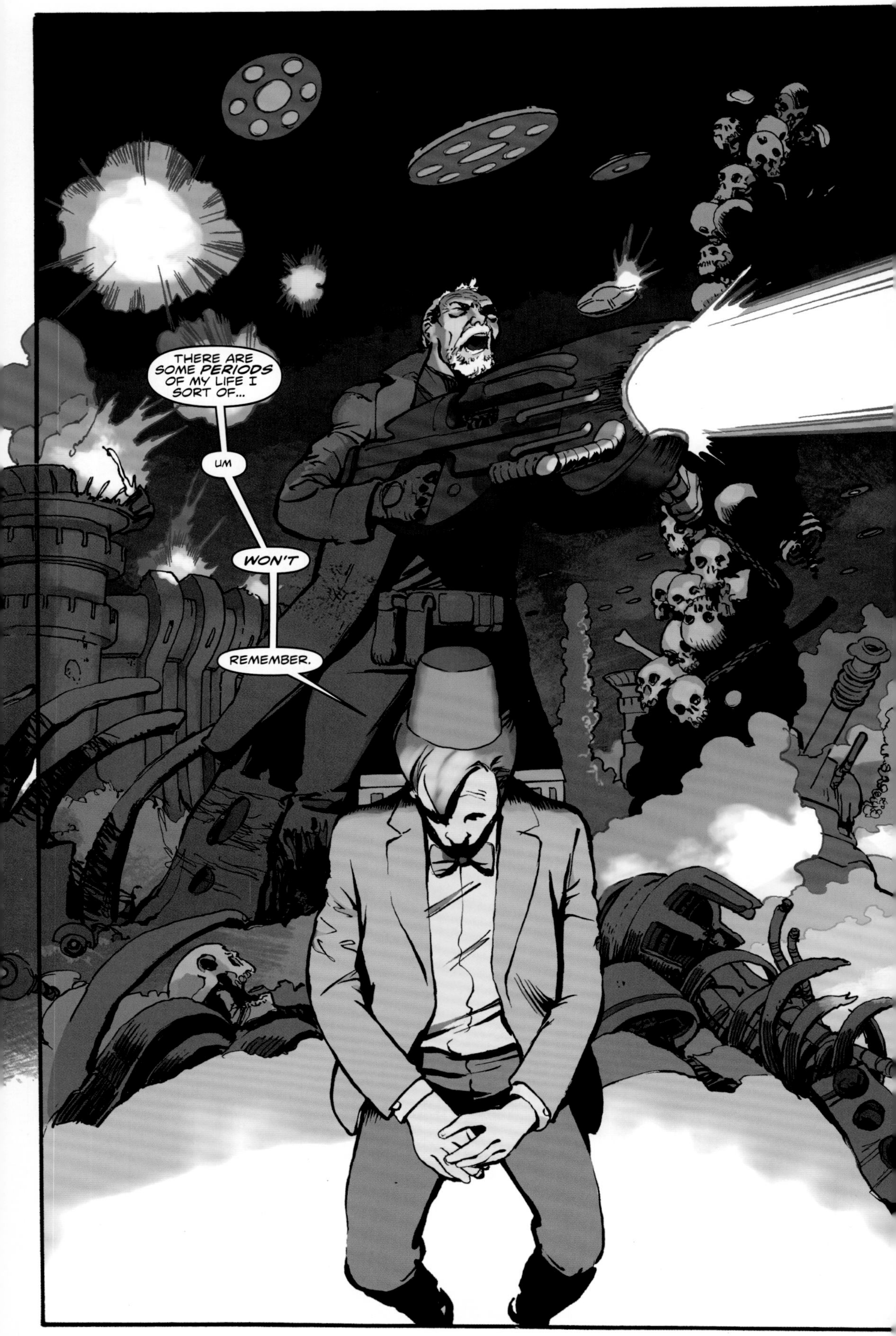
THERE ARE SOME PERIODS OF MY LIFE I SORT OF...
UM
WON'T
REMEMBER.

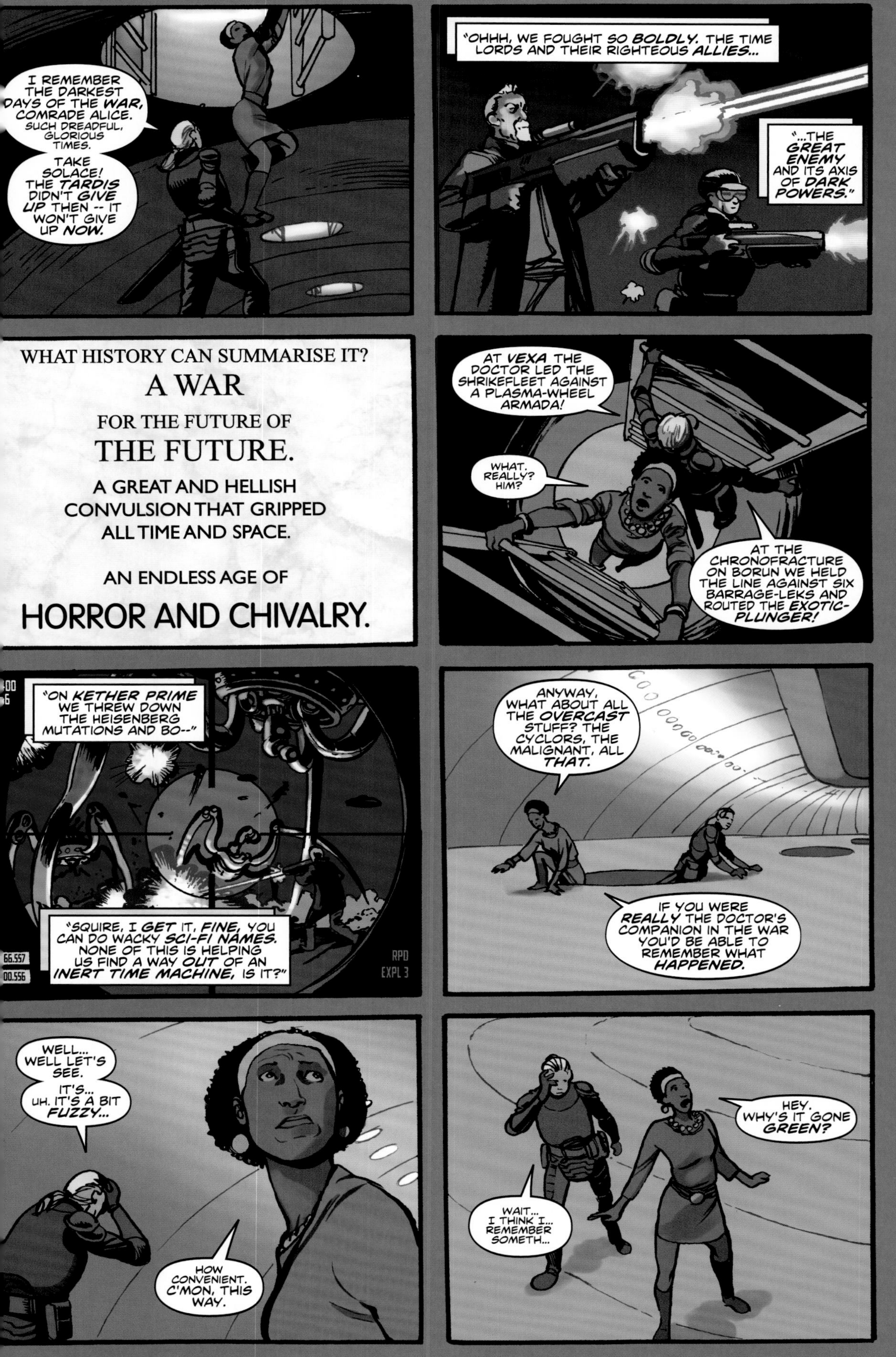
I REMEMBER THE DARKEST DAYS OF THE WAR, COMRADE ALICE. SUCH DREADFUL, GLORIOUS TIMES.
TAKE SOLACE! THE TARDIS DIDN'T GIVE UP THEN -- IT WON'T GIVE UP NOW.
"OHHH, WE FOUGHT SO BOLDLY. THE TIME LORDS AND THEIR RIGHTEOUS ALLIES...
"...THE GREAT ENEMY AND ITS AXIS OF DARK POWERS."
WHAT HISTORY CAN SUMMARISE IT?
A WAR
FOR THE FUTURE OF
THE FUTURE.
A GREAT AND HELLISH CONVULSION THAT GRIPPED ALL TIME AND SPACE.
AN ENDLESS AGE OF
HORROR AND CHIVALRY.
AT VEXA THE DOCTOR LED THE SHRIKEFLEET AGAINST A PLASMA-WHEEL ARMADA!
WHAT. REALLY? HIM?
AT THE CHRONOFRACTURE ON BORUN WE HELD THE LINE AGAINST SIX BARRAGE-LEKS AND ROUTED THE EXOTIC-PLUNGER!
"ON KETHER PRIME WE THREW DOWN THE HEISENBERG MUTATIONS AND BO--"
"SQUIRE, I GET IT, FINE, YOU CAN DO WACKY SCI-FI NAMES. NONE OF THIS IS HELPING US FIND A WAY OUT OF AN INERT TIME MACHINE, IS IT?"
66.557
00.556
RPD
EXPL 3
ANYWAY, WHAT ABOUT ALL THE OVERCAST STUFF? THE CYCLORS, THE MALIGNANT, ALL THAT.
IF YOU WERE REALLY THE DOCTOR'S COMPANION IN THE WAR YOU'D BE ABLE TO REMEMBER WHAT HAPPENED.
WELL... WELL LET'S SEE.
IT'S... UH. IT'S A BIT FUZZY...
HOW CONVENIENT. C'MON, THIS WAY.
HEY. WHY'S IT GONE GREEN?
WAIT... I THINK I... REMEMBER SOMETH...

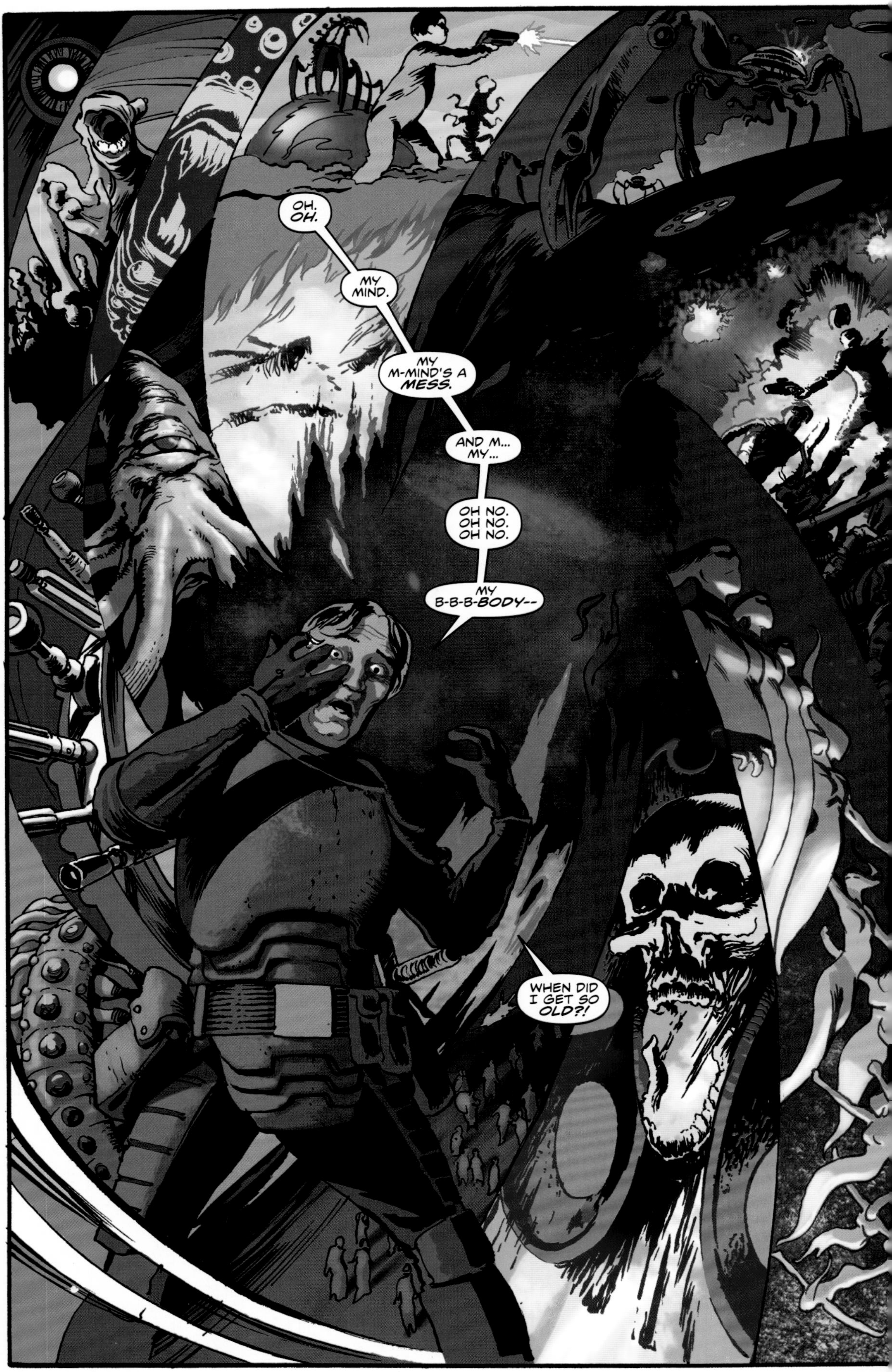
OH. OH.
MY MIND.
MY M-MIND'S A MESS.
AND M... MY...
OH NO. OH NO. OH NO.
MY B-B-B-BODY--
WHEN DID I GET SO OLD?!

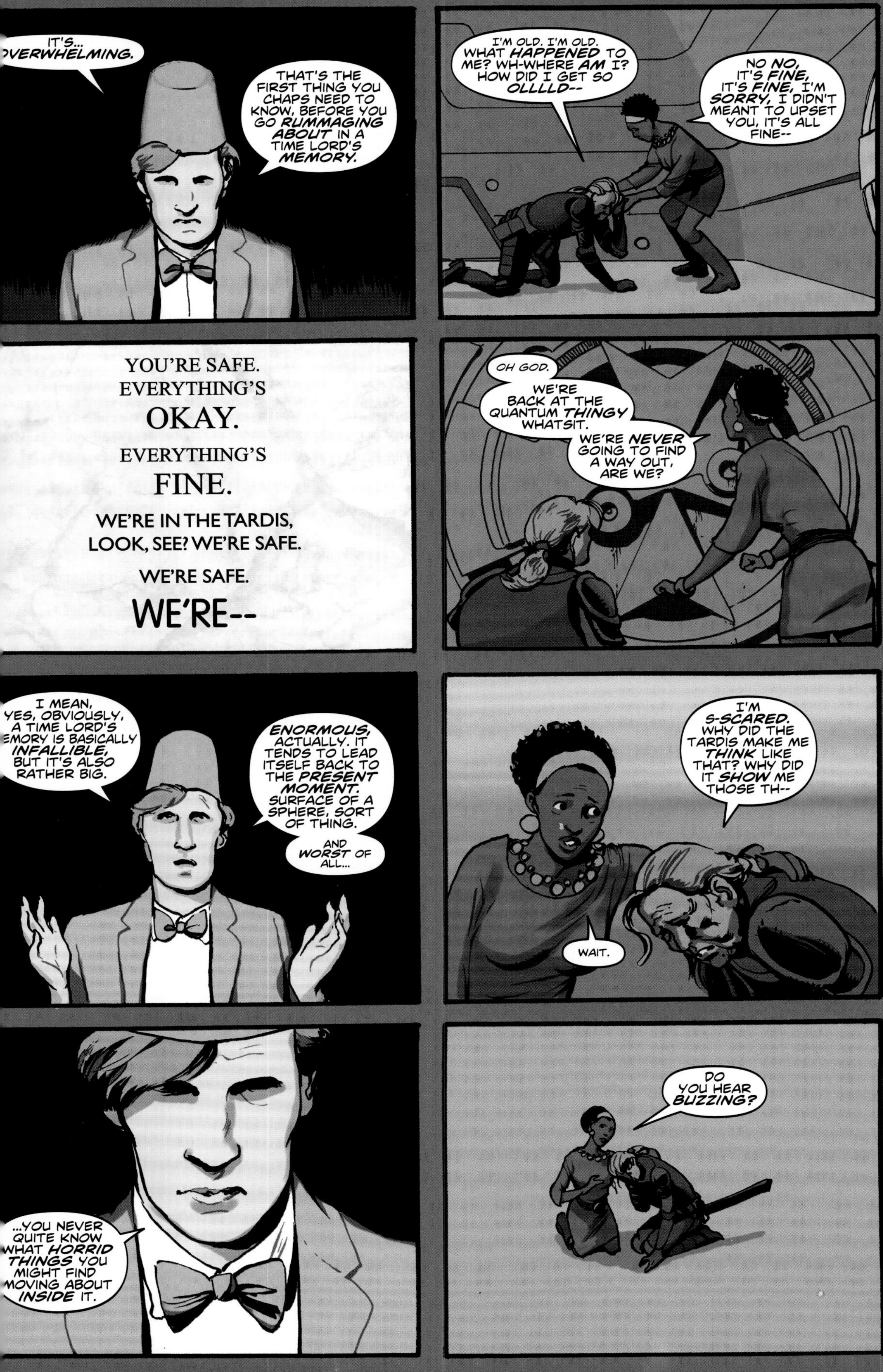
IT'S... OVERWHELMING.
THAT'S THE FIRST THING YOU CHAPS NEED TO KNOW, BEFORE YOU GO **RUMMAGING ABOUT** IN A TIME LORD'S **MEMORY.**
I'M OLD. I'M OLD. WHAT **HAPPENED** TO ME? WH-WHERE **AM** I? HOW DID I GET SO **OLLLLD--**
NO **NO,** IT'S **FINE,** IT'S **FINE,** I'M **SORRY,** I DIDN'T MEANT TO UPSET YOU, IT'S ALL FINE--
YOU'RE SAFE.
EVERYTHING'S
OKAY.
EVERYTHING'S
FINE.
WE'RE IN THE TARDIS,
LOOK, SEE? WE'RE SAFE.
WE'RE SAFE.
WE'RE--
OH GOD.
WE'RE BACK AT THE QUANTUM **THINGY** WHATSIT.
WE'RE **NEVER** GOING TO FIND A WAY OUT, ARE WE?
I MEAN, YES, OBVIOUSLY, A TIME LORD'S EMORY IS BASICALLY **INFALLIBLE,** BUT IT'S ALSO RATHER BIG.
ENORMOUS, ACTUALLY. IT TENDS TO LEAD ITSELF BACK TO THE **PRESENT MOMENT.** SURFACE OF A SPHERE, SORT OF THING.
AND **WORST** OF ALL...
I'M **S-SCARED.** WHY DID THE TARDIS MAKE ME **THINK** LIKE THAT? WHY DID IT **SHOW** ME THOSE TH--
WAIT.
...YOU NEVER QUITE KNOW WHAT **HORRID THINGS** YOU MIGHT FIND MOVING ABOUT **INSIDE** IT.
DO YOU HEAR **BUZZING?**

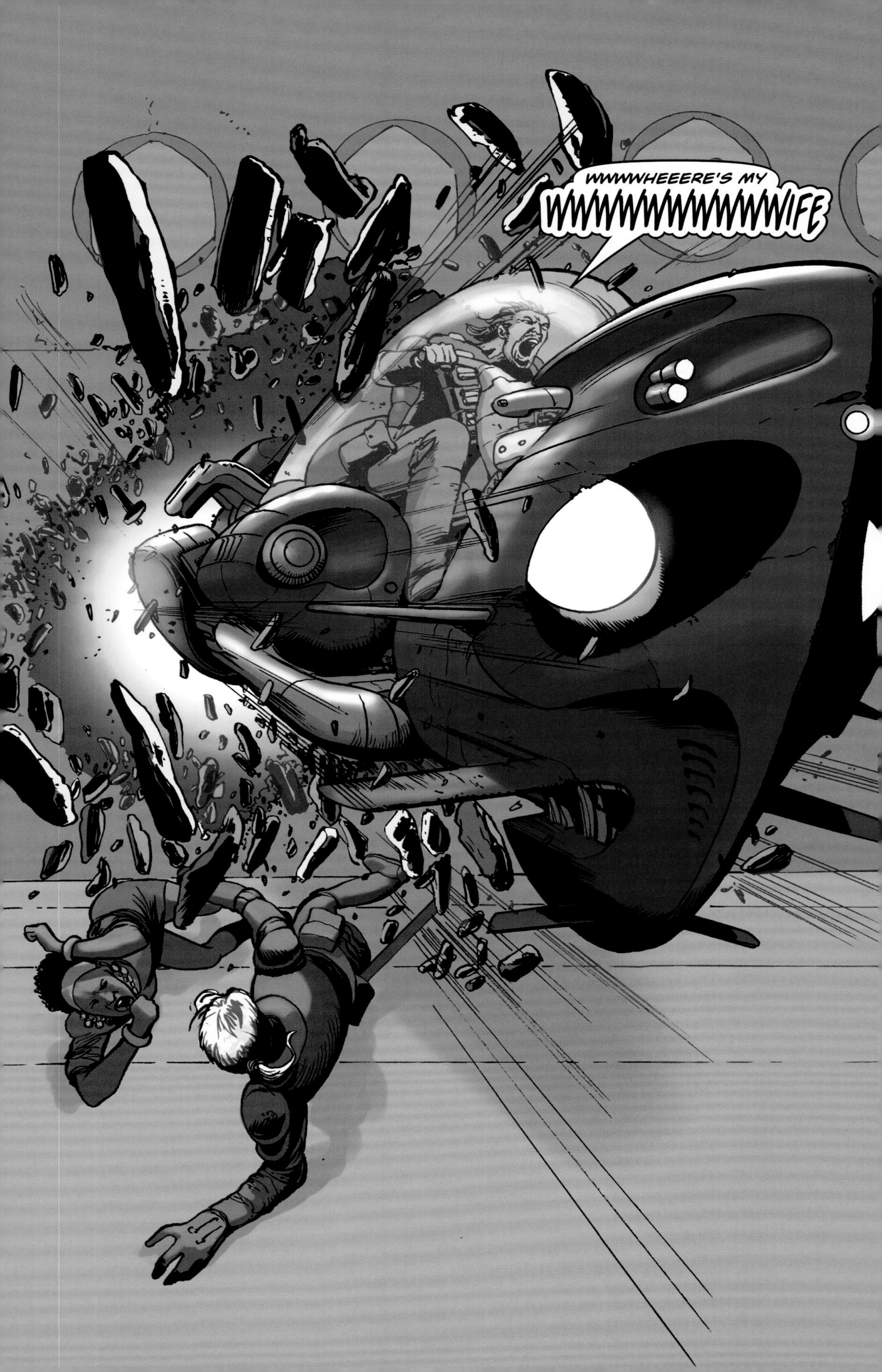
WWWWHEEERE'S MY
WWWWWWWWWWWIFE

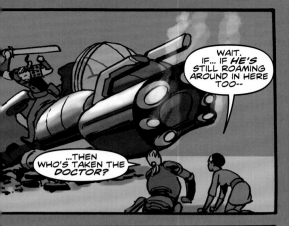

WAIT. IF... IF *HE'S* STILL ROAMING AROUND IN HERE TOO--

...THEN WHO'S TAKEN THE *DOCTOR?*

SO YOU WANT ME TO REMEMBER *THE WAR,* DO YOU?

YOU WANT ME TO THINK A LITTLE *HARDER...* TO DELVE A LITTLE *DEEPER.* WELL.

THAT, OH SHADOWY INTERROGATORS?

THAT'S
WHEN

THINGS GET

COMPLICATED.

THIS! DAMN!

MACHINE!

TOOK! MY! WIFE!

HEY! STOP IT! *ST--*

KZAAAAK

EH

...

BUT THEN IT'S NOT THE *WHOLE* WAR YOU WANT ME TO *REMEMBER* IS IT? THIS ISN'T *ABOUT* THE...THE WAY IT ENDED.

NO. YOU'RE AFTER A FUNNY LITTLE *NIBBLE* OUT ON THE *CRUST...*

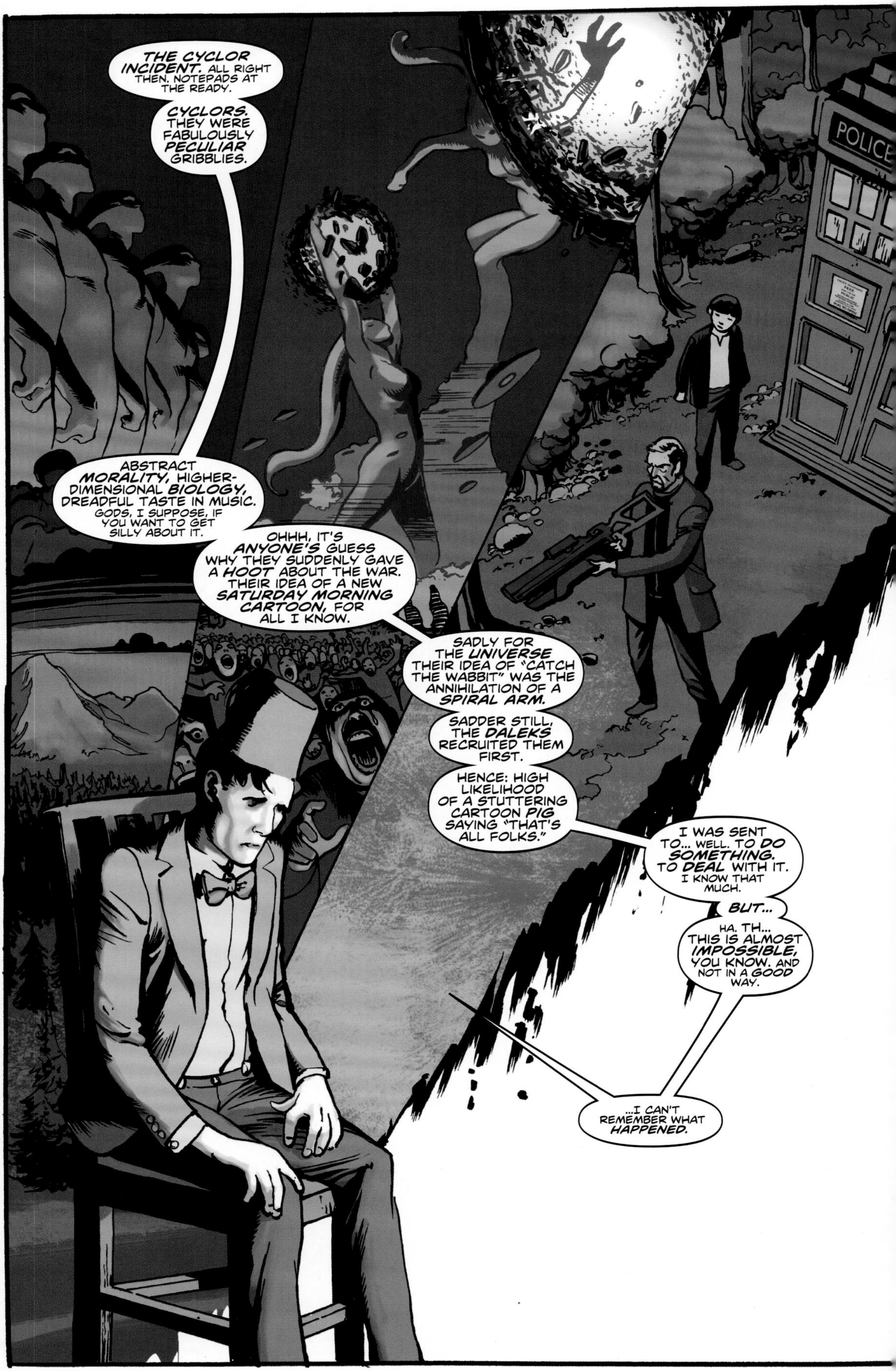
THE CYCLOR INCIDENT. ALL RIGHT THEN. NOTEPADS AT THE READY.
CYCLORS. THEY WERE FABULOUSLY PECULIAR GRIBBLIES.
ABSTRACT MORALITY, HIGHER-DIMENSIONAL BIOLOGY, DREADFUL TASTE IN MUSIC. GODS, I SUPPOSE, IF YOU WANT TO GET SILLY ABOUT IT.
OHHH, IT'S ANYONE'S GUESS WHY THEY SUDDENLY GAVE A HOOT ABOUT THE WAR. THEIR IDEA OF A NEW SATURDAY MORNING CARTOON, FOR ALL I KNOW.
SADLY FOR THE UNIVERSE THEIR IDEA OF "CATCH THE WABBIT" WAS THE ANNIHILATION OF A SPIRAL ARM.
SADDER STILL, THE DALEKS RECRUITED THEM FIRST.
HENCE: HIGH LIKELIHOOD OF A STUTTERING CARTOON PIG SAYING "THAT'S ALL FOLKS."
I WAS SENT TO... WELL. TO DO SOMETHING. TO DEAL WITH IT. I KNOW THAT MUCH.
BUT...
HA. TH... THIS IS ALMOST IMPOSSIBLE, YOU KNOW. AND NOT IN A GOOD WAY.
...I CAN'T REMEMBER WHAT HAPPENED.
POLICE

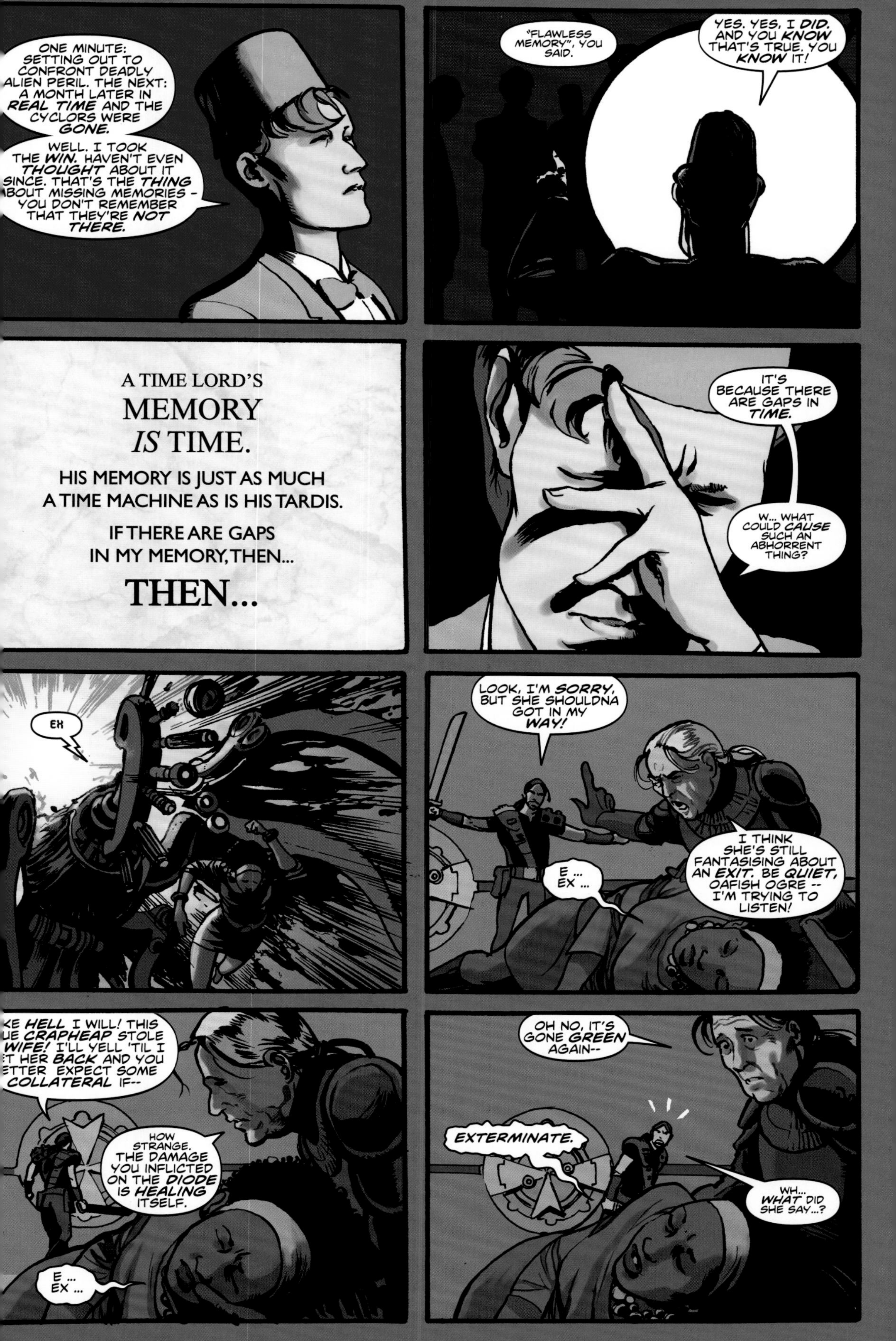
ONE MINUTE: SETTING OUT TO CONFRONT DEADLY ALIEN PERIL. THE NEXT: A MONTH LATER IN REAL TIME AND THE CYCLORS WERE GONE.
WELL. I TOOK THE WIN. HAVEN'T EVEN THOUGHT ABOUT IT SINCE. THAT'S THE THING ABOUT MISSING MEMORIES - YOU DON'T REMEMBER THAT THEY'RE NOT THERE.
"FLAWLESS MEMORY", YOU SAID.
YES. YES, I DID. AND YOU KNOW THAT'S TRUE. YOU KNOW IT!
A TIME LORD'S MEMORY IS TIME.
HIS MEMORY IS JUST AS MUCH A TIME MACHINE AS IS HIS TARDIS.
IF THERE ARE GAPS IN MY MEMORY, THEN...
THEN...
IT'S BECAUSE THERE ARE GAPS IN TIME.
W... WHAT COULD CAUSE SUCH AN ABHORRENT THING?
EX
LOOK, I'M SORRY, BUT SHE SHOULDNA GOT IN MY WAY!
E ... EX ...
I THINK SHE'S STILL FANTASISING ABOUT AN EXIT. BE QUIET, OAFISH OGRE -- I'M TRYING TO LISTEN!
KE HELL I WILL! THIS UE CRAPHEAP STOLE WIFE! I'LL YELL 'TIL I T HER BACK AND YOU ETTER EXPECT SOME COLLATERAL IF--
HOW STRANGE. THE DAMAGE YOU INFLICTED ON THE DIODE IS HEALING ITSELF.
E ... EX ...
OH NO, IT'S GONE GREEN AGAIN--
EXTERMINATE.
WH... WHAT DID SHE SAY...?

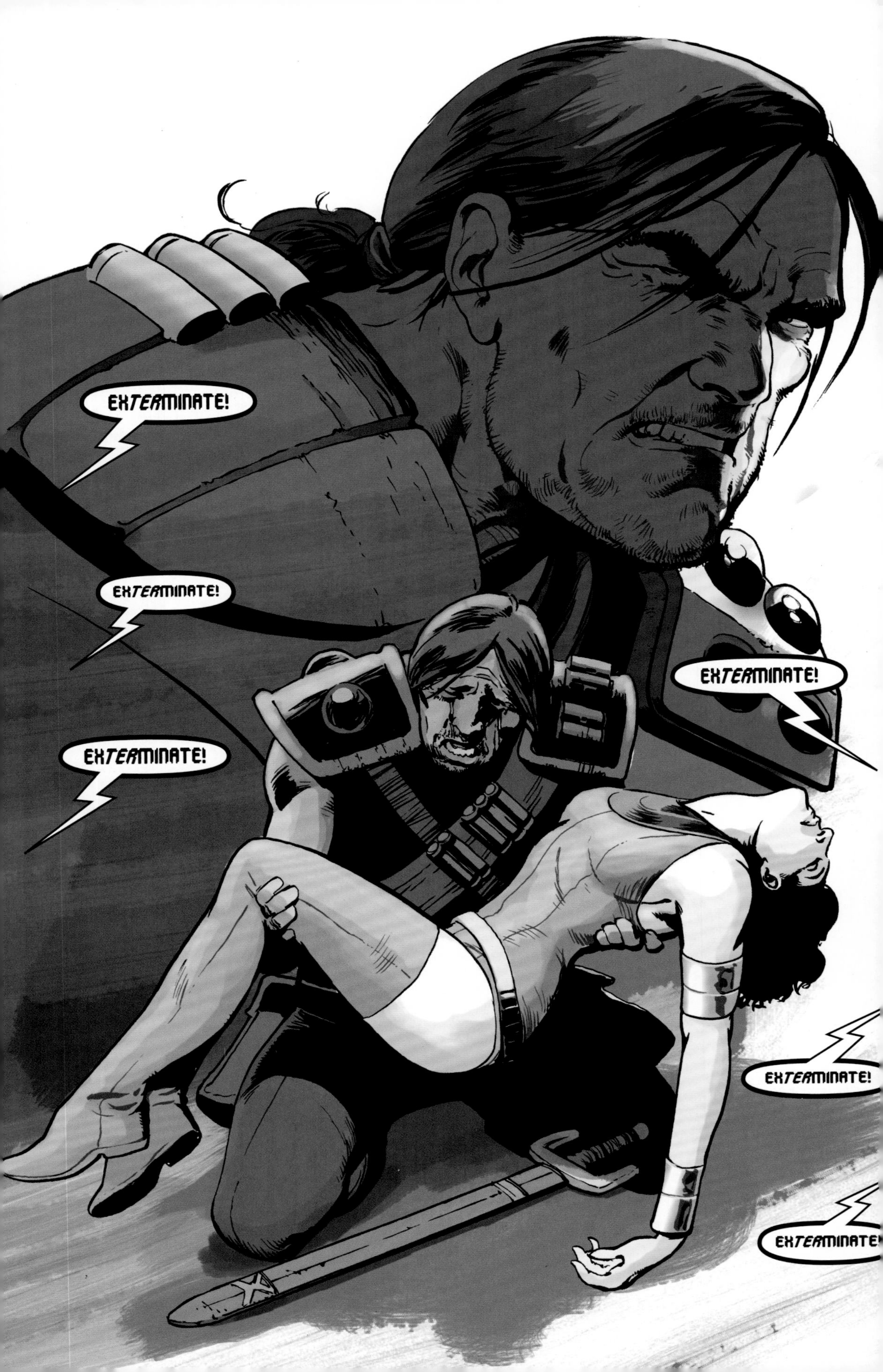
EXTERMINATE!
EXTERMINATE!
EXTERMINATE!
EXTERMINATE!
EXTERMINATE!
EXTERMINATE

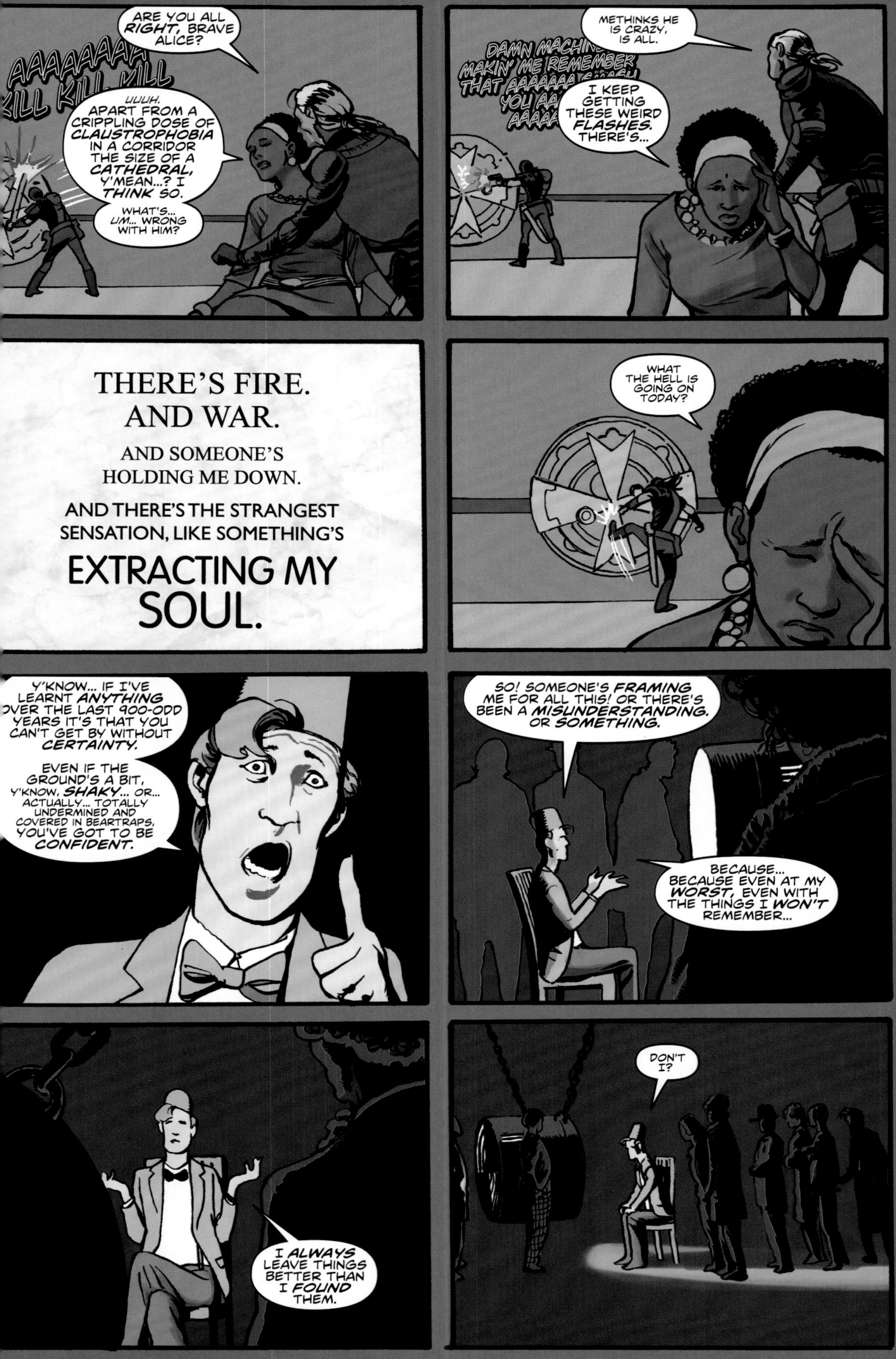

ARE YOU ALL RIGHT, BRAVE ALICE?
AAAAAAAA
ILL KILL KILL
UUUH. APART FROM A CRIPPLING DOSE OF CLAUSTROPHOBIA IN A CORRIDOR THE SIZE OF A CATHEDRAL, Y'MEAN...? I THINK SO.
WHAT'S... UM... WRONG WITH HIM?
METHINKS HE IS CRAZY, IS ALL.
MAKIN' ME REMEMBER
I KEEP GETTING THESE WEIRD FLASHES. THERE'S...
THERE'S FIRE.
AND WAR.
AND SOMEONE'S HOLDING ME DOWN.
AND THERE'S THE STRANGEST SENSATION, LIKE SOMETHING'S
EXTRACTING MY SOUL.
WHAT THE HELL IS GOING ON TODAY?
Y'KNOW... IF I'VE LEARNT ANYTHING OVER THE LAST 900-ODD YEARS IT'S THAT YOU CAN'T GET BY WITHOUT CERTAINTY.
EVEN IF THE GROUND'S A BIT, Y'KNOW, SHAKY... OR... ACTUALLY... TOTALLY UNDERMINED AND COVERED IN BEARTRAPS, YOU'VE GOT TO BE CONFIDENT.
SO! SOMEONE'S FRAMING ME FOR ALL THIS! OR THERE'S BEEN A MISUNDERSTANDING. OR SOMETHING.
BECAUSE... BECAUSE EVEN AT MY WORST, EVEN WITH THE THINGS I WON'T REMEMBER...
I ALWAYS LEAVE THINGS BETTER THAN I FOUND THEM.
DON'T I?

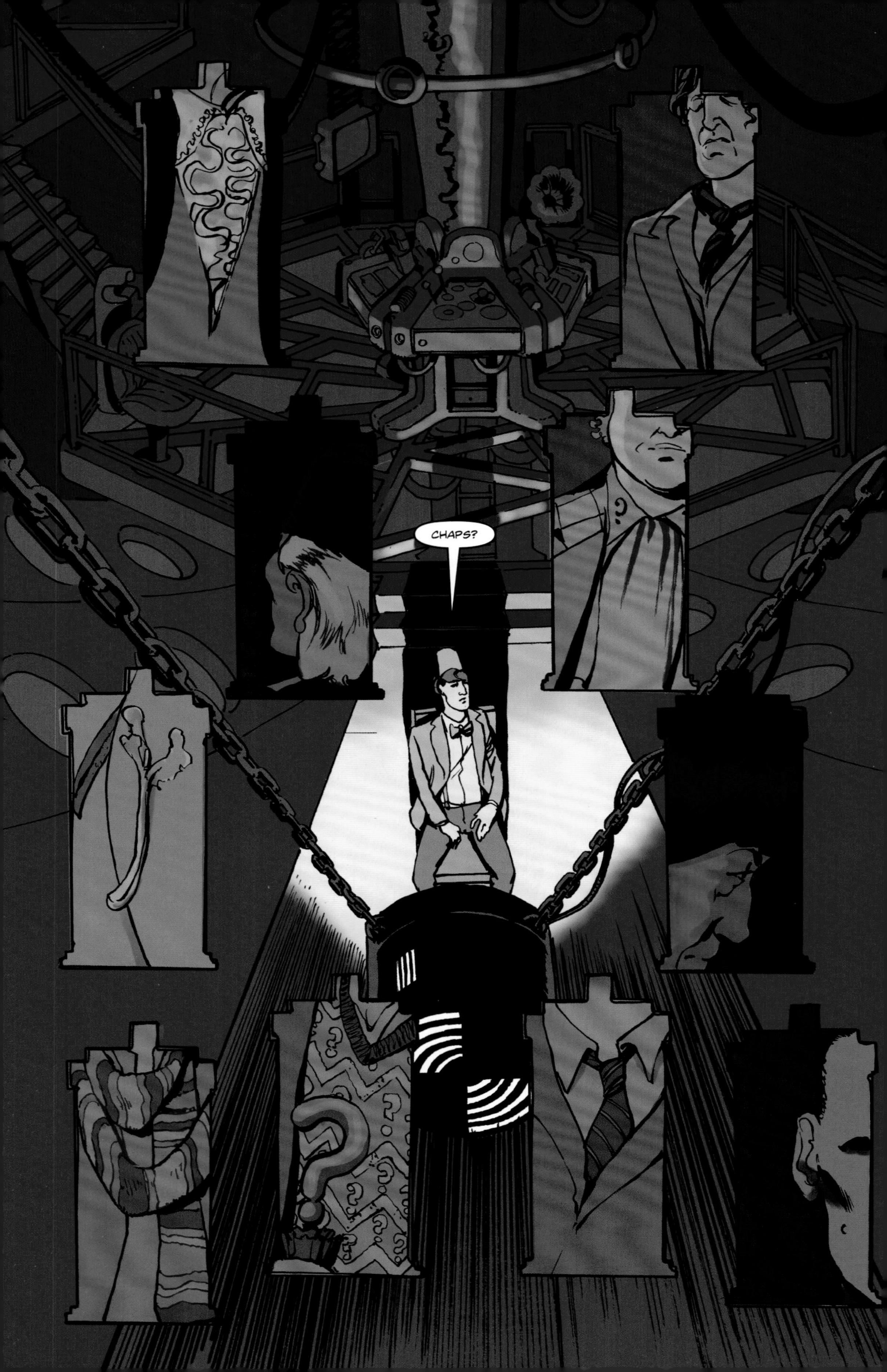
CHAPS?

OOOOOH... I BELIEVE I HAVE SOLVED THIS RIDDLE. IT'S THE TARDIS. IT'S PLAYING A GAME!

YOU KNOW WHAT IT'S LIKE!

ACTUALLY, I DON'T KN--

IT'S CLEVER. IT'S MANIPULATIVE. IT INTENDS THAT WE FIND AND RESCUE THE DOCTOR! SO WHAT DOES IT DO?

IT LACES OUR

MINDS

WITH CUNNING

PROMPTS

EXQUISITELY SELECTED TO FORGE A STALWART TEAM!

ALL PERIL SUCCUMBS BEFORE DUTY, VALOR AND

COMPANIONSHIP!

THAT IS BULL, LADY!

I AIN'T HERE TO BE ON NO STINKIN' TEAM, AN' SHOWIN' ME WHAT IT SHOWED ME JUST MAKES ME WANNA CUT IT EVEN WORSE!

I'M HERE TO GET MY WIFE AN' MY DAMN BOUNTY MONEY AND TH--

SO YOU SAY, BRAVE SAVAGE. BUT I BELIEVE THE TARDIS SEES THROUGH YOUR ROUGH EXTERIOR TO THE CHIVALROUS DO-GOODER BENEATH, AND W--

UM

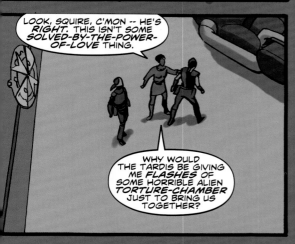

LOOK, SQUIRE, C'MON -- HE'S RIGHT. THIS ISN'T SOME SOLVED-BY-THE-POWER-OF-LOVE THING.

WHY WOULD THE TARDIS BE GIVING ME FLASHES OF SOME HORRIBLE ALIEN TORTURE-CHAMBER JUST TO BRING US TOGETHER?

MAYBE IT'S DIFFERENT FOR YOU. THAT DOOHICKY WAS BROKEN WHEN YOU GOT ZAPPED, AFTER ALL.

SORRY 'BOUT THAT.

INTERESTING POINT. WHAT WERE YOU THINKING OF AT THE TIME, ALICE?

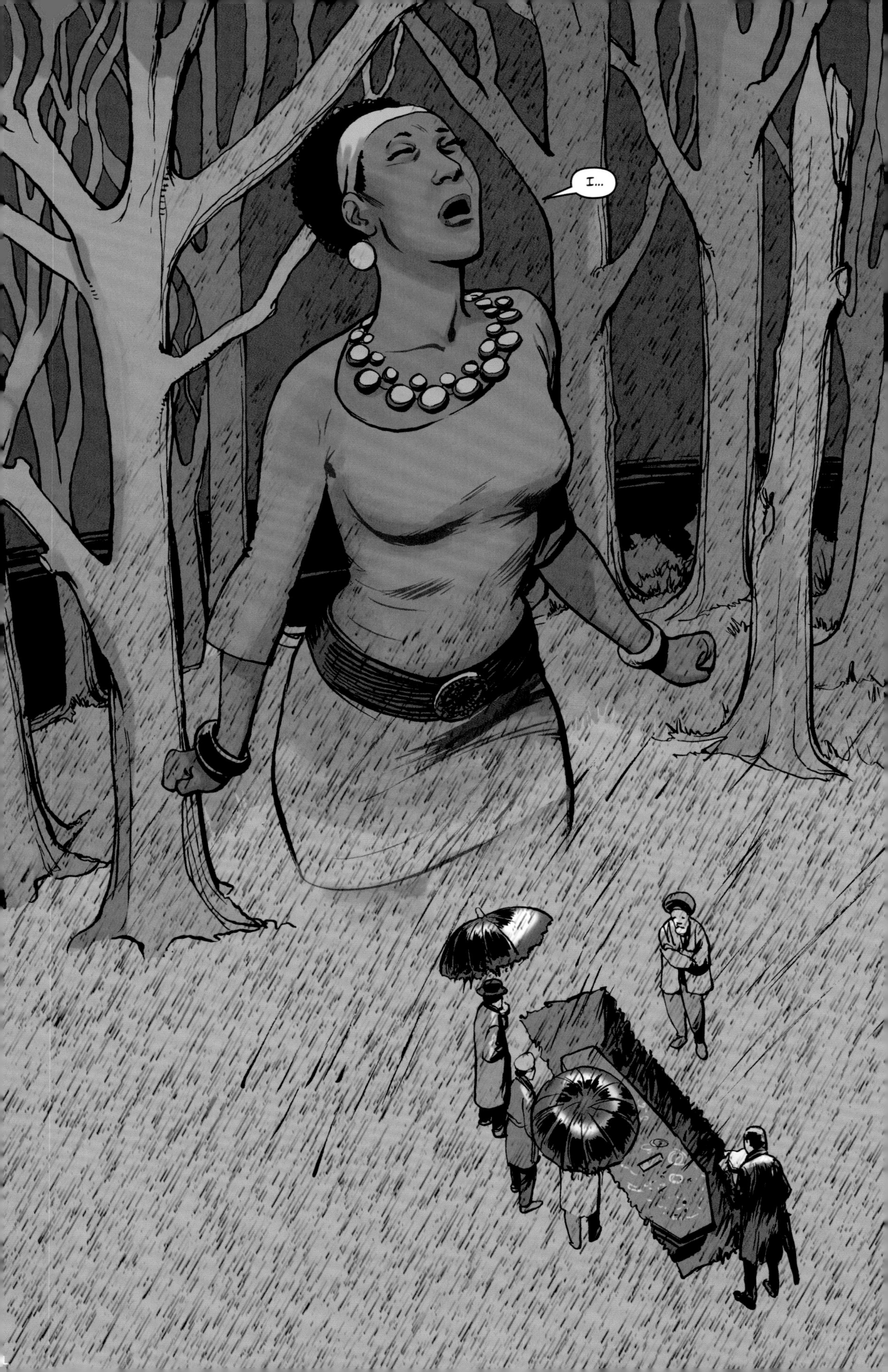
I...

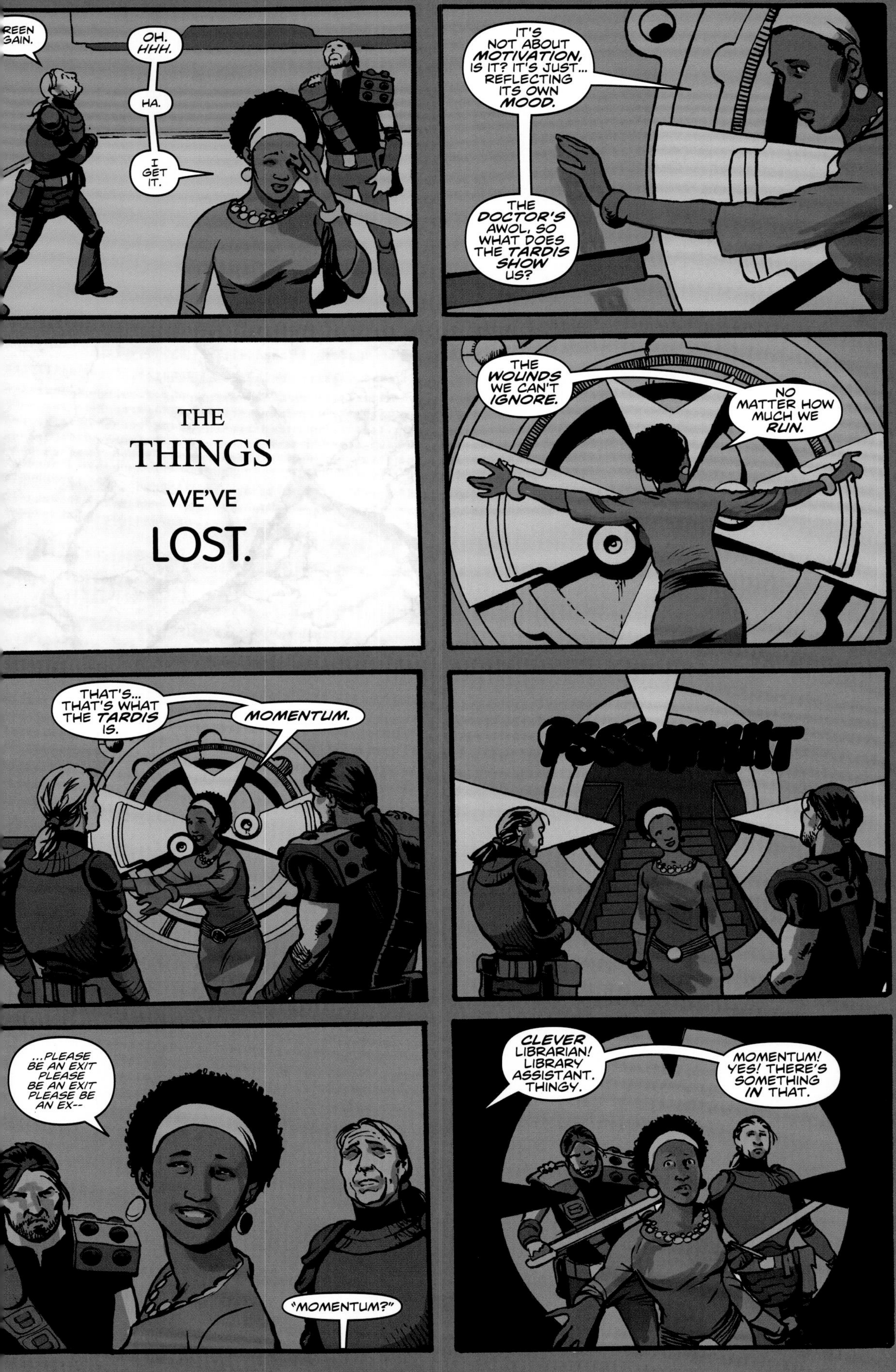

REEN
GAIN.
OH. HHH.
HA.
I GET IT.
IT'S NOT ABOUT MOTIVATION, IS IT? IT'S JUST... REFLECTING ITS OWN MOOD.
THE DOCTOR'S AWOL, SO WHAT DOES THE TARDIS SHOW US?
THE THINGS WE'VE LOST.
THE WOUNDS WE CAN'T IGNORE.
NO MATTER HOW MUCH WE RUN.
THAT'S... THAT'S WHAT THE TARDIS IS.
MOMENTUM.
...PLEASE BE AN EXIT PLEASE BE AN EXIT PLEASE BE AN EX--
"MOMENTUM?"
CLEVER LIBRARIAN! LIBRARY ASSISTANT. THINGY.
MOMENTUM! YES! THERE'S SOMETHING IN THAT.

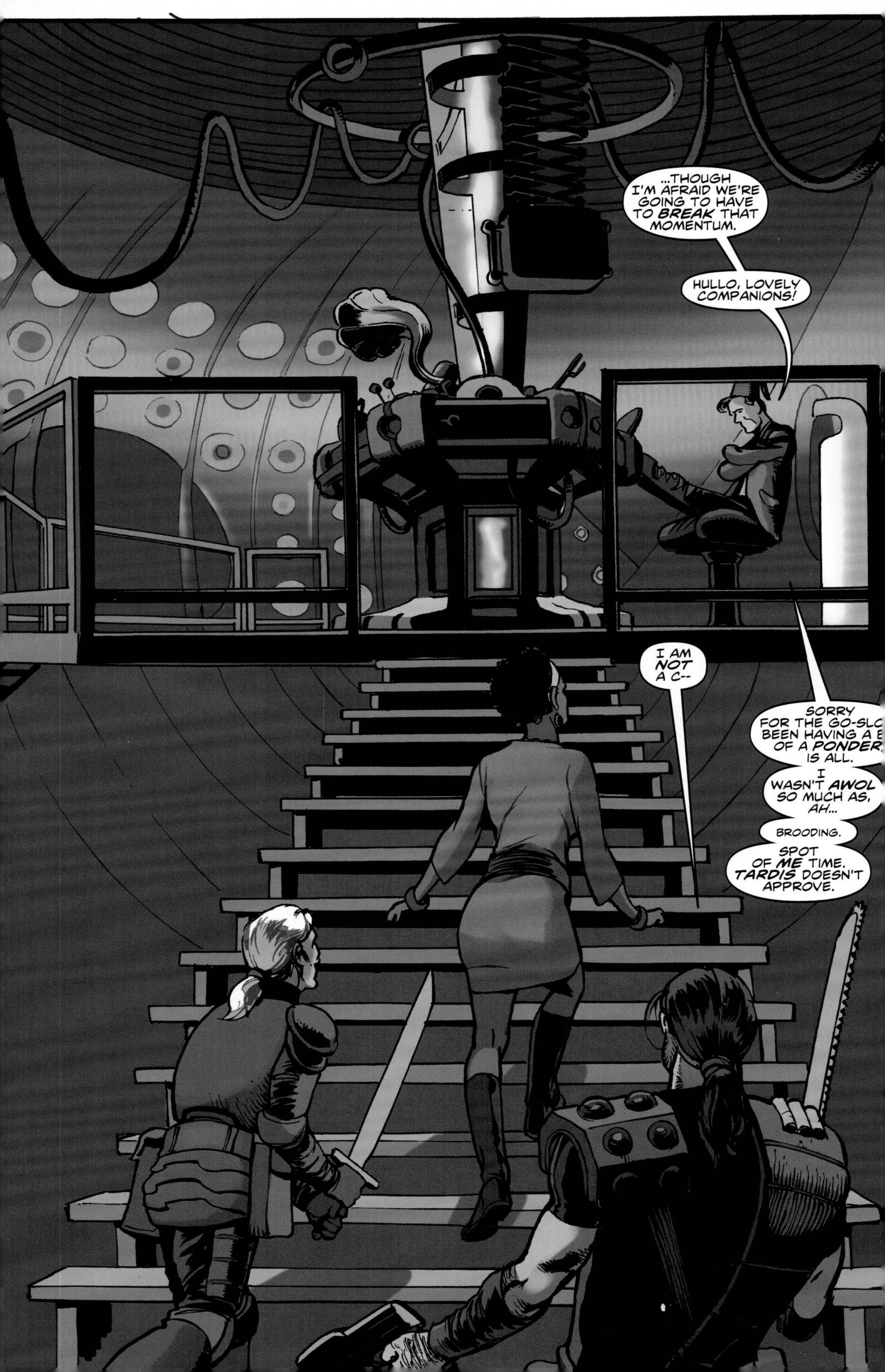
...THOUGH I'M AFRAID WE'RE GOING TO HAVE TO BREAK THAT MOMENTUM.
HULLO, LOVELY COMPANIONS!
I AM NOT A C--
SORRY FOR THE GO-SLO BEEN HAVING A B OF A PONDER, IS ALL.
I WASN'T AWOL SO MUCH AS, AH...
BROODING.
SPOT OF ME TIME. TARDIS DOESN'T APPROVE.

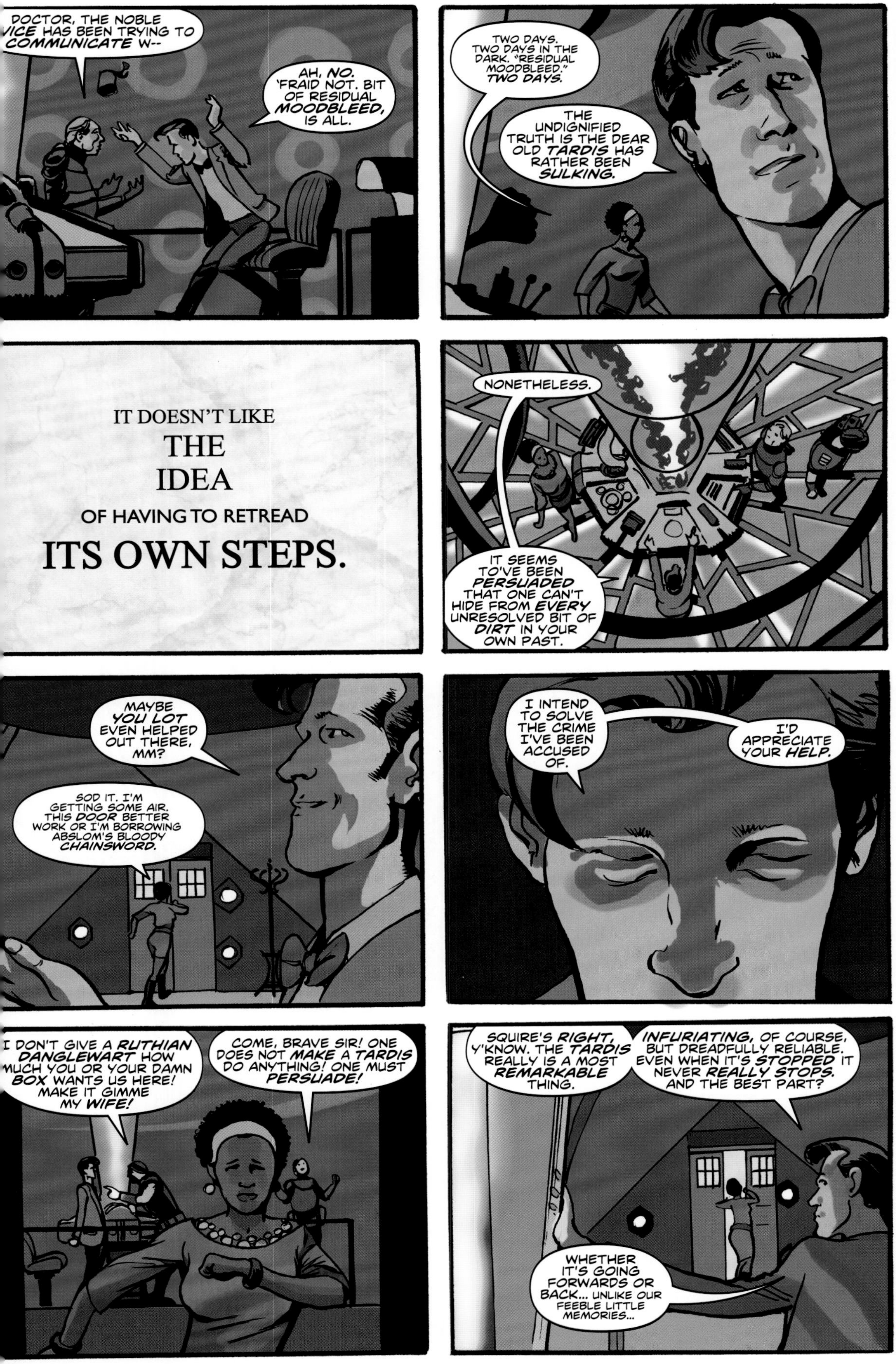
DOCTOR, THE NOBLE VICE HAS BEEN TRYING TO COMMUNICATE W--
AH, NO. 'FRAID NOT. BIT OF RESIDUAL MOODBLEED, IS ALL.
TWO DAYS. TWO DAYS IN THE DARK. "RESIDUAL MOODBLEED." TWO DAYS.
THE UNDIGNIFIED TRUTH IS THE DEAR OLD TARDIS HAS RATHER BEEN SULKING.
IT DOESN'T LIKE THE IDEA OF HAVING TO RETREAD ITS OWN STEPS.
NONETHELESS.
IT SEEMS TO'VE BEEN PERSUADED THAT ONE CAN'T HIDE FROM EVERY UNRESOLVED BIT OF DIRT IN YOUR OWN PAST.
MAYBE YOU LOT EVEN HELPED OUT THERE, MM?
SOD IT. I'M GETTING SOME AIR. THIS DOOR BETTER WORK OR I'M BORROWING ABSLOM'S BLOODY CHAINSWORD.
I INTEND TO SOLVE THE CRIME I'VE BEEN ACCUSED OF.
I'D APPRECIATE YOUR HELP.
I DON'T GIVE A RUTHIAN DANGLEWART HOW MUCH YOU OR YOUR DAMN BOX WANTS US HERE! MAKE IT GIMME MY WIFE!
COME, BRAVE SIR! ONE DOES NOT MAKE A TARDIS DO ANYTHING! ONE MUST PERSUADE!
SQUIRE'S RIGHT, Y'KNOW. THE TARDIS REALLY IS A MOST REMARKABLE THING.
INFURIATING, OF COURSE, BUT DREADFULLY RELIABLE. EVEN WHEN IT'S STOPPED IT NEVER REALLY STOPS. AND THE BEST PART?
WHETHER IT'S GOING FORWARDS OR BACK... UNLIKE OUR FEEBLE LITTLE MEMORIES...

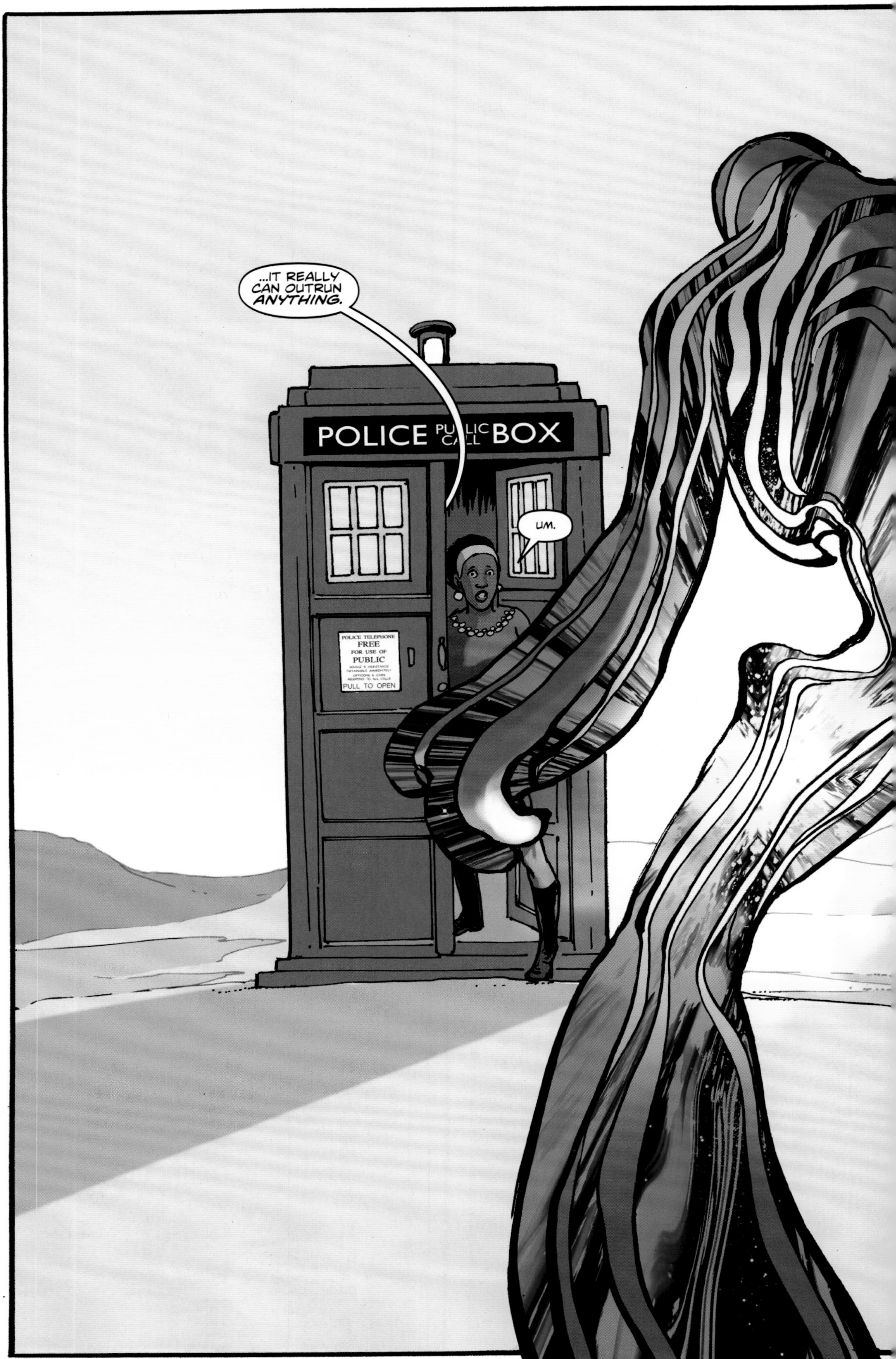
...IT REALLY CAN OUTRUN *ANYTHING.*
POLICE PUBLIC CALL BOX
UM.
POLICE TELEPHONE
FREE
FOR USE OF
PUBLIC
PULL TO OPEN

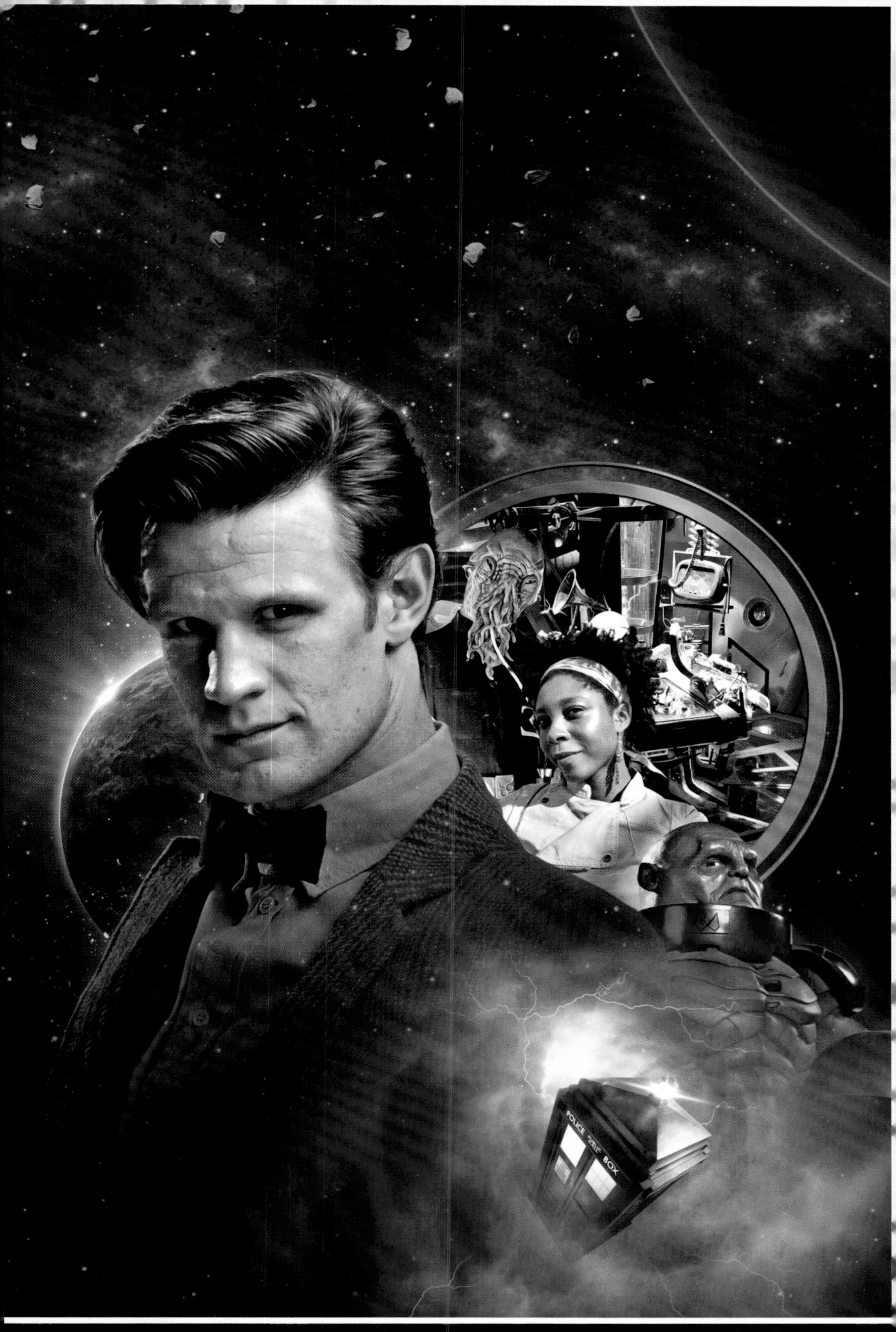
POLICE BOX

11D #2.4 Cover B: WILL BROOKS

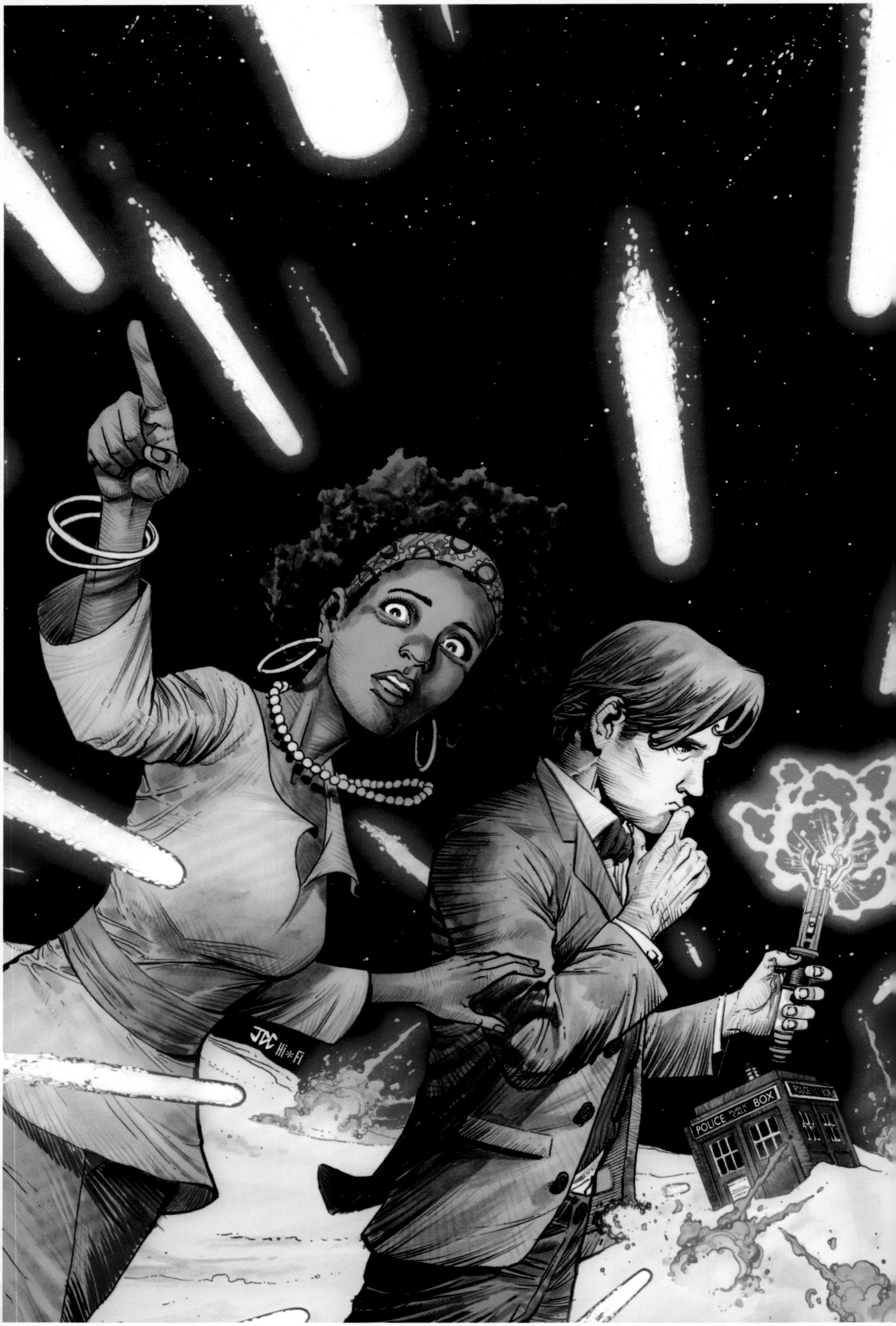
POLICE PUBLIC CALL BOX

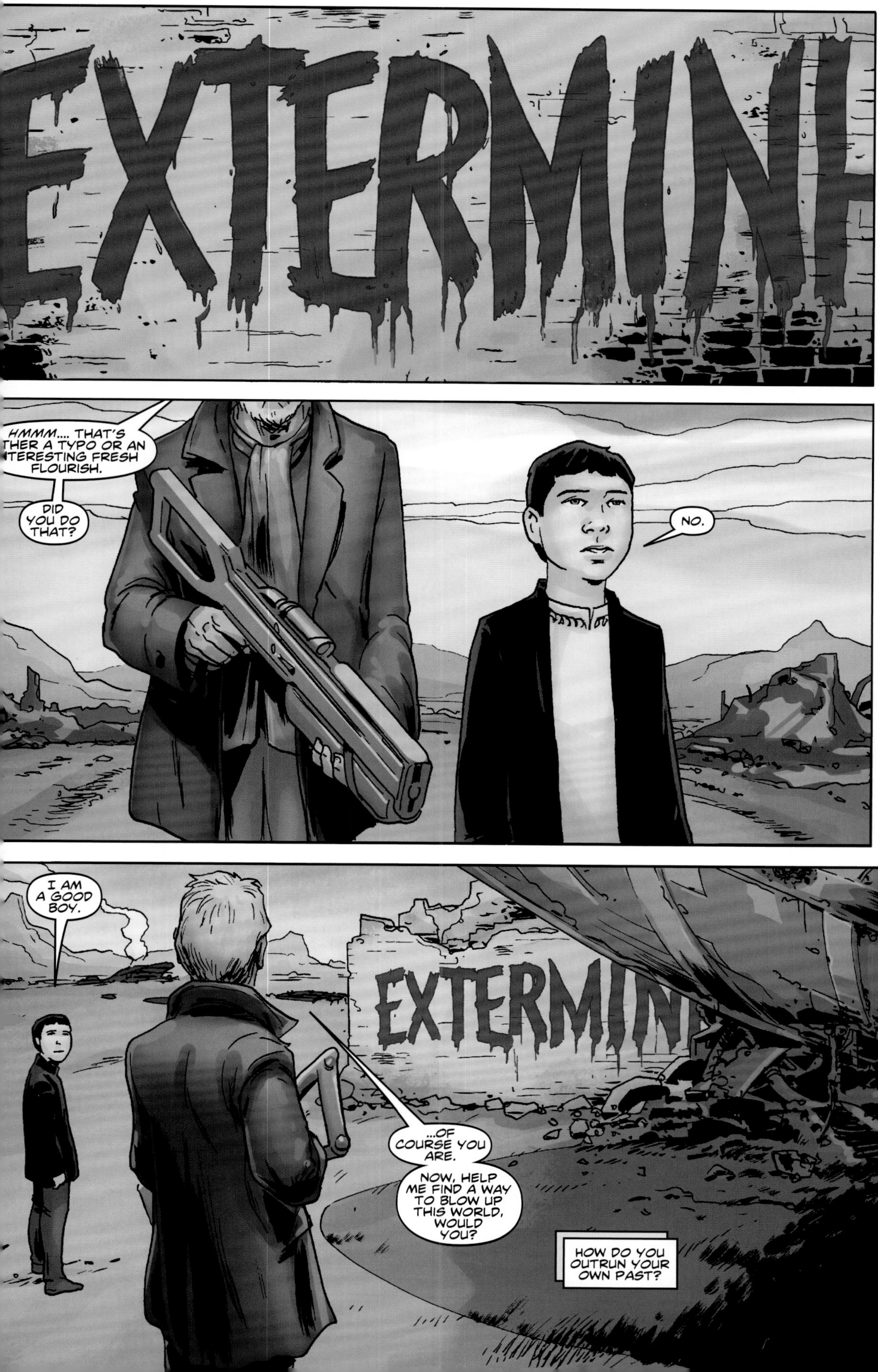
EXTERMIN
HMMM.... THAT'S THER A TYPO OR AN TERESTING FRESH FLOURISH.
DID YOU DO THAT?
NO.
I AM A GOOD BOY.
EXTERMIN
...OF COURSE YOU ARE.
NOW, HELP ME FIND A WAY TO BLOW UP THIS WORLD, WOULD YOU?
HOW DO YOU OUTRUN YOUR OWN PAST?

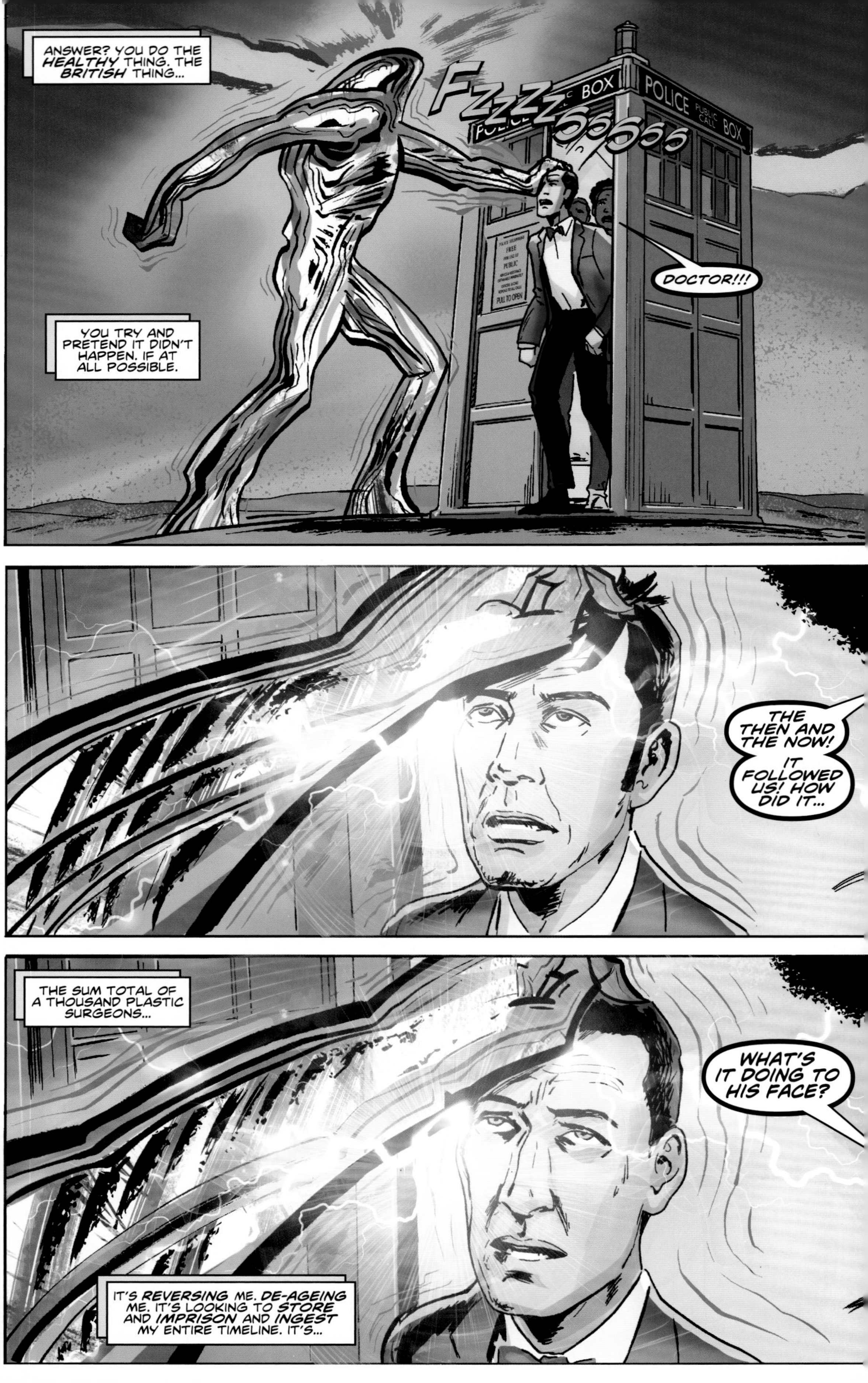
ANSWER? YOU DO THE *HEALTHY* THING. THE *BRITISH* THING...
FZZZZSSSSSS
POLICE BOX
POLICE PUBLIC CALL BOX
FREE
PUBLIC
PULL TO OPEN
DOCTOR!!!
YOU TRY AND PRETEND IT DIDN'T HAPPEN. IF AT ALL POSSIBLE.
THE THEN AND THE NOW! IT FOLLOWED US! HOW DID IT...
THE SUM TOTAL OF A THOUSAND PLASTIC SURGEONS...
WHAT'S IT DOING TO HIS FACE?
IT'S *REVERSING* ME. *DE-AGEING* ME. IT'S LOOKING TO *STORE* AND *IMPRISON* AND *INGEST* MY ENTIRE TIMELINE. IT'S...

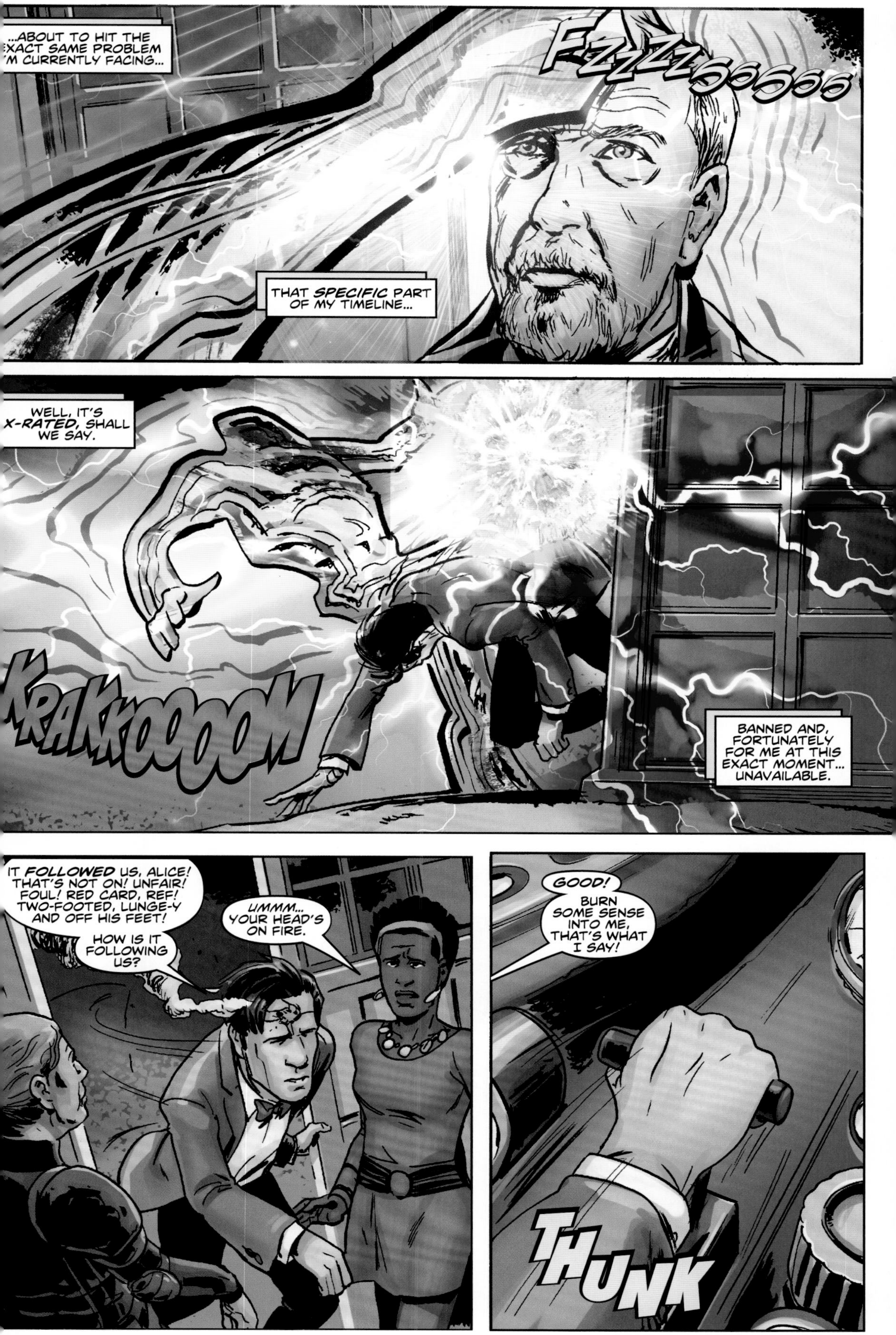
...ABOUT TO HIT THE EXACT SAME PROBLEM I'M CURRENTLY FACING...
FZZZZSSSSSS
THAT SPECIFIC PART OF MY TIMELINE...
WELL, IT'S X-RATED, SHALL WE SAY.
KRAKKOOOOM
BANNED AND, FORTUNATELY FOR ME AT THIS EXACT MOMENT... UNAVAILABLE.
IT FOLLOWED US, ALICE! THAT'S NOT ON! UNFAIR! FOUL! RED CARD, REF! TWO-FOOTED, LUNGE-Y AND OFF HIS FEET!
HOW IS IT FOLLOWING US?
UMMM... YOUR HEAD'S ON FIRE.
GOOD! BURN SOME SENSE INTO ME, THAT'S WHAT I SAY!
THUNK

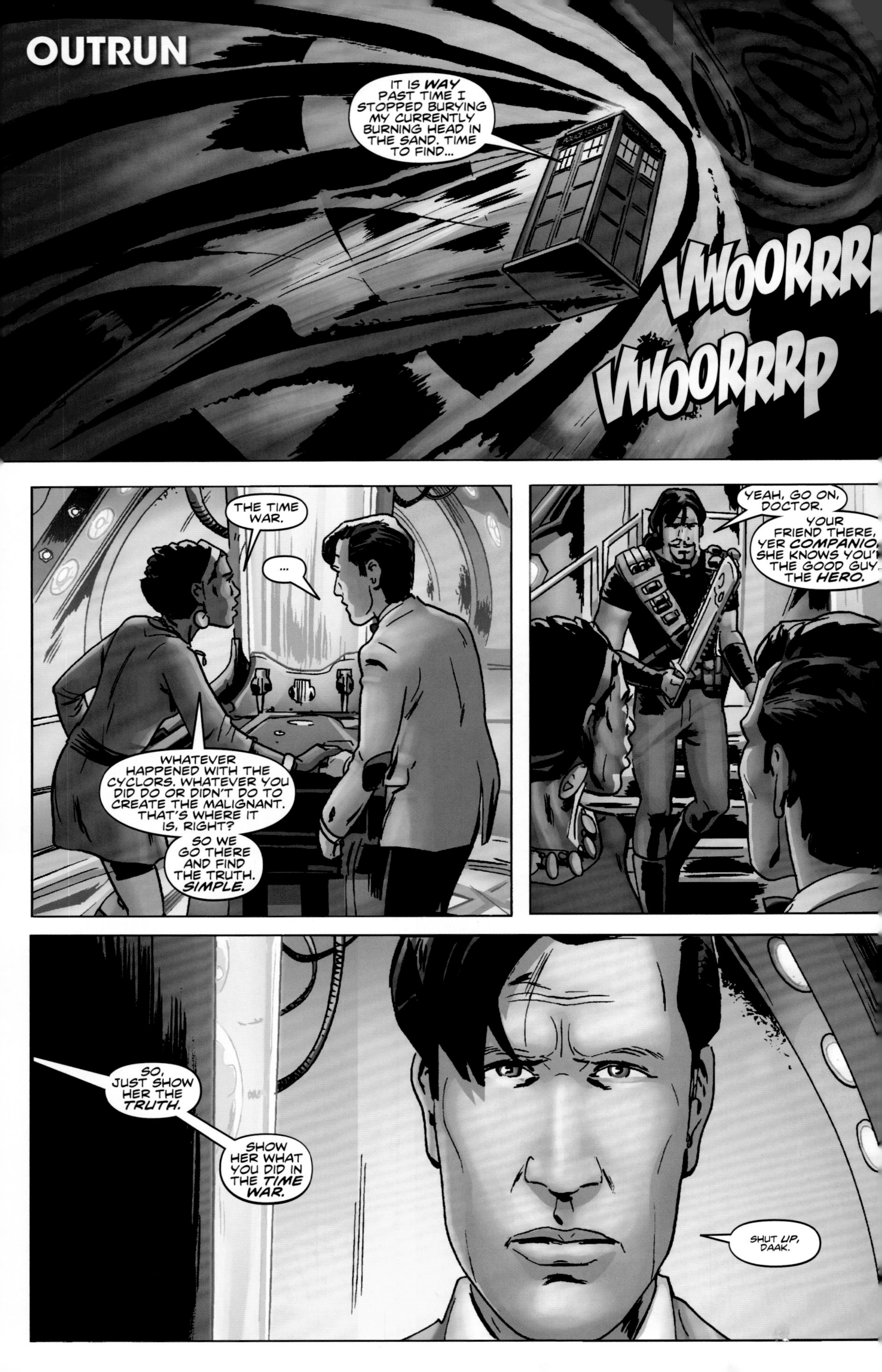
OUTRUN
IT IS WAY PAST TIME I STOPPED BURYING MY CURRENTLY BURNING HEAD IN THE SAND. TIME TO FIND...
VWOORRRP
VWOORRRP
THE TIME WAR.
...
WHATEVER HAPPENED WITH THE CYCLORS. WHATEVER YOU DID DO OR DIDN'T DO TO CREATE THE MALIGNANT. THAT'S WHERE IT IS, RIGHT?
SO WE GO THERE AND FIND THE TRUTH. SIMPLE.
YEAH, GO ON, DOCTOR.
YOUR FRIEND THERE, YER COMPANIO SHE KNOWS YOU' THE GOOD GUY THE HERO.
SO, JUST SHOW HER THE TRUTH.
SHOW HER WHAT YOU DID IN THE TIME WAR.
SHUT UP, DAAK.

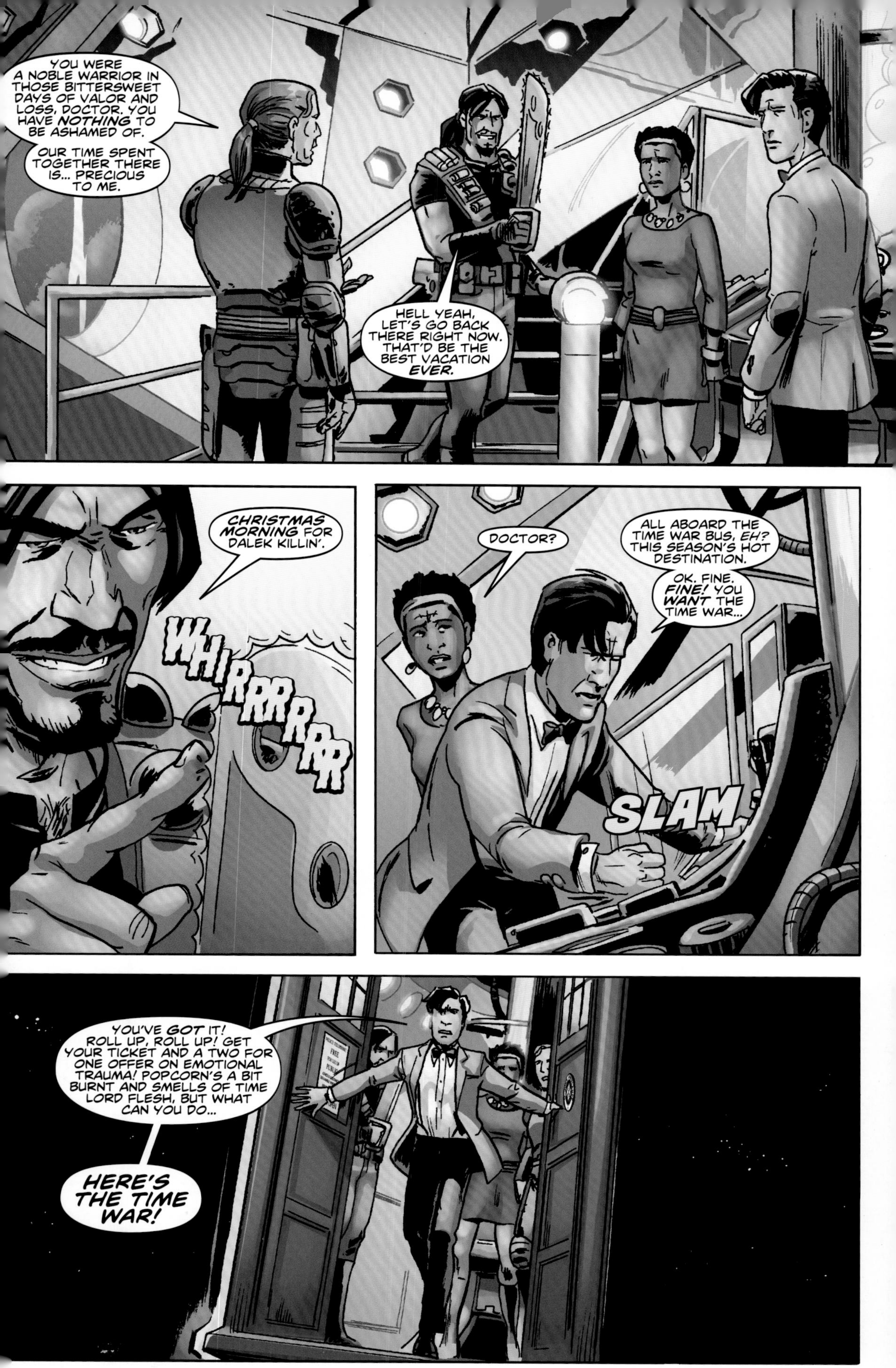
YOU WERE A NOBLE WARRIOR IN THOSE BITTERSWEET DAYS OF VALOR AND LOSS, DOCTOR. YOU HAVE *NOTHING* TO BE ASHAMED OF.
OUR TIME SPENT TOGETHER THERE IS... PRECIOUS TO ME.
HELL YEAH, LET'S GO BACK THERE RIGHT NOW. THAT'D BE THE BEST VACATION *EVER.*
CHRISTMAS MORNING FOR DALEK KILLIN'.
WHIRRRRRRRR
DOCTOR?
ALL ABOARD THE TIME WAR BUS, *EH?* THIS SEASON'S HOT DESTINATION.
OK. FINE. *FINE!* YOU *WANT* THE TIME WAR...
SLAM
YOU'VE *GOT* IT! ROLL UP, ROLL UP! GET YOUR TICKET AND A TWO FOR ONE OFFER ON EMOTIONAL TRAUMA! POPCORN'S A BIT BURNT AND SMELLS OF TIME LORD FLESH, BUT WHAT CAN YOU DO...
HERE'S THE TIME WAR!

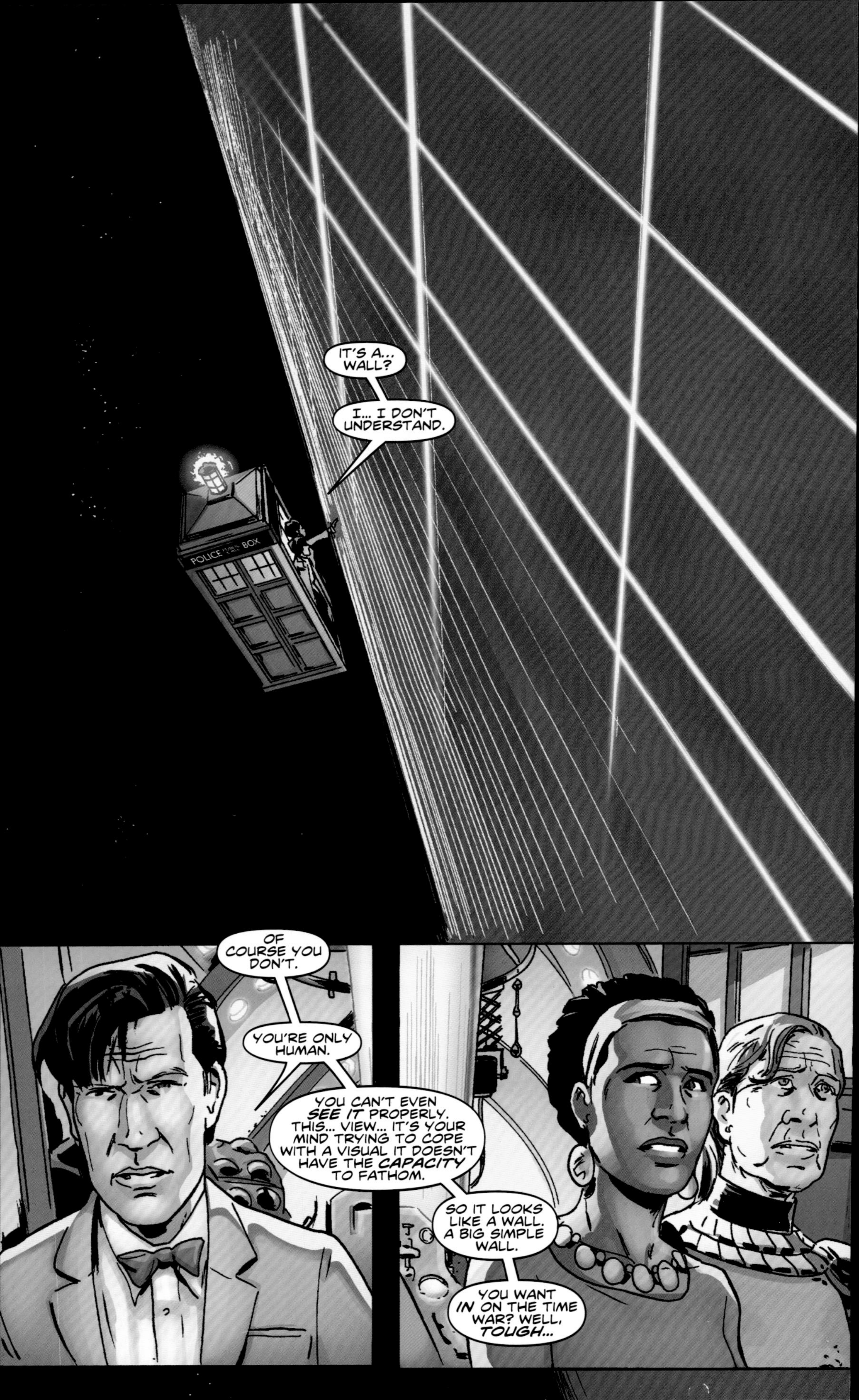

IT'S A... WALL?
I... I DON'T UNDERSTAND.
POLICE BOX
OF COURSE YOU DON'T.
YOU'RE ONLY HUMAN.
YOU CAN'T EVEN *SEE IT* PROPERLY. THIS... VIEW... IT'S YOUR MIND TRYING TO COPE WITH A VISUAL IT DOESN'T HAVE THE *CAPACITY* TO FATHOM.
SO IT LOOKS LIKE A WALL. A BIG SIMPLE WALL.
YOU WANT *IN* ON THE TIME WAR? WELL, *TOUGH...*

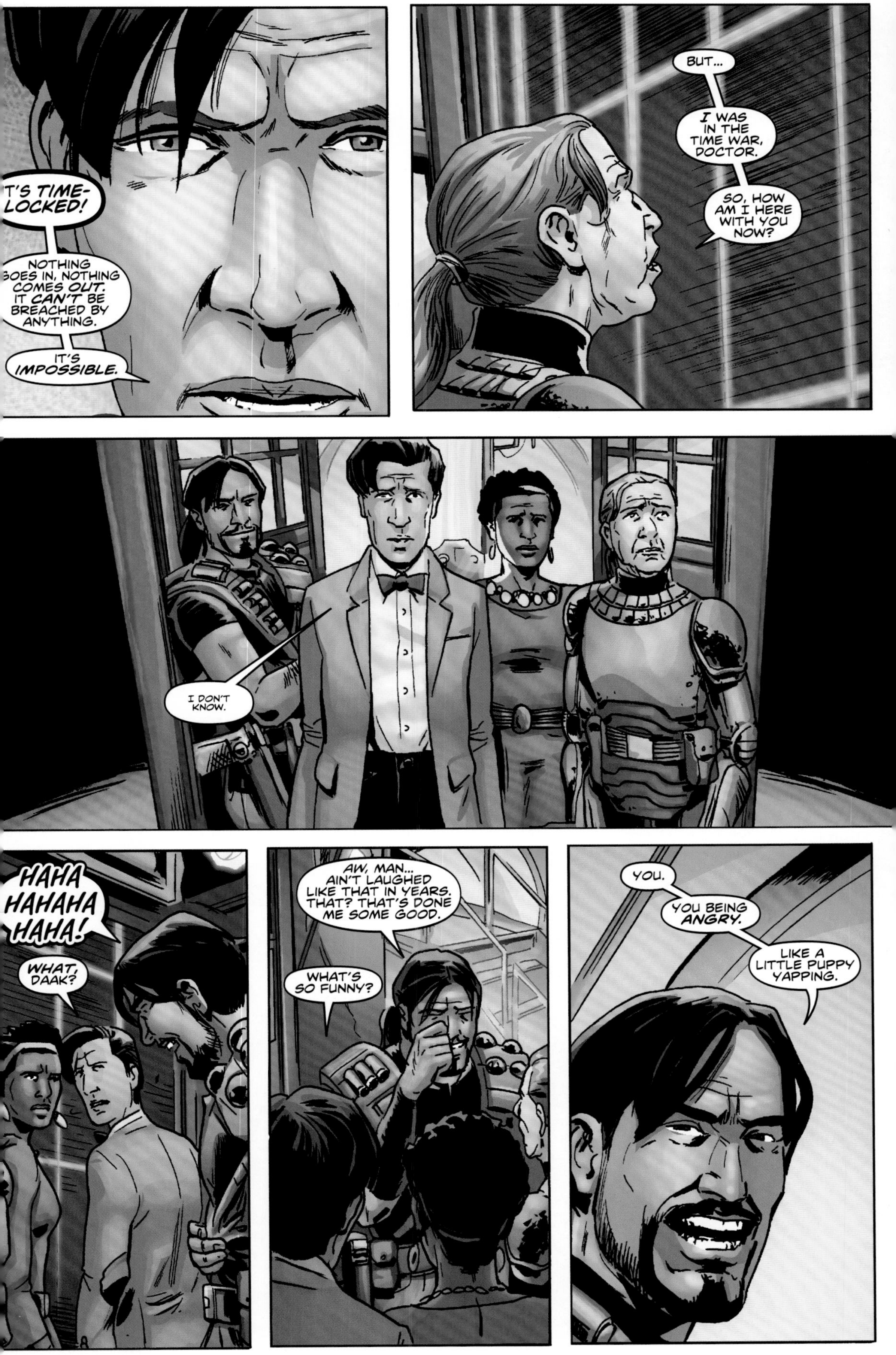
IT'S TIME-LOCKED!
NOTHING GOES IN, NOTHING COMES OUT. IT CAN'T BE BREACHED BY ANYTHING.
IT'S IMPOSSIBLE.
BUT...
I WAS IN THE TIME WAR, DOCTOR.
SO, HOW AM I HERE WITH YOU NOW?
I DON'T KNOW.
HAHA HAHAHA HAHA!
WHAT, DAAK?
AW, MAN... AIN'T LAUGHED LIKE THAT IN YEARS. THAT? THAT'S DONE ME SOME GOOD.
WHAT'S SO FUNNY?
YOU.
YOU BEING ANGRY.
LIKE A LITTLE PUPPY YAPPING.

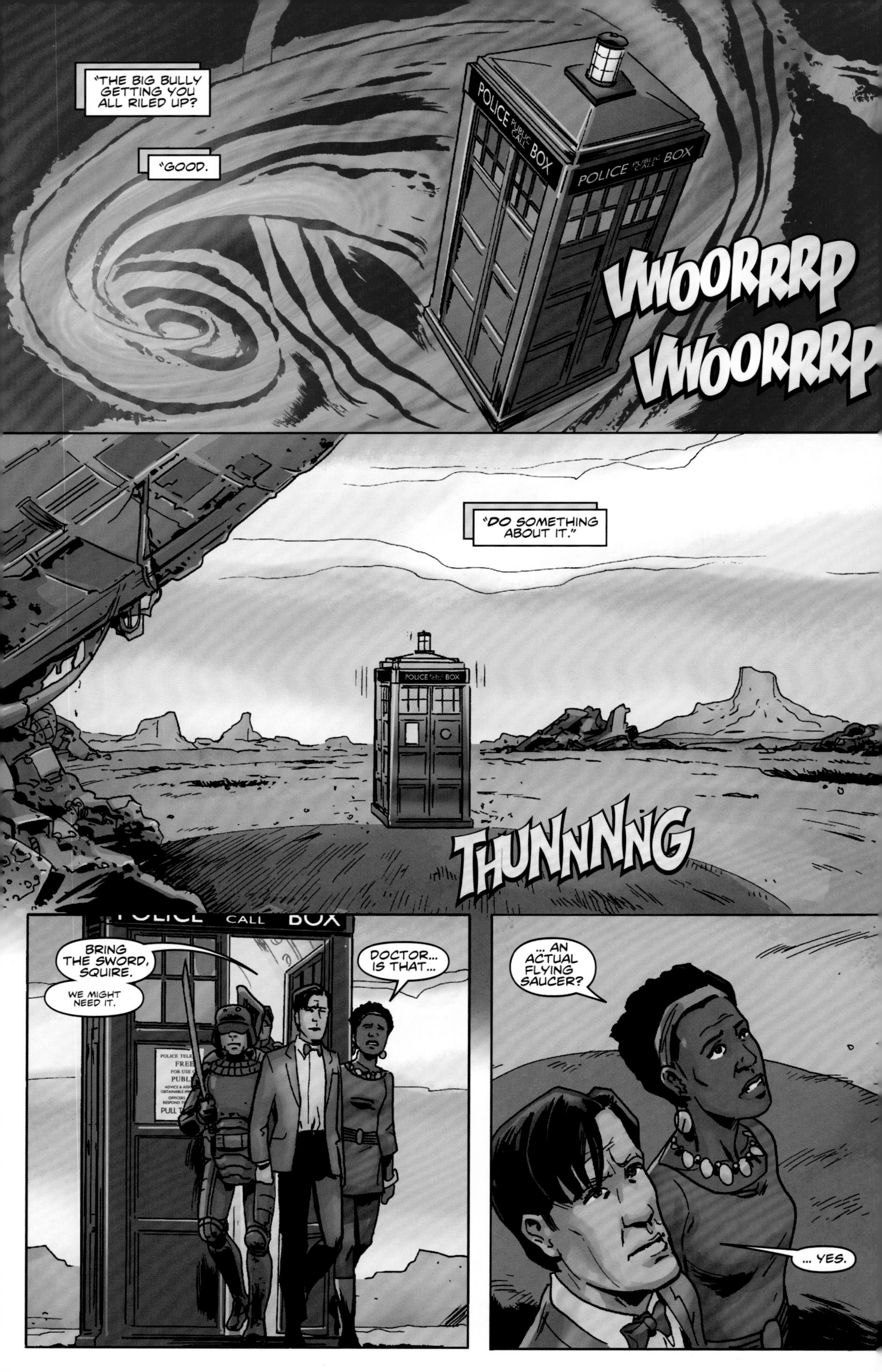
"THE BIG BULLY GETTING YOU ALL RILED UP?
"GOOD.
POLICE PUBLIC CALL BOX
VWOORRRP
VWOORRRP
"DO SOMETHING ABOUT IT."
THUNNNNG
BRING THE SWORD, SQUIRE.
WE MIGHT NEED IT.
DOCTOR... IS THAT...
... AN ACTUAL FLYING SAUCER?
... YES.

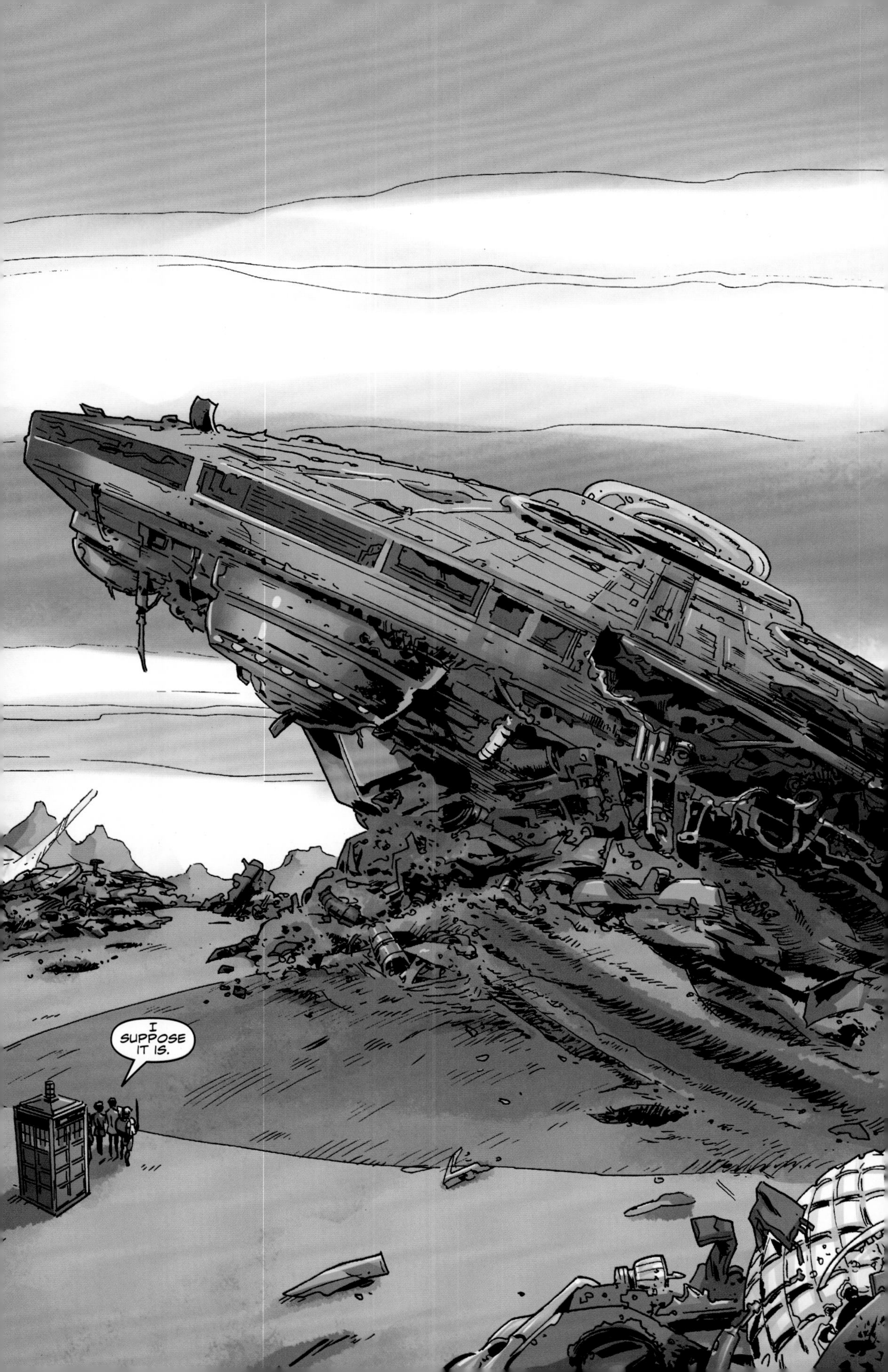
I SUPPOSE IT IS.

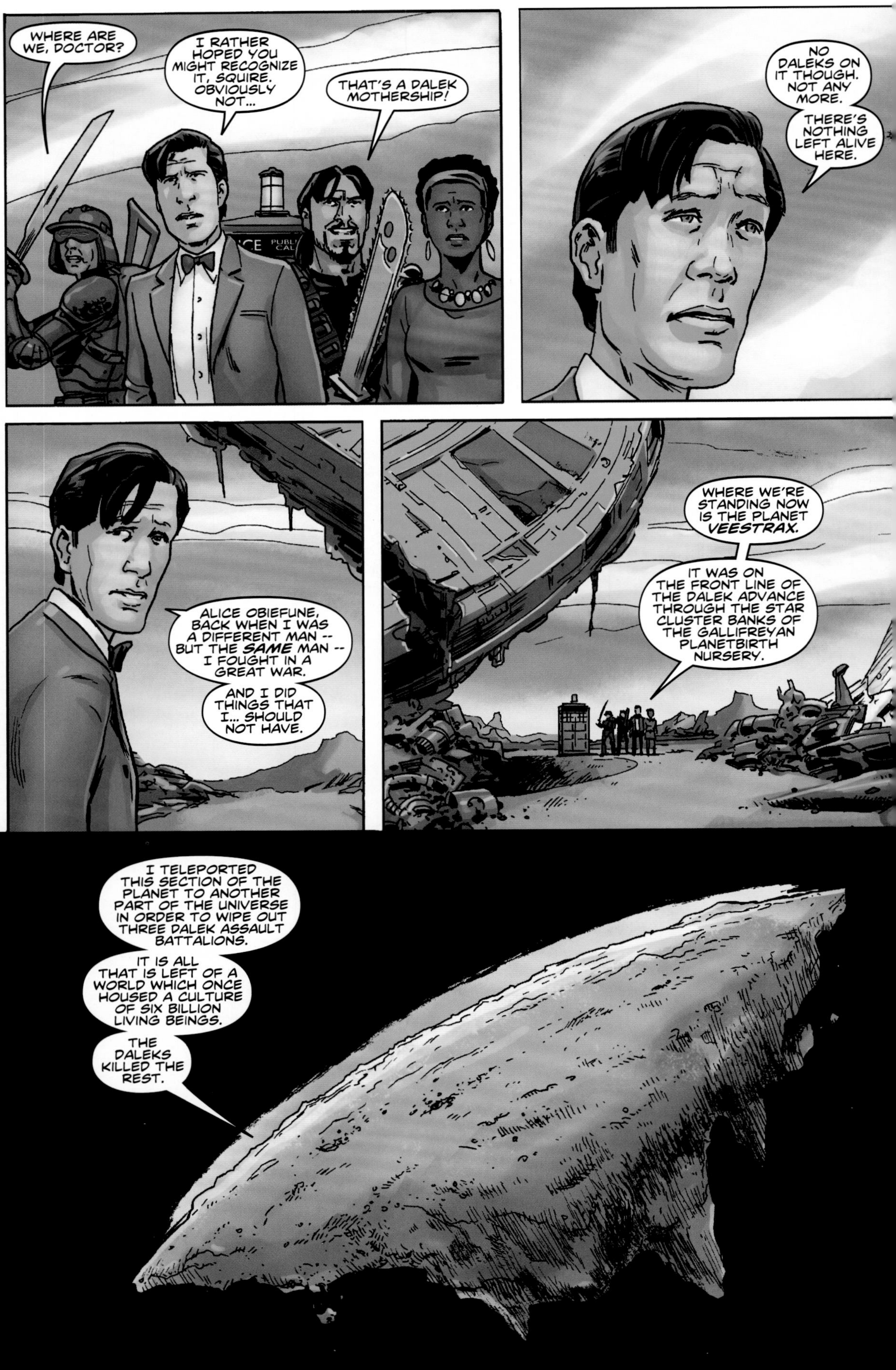
WHERE ARE WE, DOCTOR?
I RATHER HOPED YOU MIGHT RECOGNIZE IT, SQUIRE. OBVIOUSLY NOT...
THAT'S A DALEK MOTHERSHIP!
NO DALEKS ON IT THOUGH. NOT ANY MORE.
THERE'S NOTHING LEFT ALIVE HERE.
ALICE OBIEFUNE, BACK WHEN I WAS A DIFFERENT MAN -- BUT THE SAME MAN -- I FOUGHT IN A GREAT WAR.
AND I DID THINGS THAT I... SHOULD NOT HAVE.
WHERE WE'RE STANDING NOW IS THE PLANET VEESTRAX.
IT WAS ON THE FRONT LINE OF THE DALEK ADVANCE THROUGH THE STAR CLUSTER BANKS OF THE GALLIFREYAN PLANETBIRTH NURSERY.
I TELEPORTED THIS SECTION OF THE PLANET TO ANOTHER PART OF THE UNIVERSE IN ORDER TO WIPE OUT THREE DALEK ASSAULT BATTALIONS.
IT IS ALL THAT IS LEFT OF A WORLD WHICH ONCE HOUSED A CULTURE OF SIX BILLION LIVING BEINGS.
THE DALEKS KILLED THE REST.

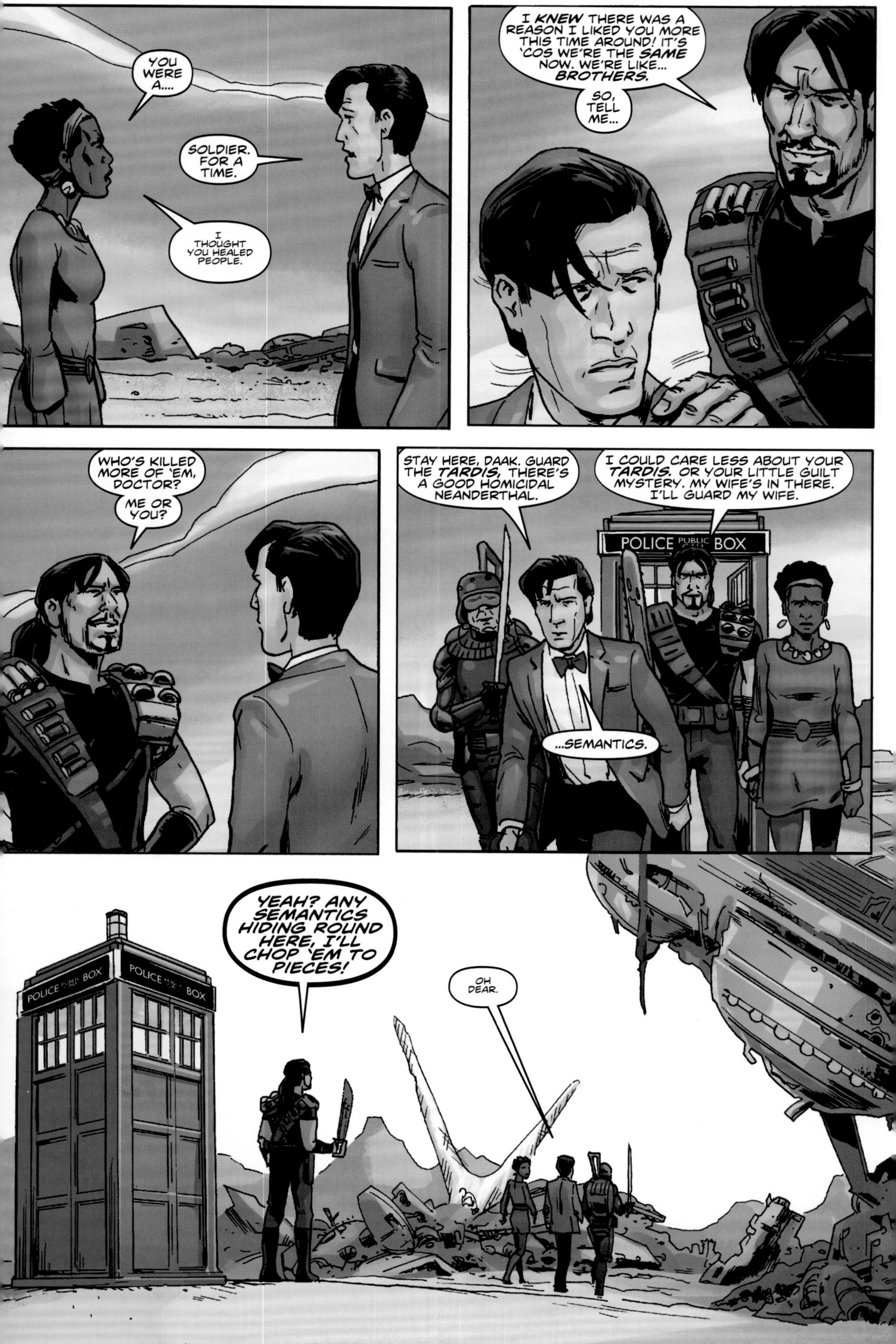
YOU WERE A....
SOLDIER. FOR A TIME.
I THOUGHT YOU HEALED PEOPLE.
I KNEW THERE WAS A REASON I LIKED YOU MORE THIS TIME AROUND! IT'S 'COS WE'RE THE SAME NOW. WE'RE LIKE... BROTHERS.
SO, TELL ME...
WHO'S KILLED MORE OF 'EM, DOCTOR?
ME OR YOU?
STAY HERE, DAAK. GUARD THE TARDIS, THERE'S A GOOD HOMICIDAL NEANDERTHAL.
I COULD CARE LESS ABOUT YOUR TARDIS. OR YOUR LITTLE GUILT MYSTERY. MY WIFE'S IN THERE. I'LL GUARD MY WIFE.
POLICE PUBLIC CALL BOX
...SEMANTICS.
YEAH? ANY SEMANTICS HIDING ROUND HERE, I'LL CHOP 'EM TO PIECES!
OH DEAR.
POLICE PUBLIC CALL BOX
POLICE PUBLIC CALL BOX

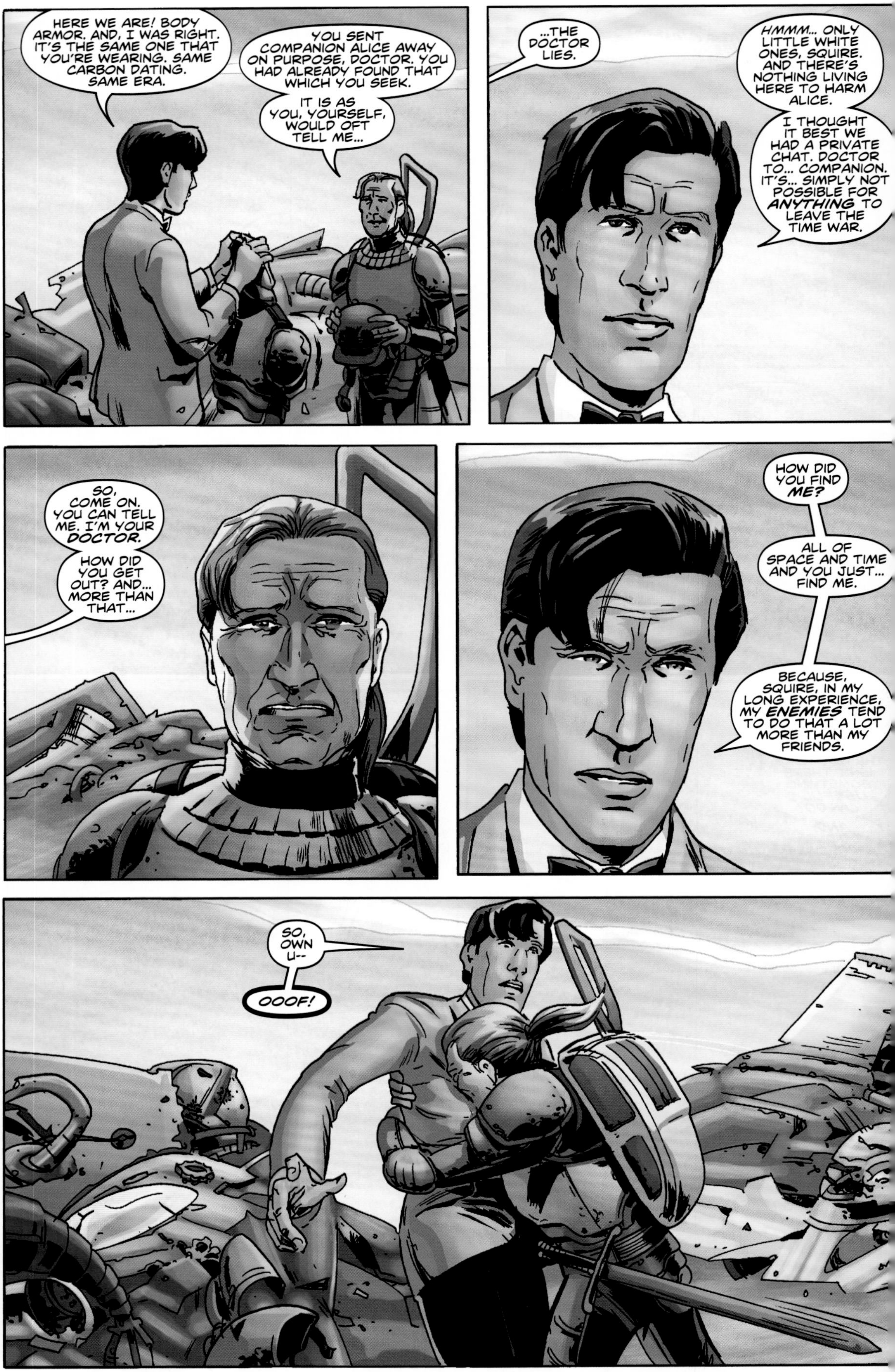
HERE WE ARE! BODY ARMOR. AND, I WAS RIGHT. IT'S THE SAME ONE THAT YOU'RE WEARING. SAME CARBON DATING. SAME ERA.
YOU SENT COMPANION ALICE AWAY ON PURPOSE, DOCTOR. YOU HAD ALREADY FOUND THAT WHICH YOU SEEK.
IT IS AS YOU, YOURSELF, WOULD OFT TELL ME...
...THE DOCTOR LIES.
HMMM... ONLY LITTLE WHITE ONES, SQUIRE. AND THERE'S NOTHING LIVING HERE TO HARM ALICE.
I THOUGHT IT BEST WE HAD A PRIVATE CHAT. DOCTOR TO... COMPANION. IT'S... SIMPLY NOT POSSIBLE FOR ANYTHING TO LEAVE THE TIME WAR.
SO, COME ON. YOU CAN TELL ME. I'M YOUR DOCTOR.
HOW DID YOU GET OUT? AND... MORE THAN THAT...
HOW DID YOU FIND ME?
ALL OF SPACE AND TIME AND YOU JUST... FIND ME.
BECAUSE, SQUIRE, IN MY LONG EXPERIENCE, MY ENEMIES TEND TO DO THAT A LOT MORE THAN MY FRIENDS.
SO, OWN U--
OOOF!

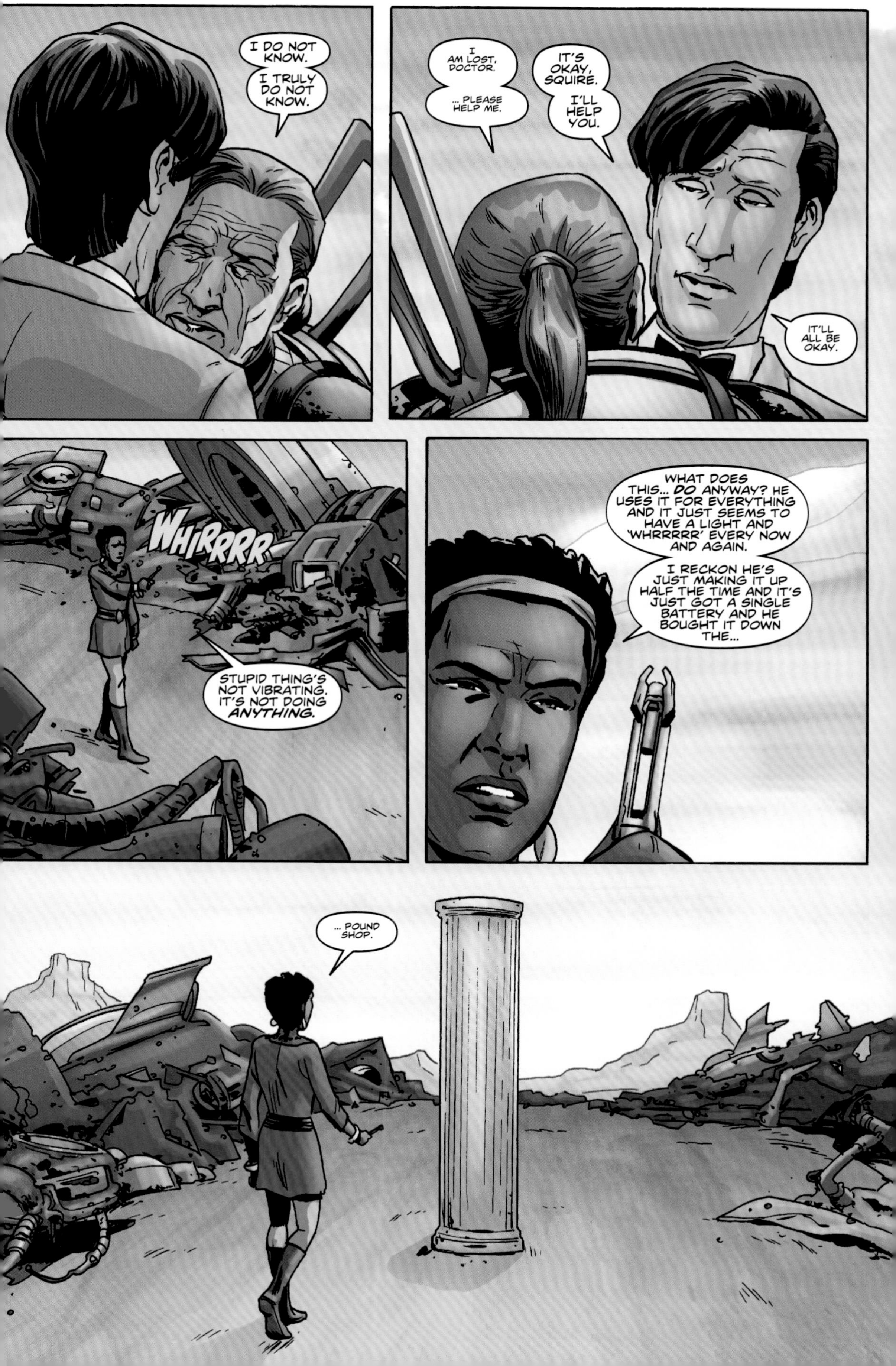
I DO NOT KNOW.
I TRULY DO NOT KNOW.
I AM LOST, DOCTOR.
... PLEASE HELP ME.
IT'S OKAY, SQUIRE.
I'LL HELP YOU.
IT'LL ALL BE OKAY.
WHIRRRR
STUPID THING'S NOT VIBRATING. IT'S NOT DOING *ANYTHING.*
WHAT DOES THIS... *DO* ANYWAY? HE USES IT FOR EVERYTHING AND IT JUST SEEMS TO HAVE A LIGHT AND 'WHRRRRR' EVERY NOW AND AGAIN.
I RECKON HE'S JUST MAKING IT UP HALF THE TIME AND IT'S JUST GOT A SINGLE BATTERY AND HE BOUGHT IT DOWN THE...
... POUND SHOP.

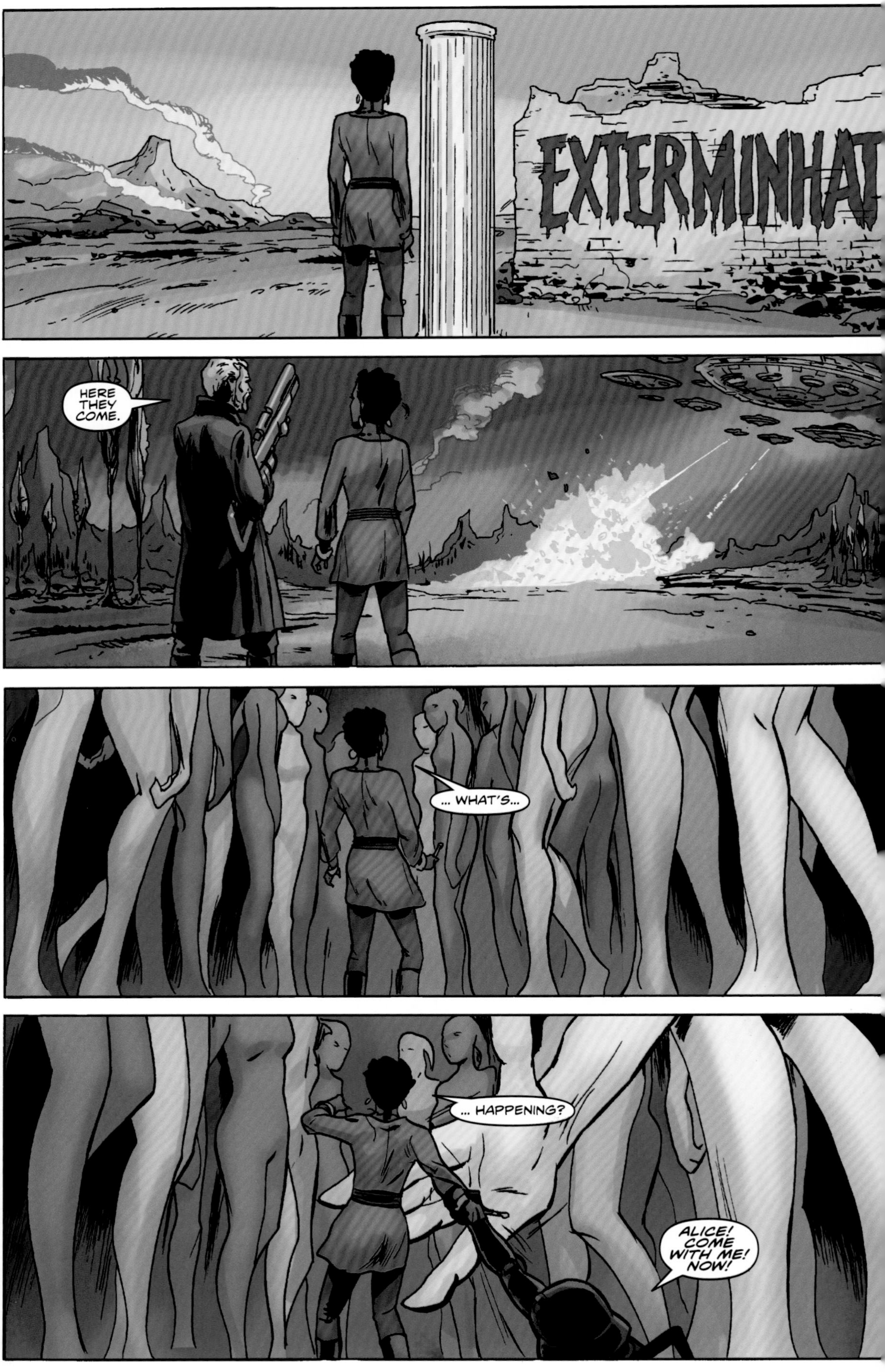
EXTERMINHAT
HERE THEY COME.
... WHAT'S...
... HAPPENING?
ALICE! COME WITH ME! NOW!

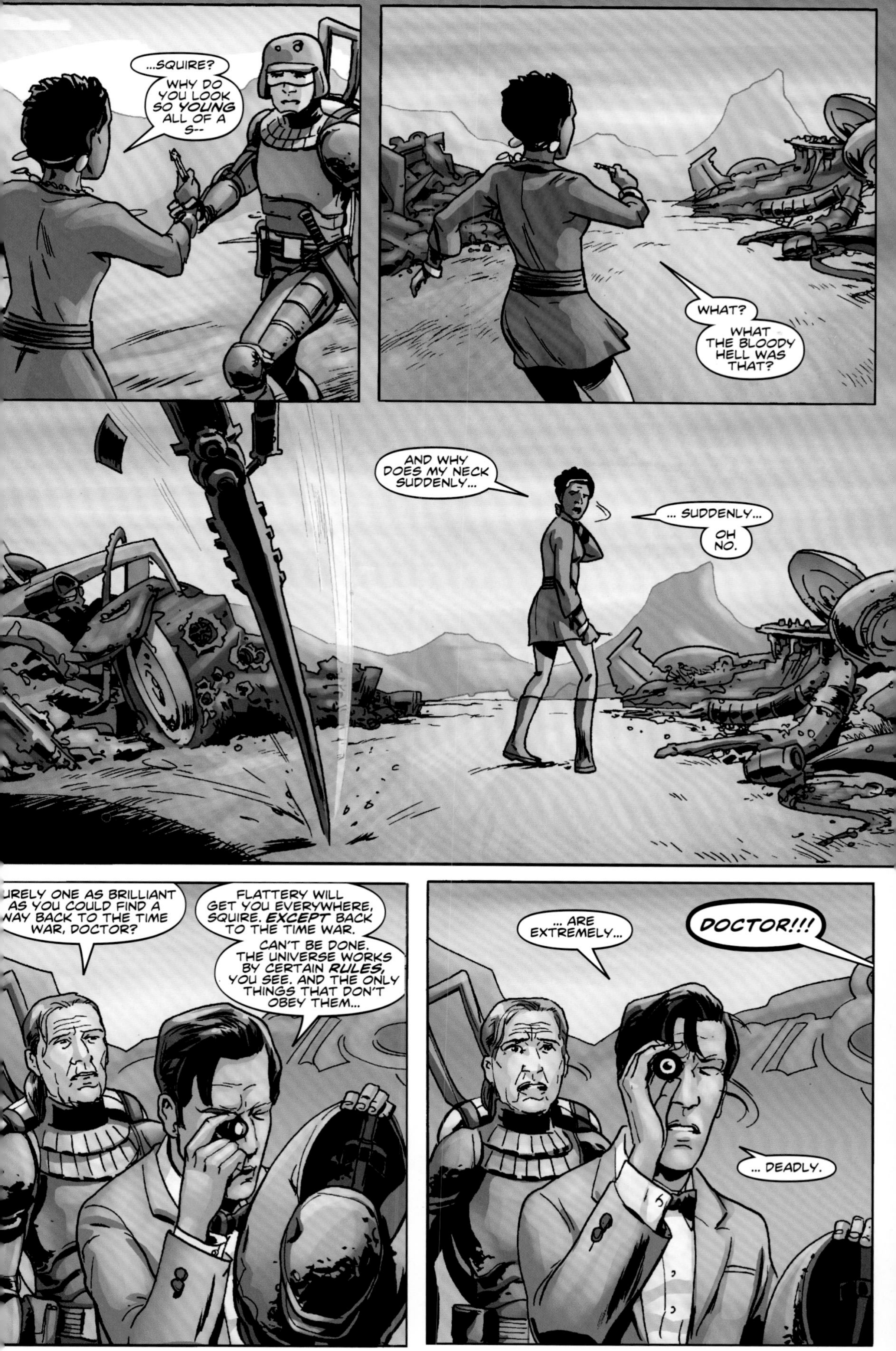
...SQUIRE?
WHY DO YOU LOOK SO YOUNG ALL OF A S--
WHAT?
WHAT THE BLOODY HELL WAS THAT?
AND WHY DOES MY NECK SUDDENLY...
... SUDDENLY...
OH NO.
URELY ONE AS BRILLIANT AS YOU COULD FIND A WAY BACK TO THE TIME WAR, DOCTOR?
FLATTERY WILL GET YOU EVERYWHERE, SQUIRE. EXCEPT BACK TO THE TIME WAR.
CAN'T BE DONE. THE UNIVERSE WORKS BY CERTAIN RULES, YOU SEE. AND THE ONLY THINGS THAT DON'T OBEY THEM...
... ARE EXTREMELY...
DOCTOR!!!
... DEADLY.

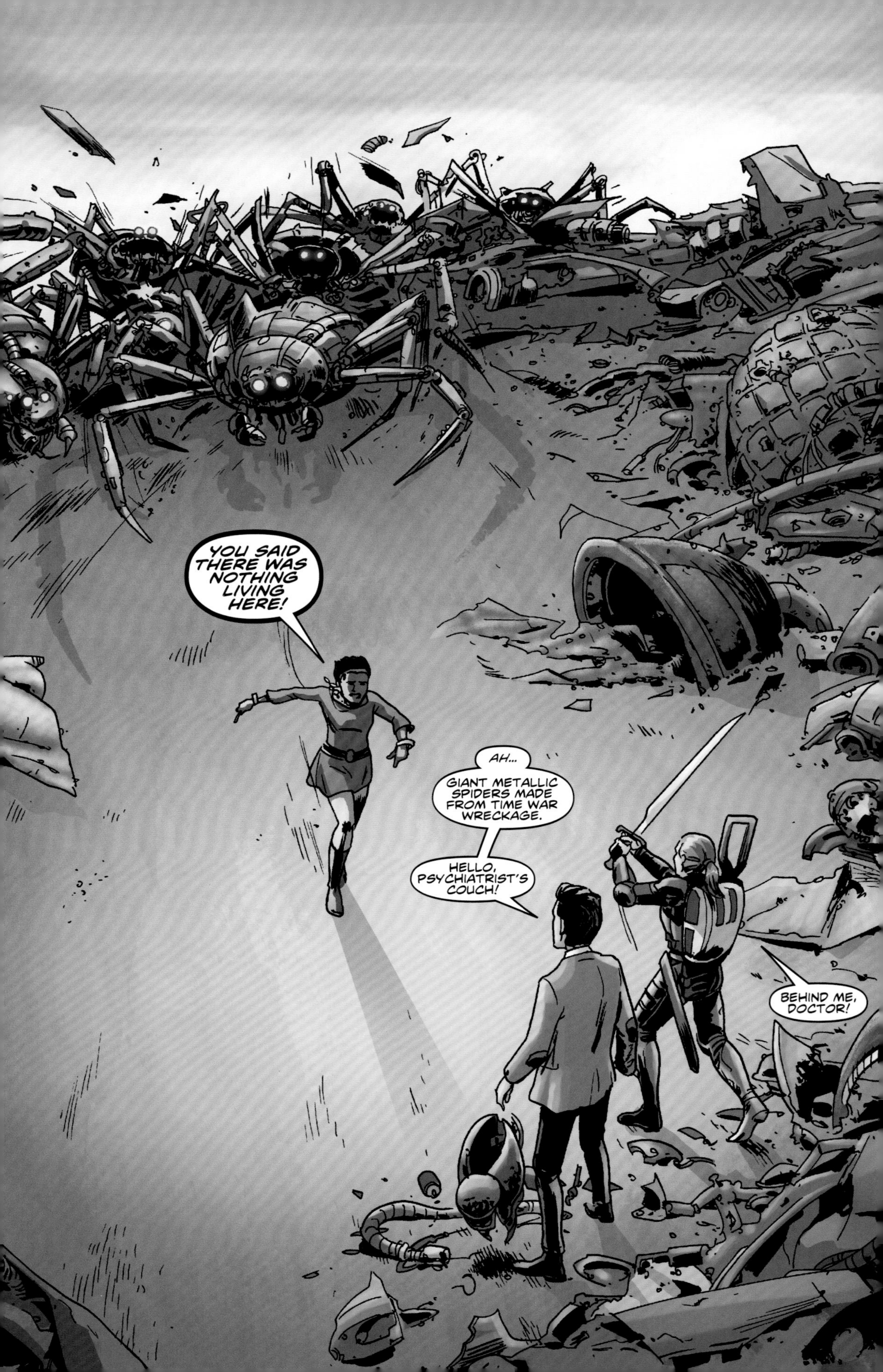
YOU SAID THERE WAS NOTHING LIVING HERE!
AH...
GIANT METALLIC SPIDERS MADE FROM TIME WAR WRECKAGE.
HELLO, PSYCHIATRIST'S COUCH!
BEHIND ME, DOCTOR!

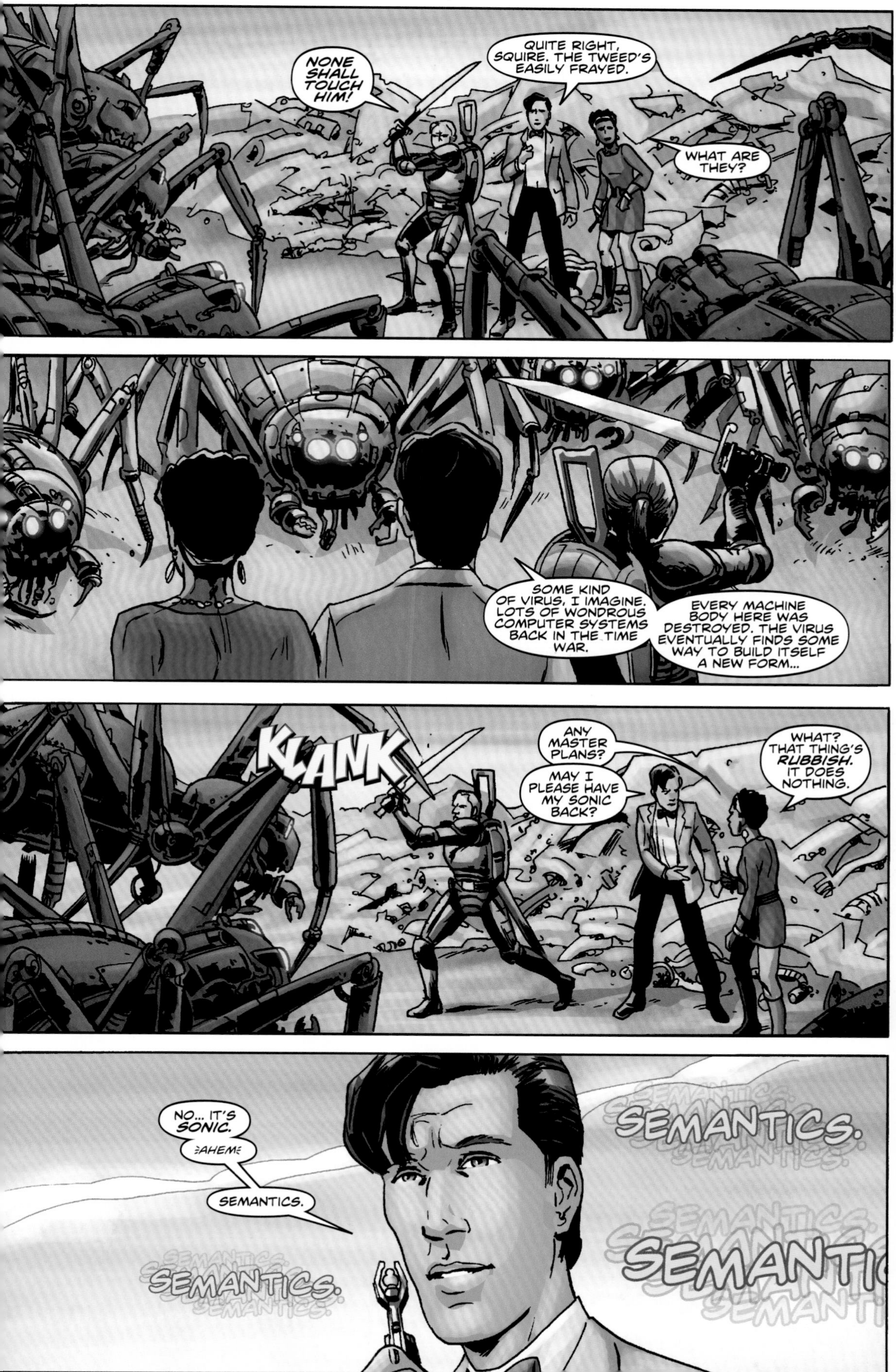
NONE SHALL TOUCH HIM!
QUITE RIGHT, SQUIRE. THE TWEED'S EASILY FRAYED.
WHAT ARE THEY?
SOME KIND OF VIRUS, I IMAGINE. LOTS OF WONDROUS COMPUTER SYSTEMS BACK IN THE TIME WAR.
EVERY MACHINE BODY HERE WAS DESTROYED. THE VIRUS EVENTUALLY FINDS SOME WAY TO BUILD ITSELF A NEW FORM...
KLANK
ANY MASTER PLANS?
MAY I PLEASE HAVE MY SONIC BACK?
WHAT? THAT THING'S RUBBISH. IT DOES NOTHING.
NO... IT'S SONIC.
AHEM
SEMANTICS.
SEMANTICS.
SEMANTICS.
SEMANTIC

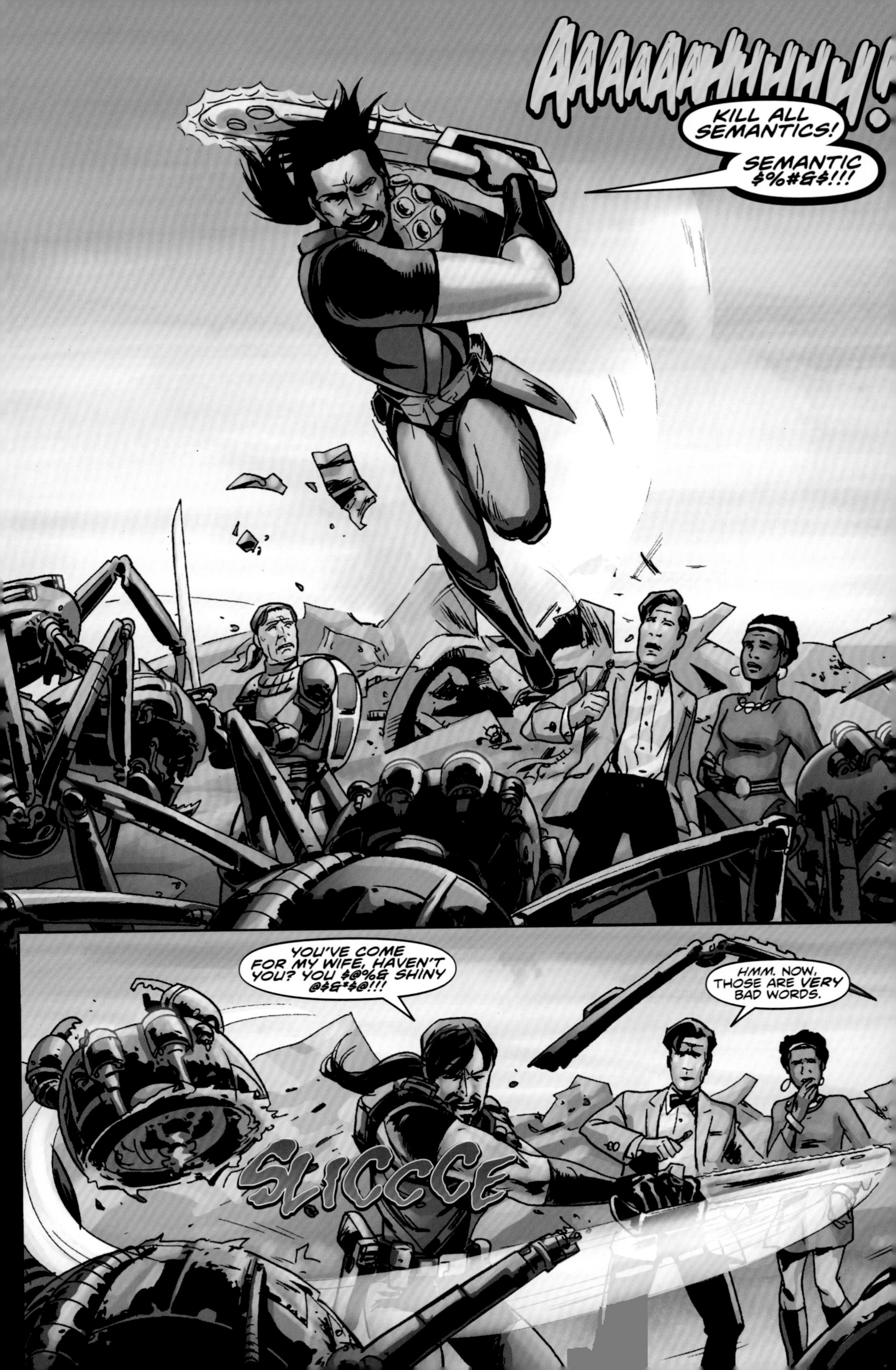
AAAAAAHHHHH!
KILL ALL SEMANTICS!
SEMANTIC $%#&$!!!
YOU'VE COME FOR MY WIFE, HAVEN'T YOU? YOU $@%& SHINY @$&*$@!!!
HMM. NOW, THOSE ARE VERY BAD WORDS.
SLICCCE

YES, ABSLOM! THE SQUIRE SHALL JOIN YOU IN ROUTING THE VILE SEMANTIC HORDE!!

THEY... ERM... WELL, SHE'S...

THIS IS QUITE ANNOYING FOR A LIBRARY ASSISTANT, YOU KNOW.

[DO]N'T LET PEDANTRY GET [IN T]HE WAY OF A GOOD SAVE, [LIK]E OBIEFUNE. I'M SORRY I [WA]S RUDE TO YOU AND SAID YOU WERE HUMAN.

I HAD A VISION, DOCTOR. AND I'VE READ ENOUGH BOOKS TO NOT TRUST IN COINCIDENCE.

I SAW YOU. BACK THEN. YOU HAD THE GUN. AND THE BEARD.

AND I SAW THE CYCLORS. I WAS *THERE*, DOCTOR. IT WAS REAL. SOMEHOW.

WHAT ELSE DID YOU SEE? THINK, ALICE. DETAILS! IT MIGHT BE IMPORTANT.

THE SQUIRE. BUT SHE WAS YOUNGER. SHE *WAS* THERE. IN THE TIME WAR.

THERE WAS SOME GRAFFITI ON A WALL. "EXTERMIN*HATE*?"

... EXTERMIN*HATE*?

AND THERE WAS THE *WEIRDEST* THING. IT MADE NO SENSE.

THIS LONE WHITE PILLAR WAS THERE. LIKE SOMETHING OUT OF THE COLISEUM. NO BUILDING WRECKAGE AROUND IT THOUGH.

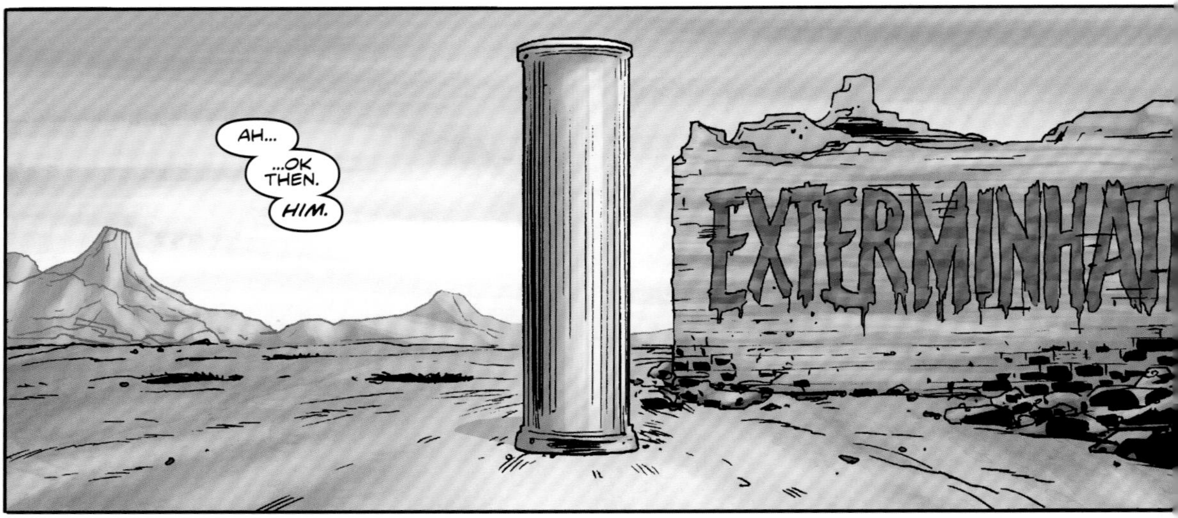
AH...
...OK THEN.
HIM.
EXTERMINHATE

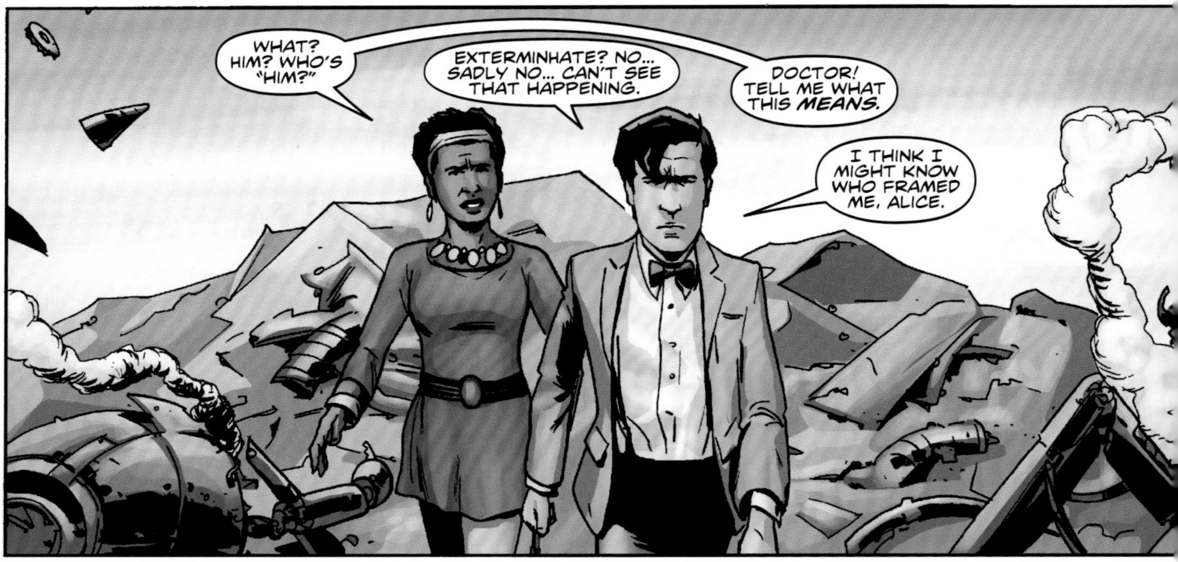
DOCTOR! TELL ME WHAT THIS MEANS.
EXTERMINHATE? NO... SADLY NO... CAN'T SEE THAT HAPPENING.
WHAT? HIM? WHO'S "HIM?"
I THINK I MIGHT KNOW WHO FRAMED ME, ALICE.

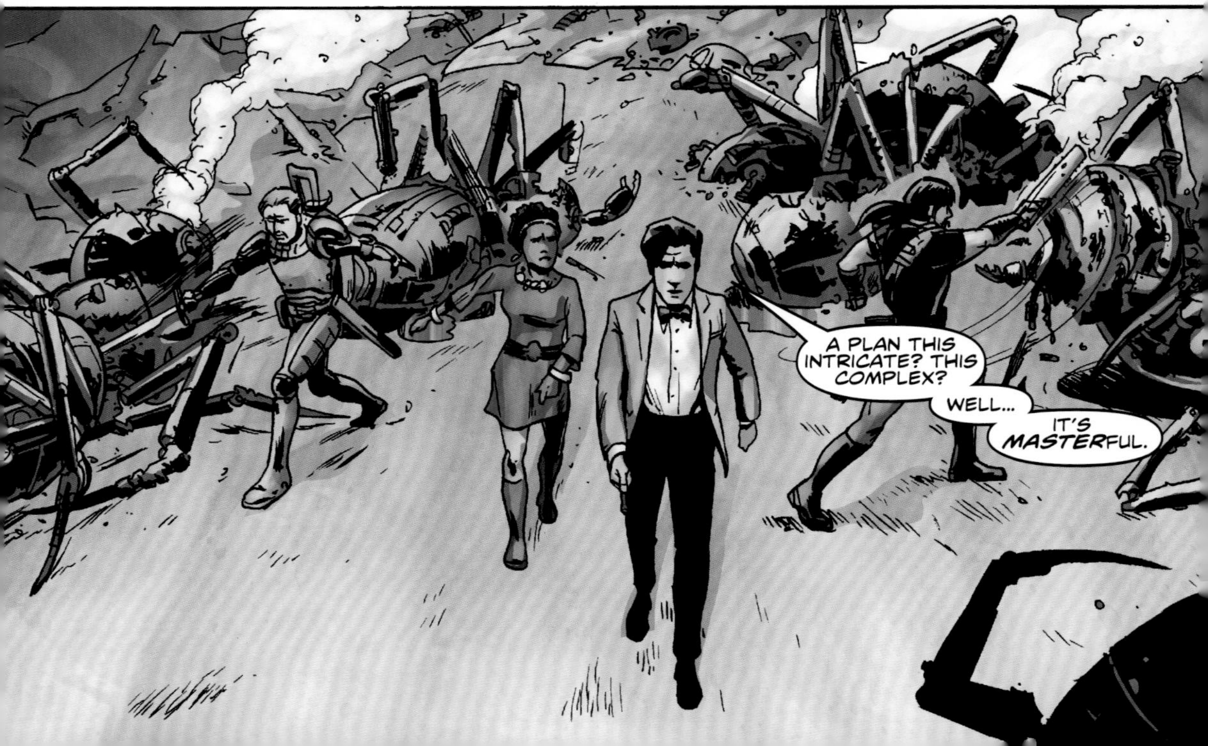
A PLAN THIS INTRICATE? THIS COMPLEX?
WELL...
IT'S MASTERFUL.

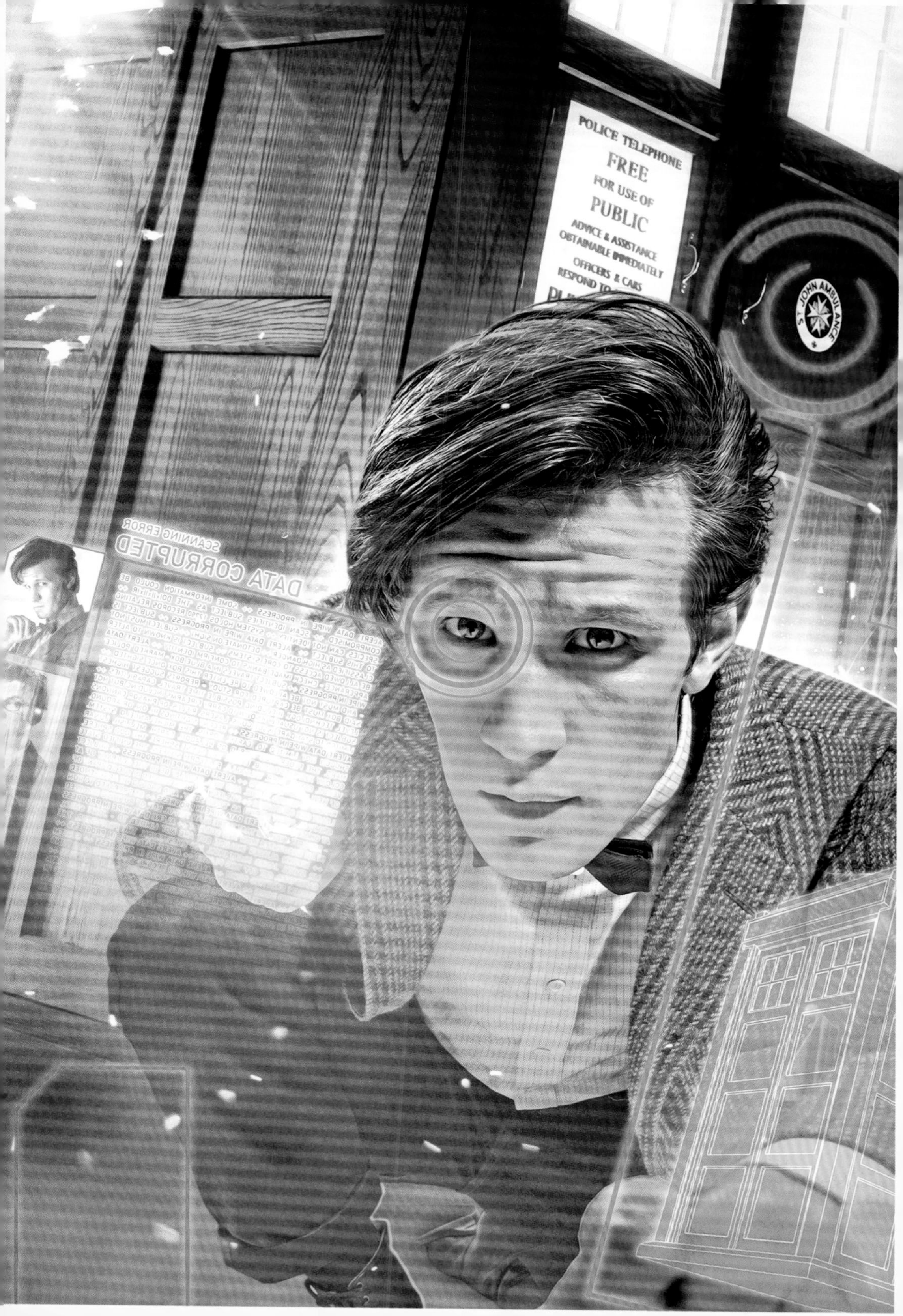
POLICE TELEPHONE
FREE
FOR USE OF
PUBLIC
ADVICE & ASSISTANCE
OBTAINABLE IMMEDIATELY
OFFICERS & CARS
ST JOHN AMBULANCE
SCANNING ERROR
DATA CORRUPTED

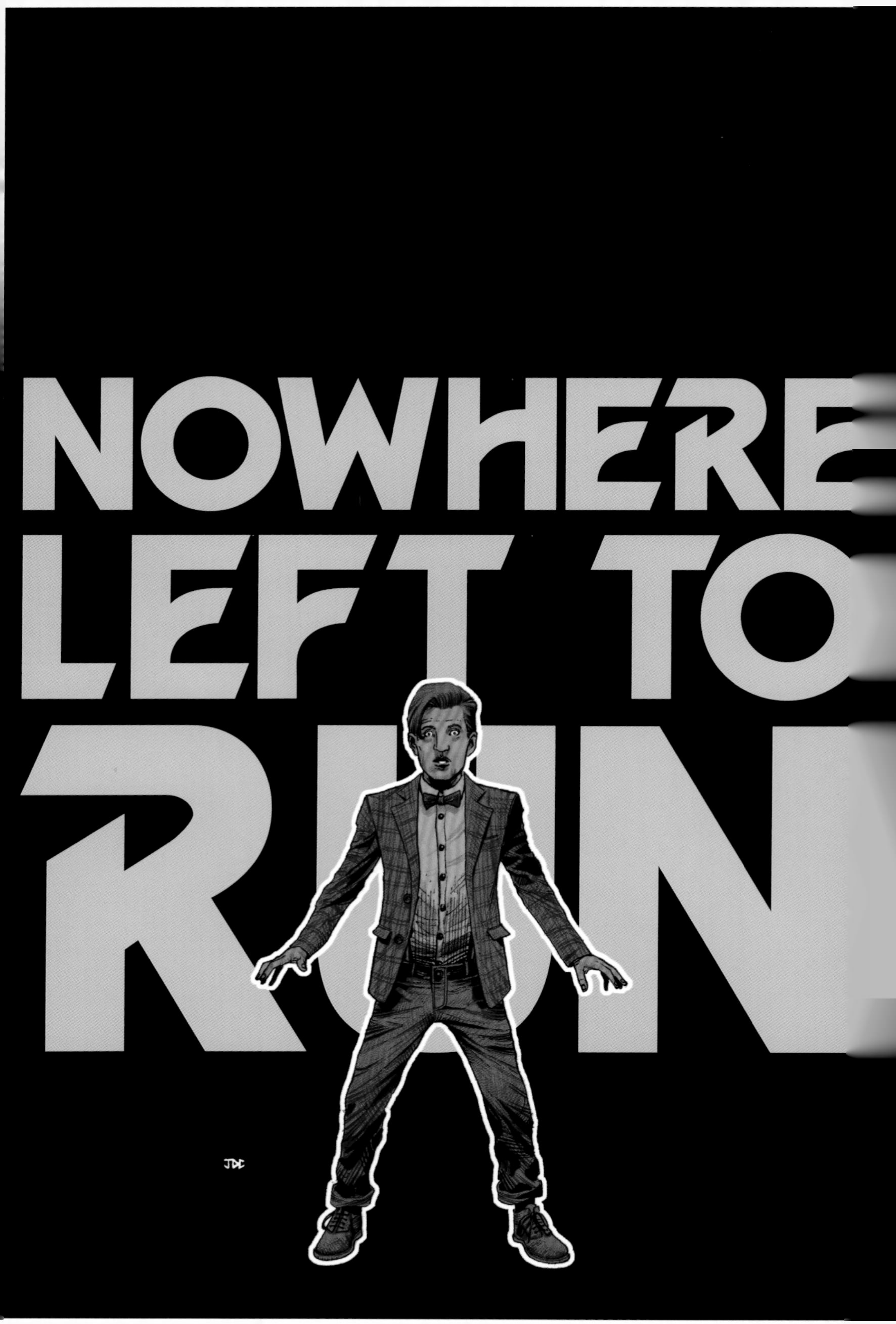
NOWHERE
LEFT TO
RUN
JDC

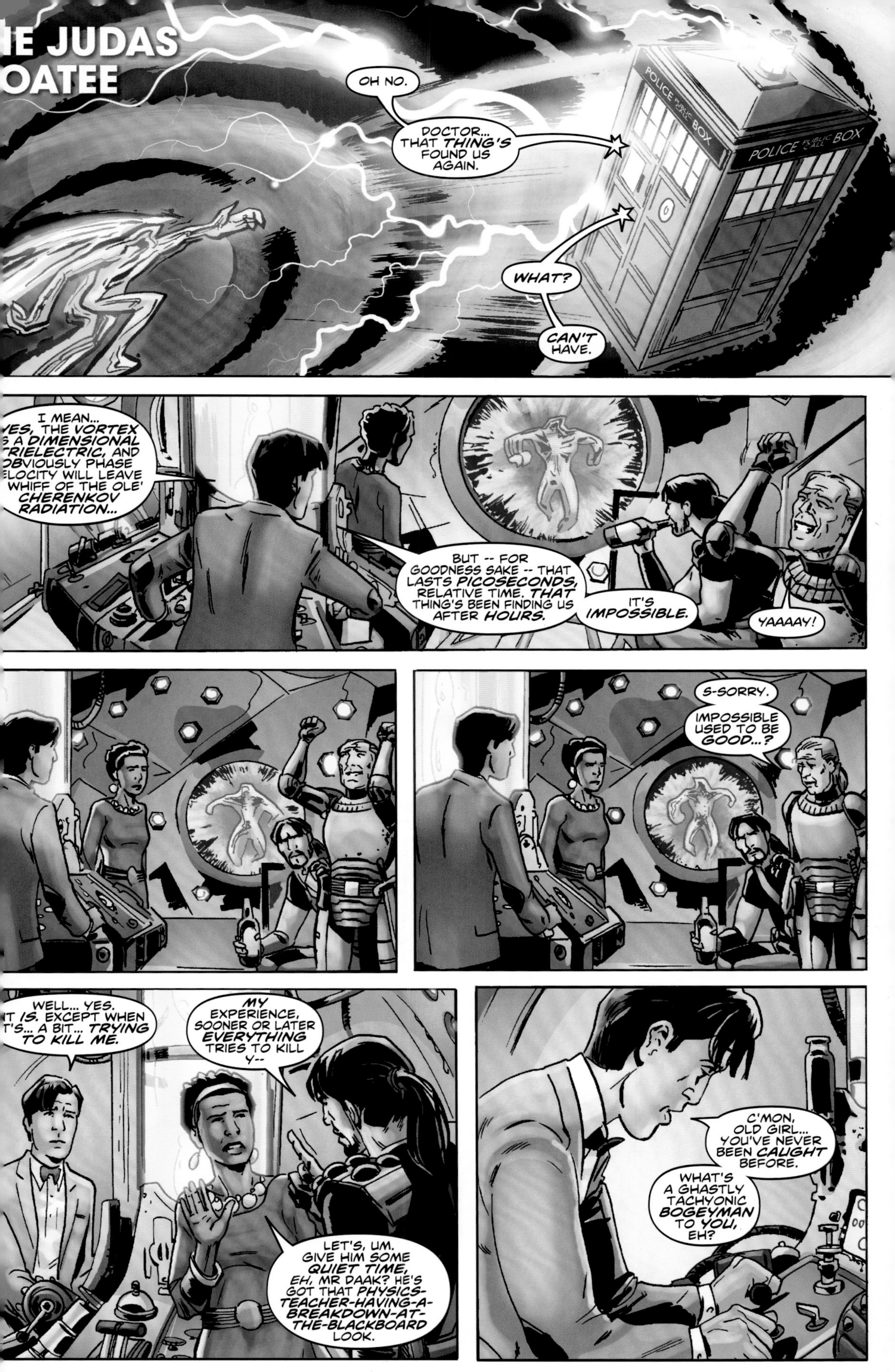
IE JUDAS
OATEE
OH NO.
DOCTOR... THAT THING'S FOUND US AGAIN.
WHAT?
CAN'T HAVE.
I MEAN... YES, THE VORTEX S A DIMENSIONAL TRIELECTRIC, AND OBVIOUSLY PHASE ELOCITY WILL LEAVE WHIFF OF THE OLE' CHERENKOV RADIATION...
BUT -- FOR GOODNESS SAKE -- THAT LASTS PICOSECONDS, RELATIVE TIME. THAT THING'S BEEN FINDING US AFTER HOURS.
IT'S IMPOSSIBLE.
YAAAAY!
S-SORRY.
IMPOSSIBLE USED TO BE GOOD...?
WELL... YES. T IS. EXCEPT WHEN T'S... A BIT... TRYING TO KILL ME.
MY EXPERIENCE, SOONER OR LATER EVERYTHING TRIES TO KILL Y--
LET'S, UM. GIVE HIM SOME QUIET TIME, EH, MR DAAK? HE'S GOT THAT PHYSICS-TEACHER-HAVING-A-BREAKDOWN-AT-THE-BLACKBOARD LOOK.
C'MON, OLD GIRL... YOU'VE NEVER BEEN CAUGHT BEFORE.
WHAT'S A GHASTLY TACHYONIC BOGEYMAN TO YOU, EH?

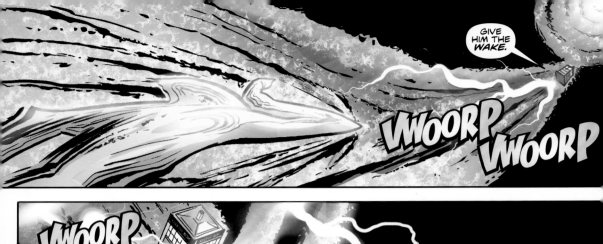

GIVE HIM THE **WAKE**.

VVOORP VVOORP

VVOORP

VVOORP

VVOORP AAAA

THUDD

AH.

SMIDGE **OVERZEALOUS**, PERHAPS, BUT...

SHE'S STILL **GOT** IT.

AND **LOOK!** LIIIIIIIFE!

RRRR. LAST FELLER I MET THIS **CHEERY**, I FIGURED IT FOR A **BRAIN-BLOCK** AND PERFORMED **SURGERY**. HE **ALWAYS** LIKE THIS?

ALMOST **NEVER**.

ALMOST **ALWAYS**.

COME ALONG, CHILDREN! TIGHT **SCHEDULE!** THINGS TO SEE!

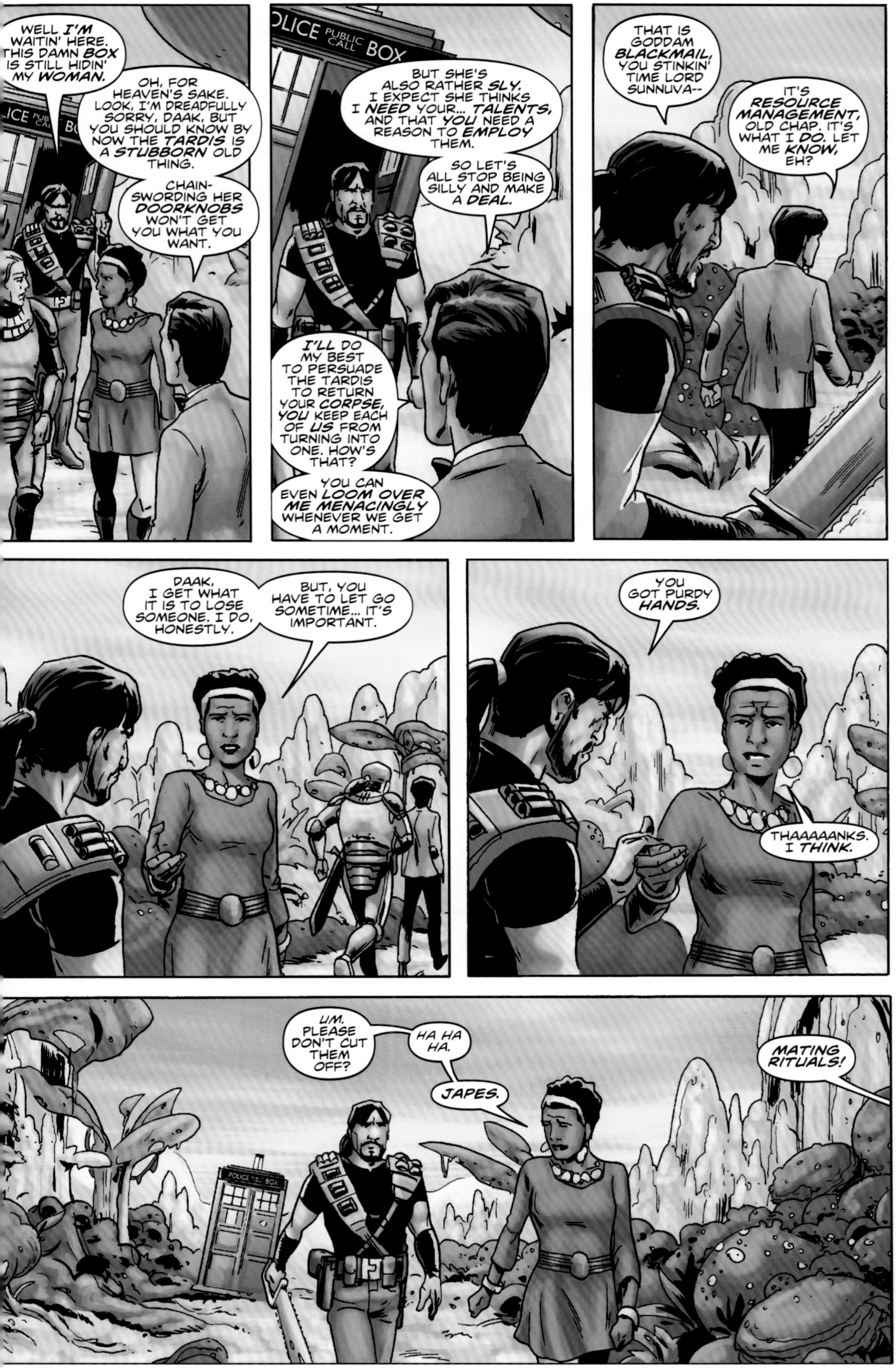
WELL I'M WAITIN' HERE. THIS DAMN BOX IS STILL HIDIN' MY WOMAN.
OH, FOR HEAVEN'S SAKE. LOOK, I'M DREADFULLY SORRY, DAAK, BUT YOU SHOULD KNOW BY NOW THE TARDIS IS A STUBBORN OLD THING.
CHAIN-SWORDING HER DOORKNOBS WON'T GET YOU WHAT YOU WANT.
POLICE PUBLIC CALL BOX
BUT SHE'S ALSO RATHER SLY. I EXPECT SHE THINKS I NEED YOUR... TALENTS, AND THAT YOU NEED A REASON TO EMPLOY THEM.
SO LET'S ALL STOP BEING SILLY AND MAKE A DEAL.
I'LL DO MY BEST TO PERSUADE THE TARDIS TO RETURN YOUR CORPSE, YOU KEEP EACH OF US FROM TURNING INTO ONE. HOW'S THAT?
YOU CAN EVEN LOOM OVER ME MENACINGLY WHENEVER WE GET A MOMENT.
THAT IS GODDAM BLACKMAIL, YOU STINKIN' TIME LORD SUNNUVA--
IT'S RESOURCE MANAGEMENT, OLD CHAP. IT'S WHAT I DO. LET ME KNOW, EH?
DAAK, I GET WHAT IT IS TO LOSE SOMEONE. I DO, HONESTLY.
BUT, YOU HAVE TO LET GO SOMETIME... IT'S IMPORTANT.
YOU GOT PURDY HANDS.
THAAAAANKS. I THINK.
UM. PLEASE DON'T CUT THEM OFF?
HA HA HA.
JAPES.
MATING RITUALS!

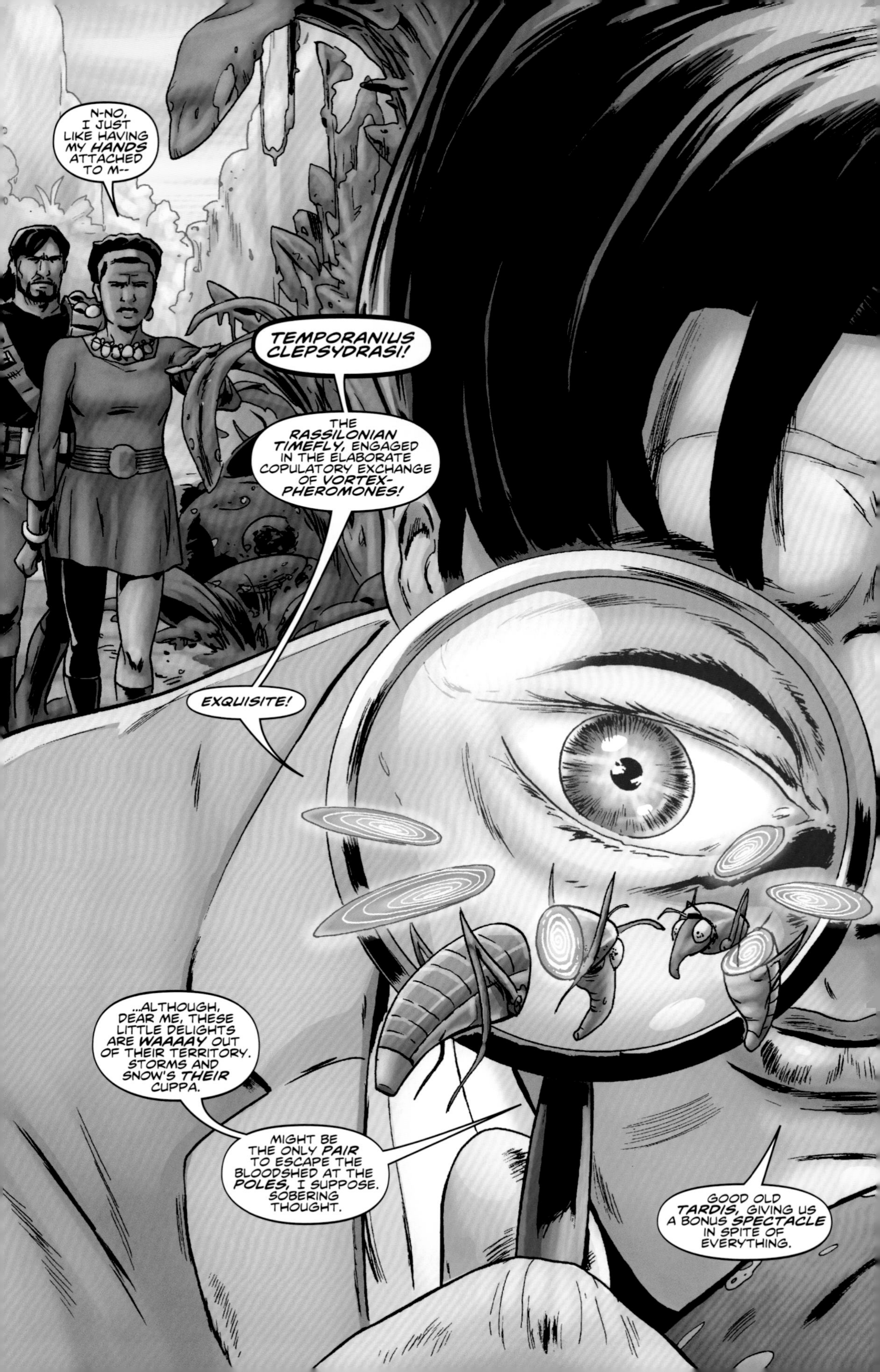
N-NO, I JUST LIKE HAVING MY HANDS ATTACHED TO M--
TEMPORANIUS CLEPSYDRASI!
THE RASSILONIAN TIMEFLY, ENGAGED IN THE ELABORATE COPULATORY EXCHANGE OF VORTEX-PHEROMONES!
EXQUISITE!
...ALTHOUGH, DEAR ME, THESE LITTLE DELIGHTS ARE WAAAAY OUT OF THEIR TERRITORY. STORMS AND SNOW'S THEIR CUPPA.
MIGHT BE THE ONLY PAIR TO ESCAPE THE BLOODSHED AT THE POLES, I SUPPOSE. SOBERING THOUGHT.
GOOD OLD TARDIS, GIVING US A BONUS SPECTACLE IN SPITE OF EVERYTHING.

BLOODSHED?

VORTEX PHEROMONES?

ARE YOU *BLUSHING*, LIBRARIAN?

...O, WHY WOULD BE B-- *WAIT* -- "BONUS"?

...SO... THIS ...GN'T WHAT WE CAME TO SEE?

NOW *LOOKIT*, ABOUT THIS *BLOODSHED*--

AND... DID YOU ...RULY SAY "*VORTEX ...HEROMONES*"? ...'VE NEVER *HEARD* ...F SUCH A THING.

OH *GOSH*, YES. THESE LITTLE DEVILS HAD A *TERRIBLE* TIME. HUNTED *MERCILESSLY*, AND THAT'S EVEN *BEFORE* THE RECENT... AH--

--*BLOODSHED*, YOU DEFINITELY SAID *BLOODSHED*.

IT'S THEIR *SHELLS*, Y'SEE?

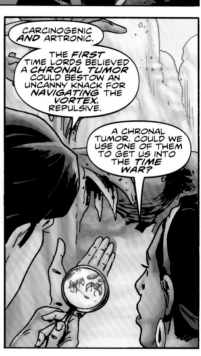

CARCINOGENIC *AND* ARTRONIC.

THE *FIRST* TIME LORDS BELIEVED A *CHRONAL TUMOR* COULD BESTOW AN UNCANNY KNACK FOR *NAVIGATING* THE *VORTEX*. REPULSIVE.

A *CHRONAL TUMOR*. COULD WE USE ONE OF THEM TO GET US INTO THE *TIME WAR*?

YOU'RE LEARNING QUICK, LIBRARY ASSISTANT. YES, SOMEONE PROBABLY *COULD*, IF THEY DIDN'T MIND BEING NEUROLOGICALLY *PULVERIZED*.

BUT ALICE, EVEN IF I *WAS* WILLING TO HAVE MY *BRAIN* SMEARED ACROSS THE NTH-DIMENSION -- NO, TA -- I COULDN'T DO IT.

CROSS MY OWN *TIMESTREAM* AND REALITY GOES *KABOOM*. YOU'D ALL BE JUST AS DOOMED AS *THESE* POOR THINGS.

...*DOOMED* BECAUSE OF... THE *BLOODSHED*?

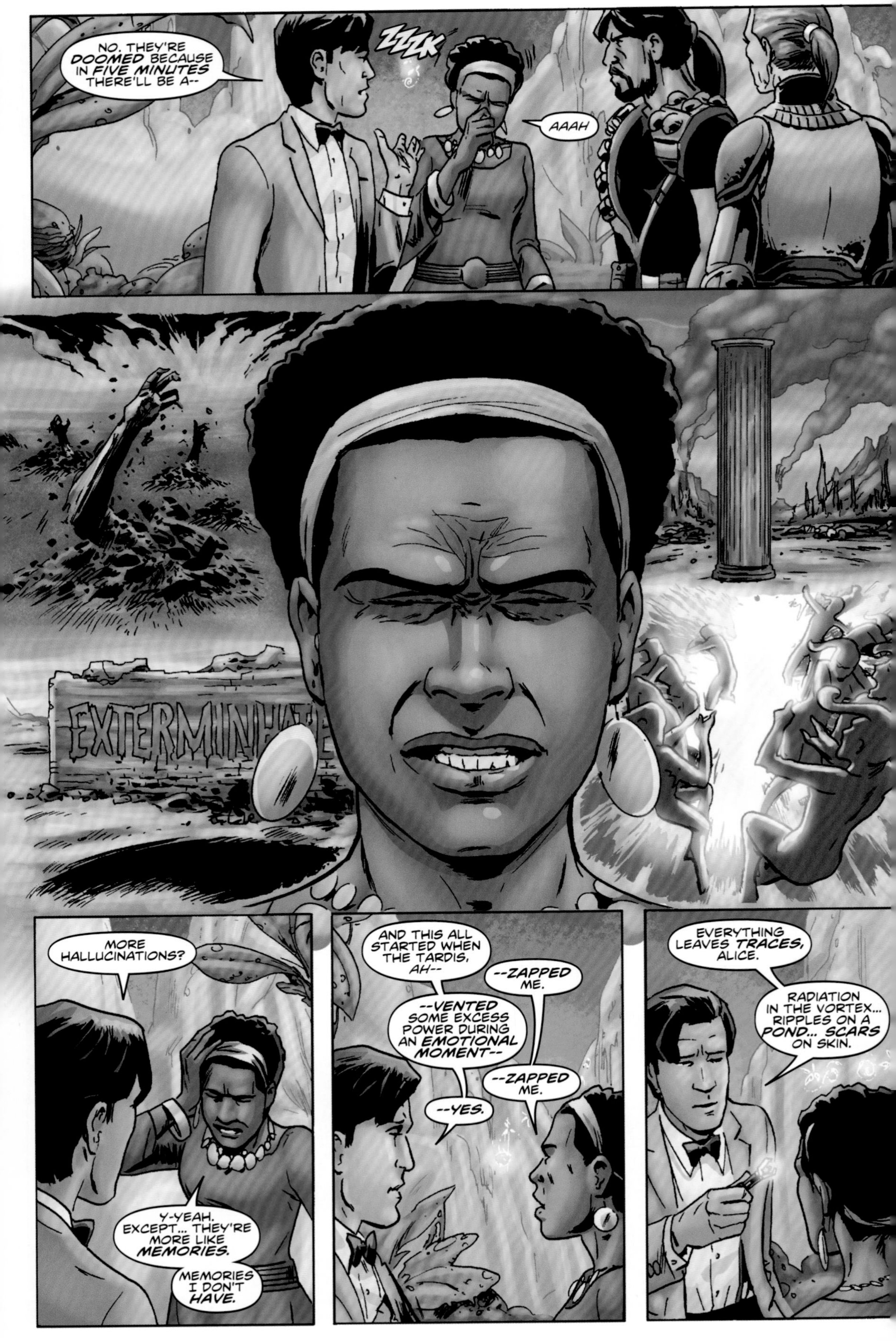

NO. THEY'RE DOOMED BECAUSE IN FIVE MINUTES THERE'LL BE A--
ZZZK
AAAH
EXTERMINATE
MORE HALLUCINATIONS?
Y-YEAH. EXCEPT... THEY'RE MORE LIKE MEMORIES.
MEMORIES I DON'T HAVE.
AND THIS ALL STARTED WHEN THE TARDIS, AH--
--ZAPPED ME.
--VENTED SOME EXCESS POWER DURING AN EMOTIONAL MOMENT--
--ZAPPED ME.
--YES.
EVERYTHING LEAVES TRACES, ALICE.
RADIATION IN THE VORTEX... RIPPLES ON A POND... SCARS ON SKIN.

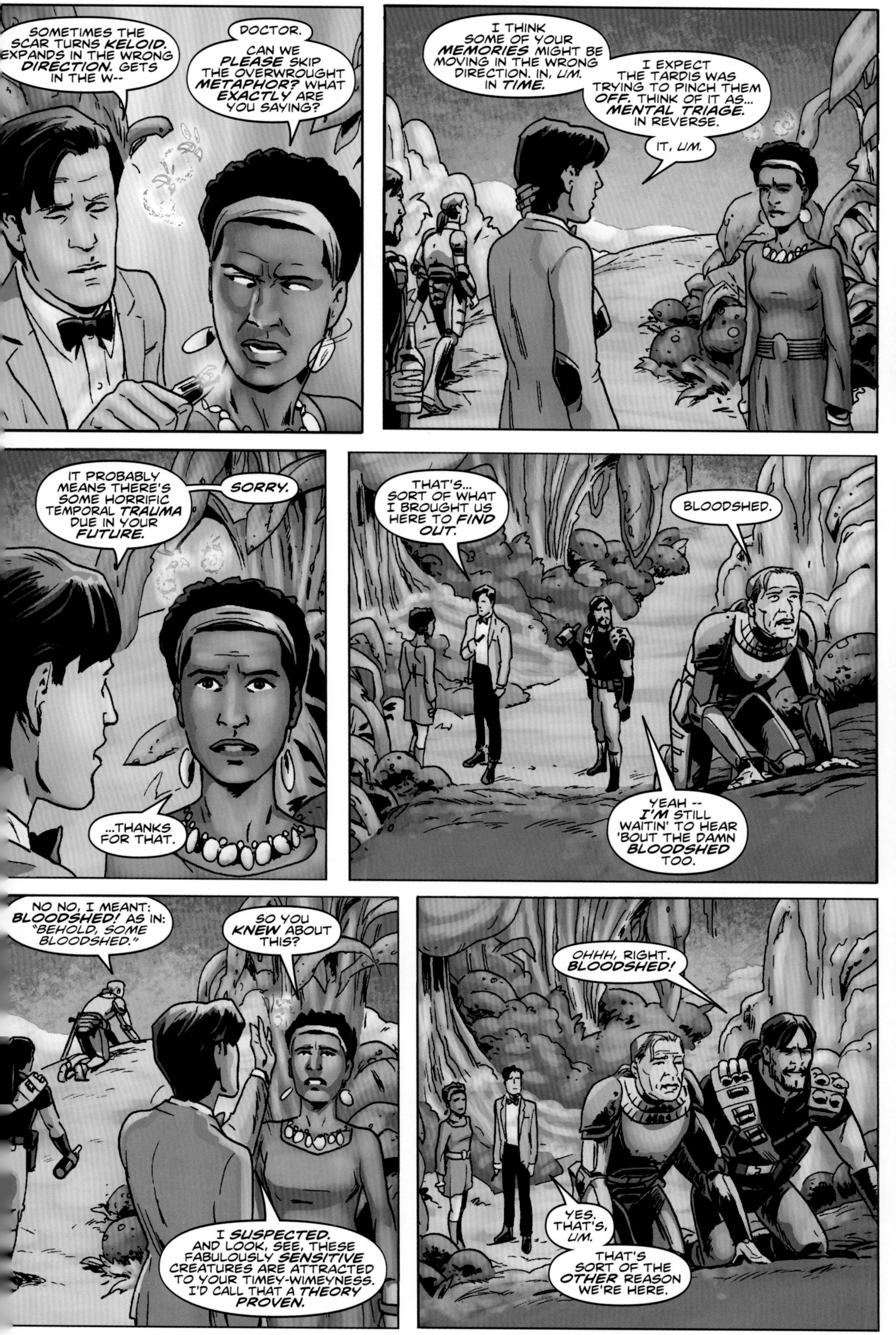
SOMETIMES THE SCAR TURNS KELOID. EXPANDS IN THE WRONG DIRECTION. GETS IN THE W--
DOCTOR.
CAN WE PLEASE SKIP THE OVERWROUGHT METAPHOR? WHAT EXACTLY ARE YOU SAYING?
I THINK SOME OF YOUR MEMORIES MIGHT BE MOVING IN THE WRONG DIRECTION. IN, UM. IN TIME.
I EXPECT THE TARDIS WAS TRYING TO PINCH THEM OFF. THINK OF IT AS... MENTAL TRIAGE. IN REVERSE.
IT, UM.
IT PROBABLY MEANS THERE'S SOME HORRIFIC TEMPORAL TRAUMA DUE IN YOUR FUTURE.
SORRY.
...THANKS FOR THAT.
THAT'S... SORT OF WHAT I BROUGHT US HERE TO FIND OUT.
BLOODSHED.
YEAH -- I'M STILL WAITIN' TO HEAR 'BOUT THE DAMN BLOODSHED TOO.
NO NO, I MEANT: BLOODSHED! AS IN: "BEHOLD, SOME BLOODSHED."
SO YOU KNEW ABOUT THIS?
I SUSPECTED. AND LOOK, SEE, THESE FABULOUSLY SENSITIVE CREATURES ARE ATTRACTED TO YOUR TIMEY-WIMEYNESS. I'D CALL THAT A THEORY PROVEN.
OHHH, RIGHT. BLOODSHED!
YES. THAT'S, UM.
THAT'S SORT OF THE OTHER REASON WE'RE HERE.

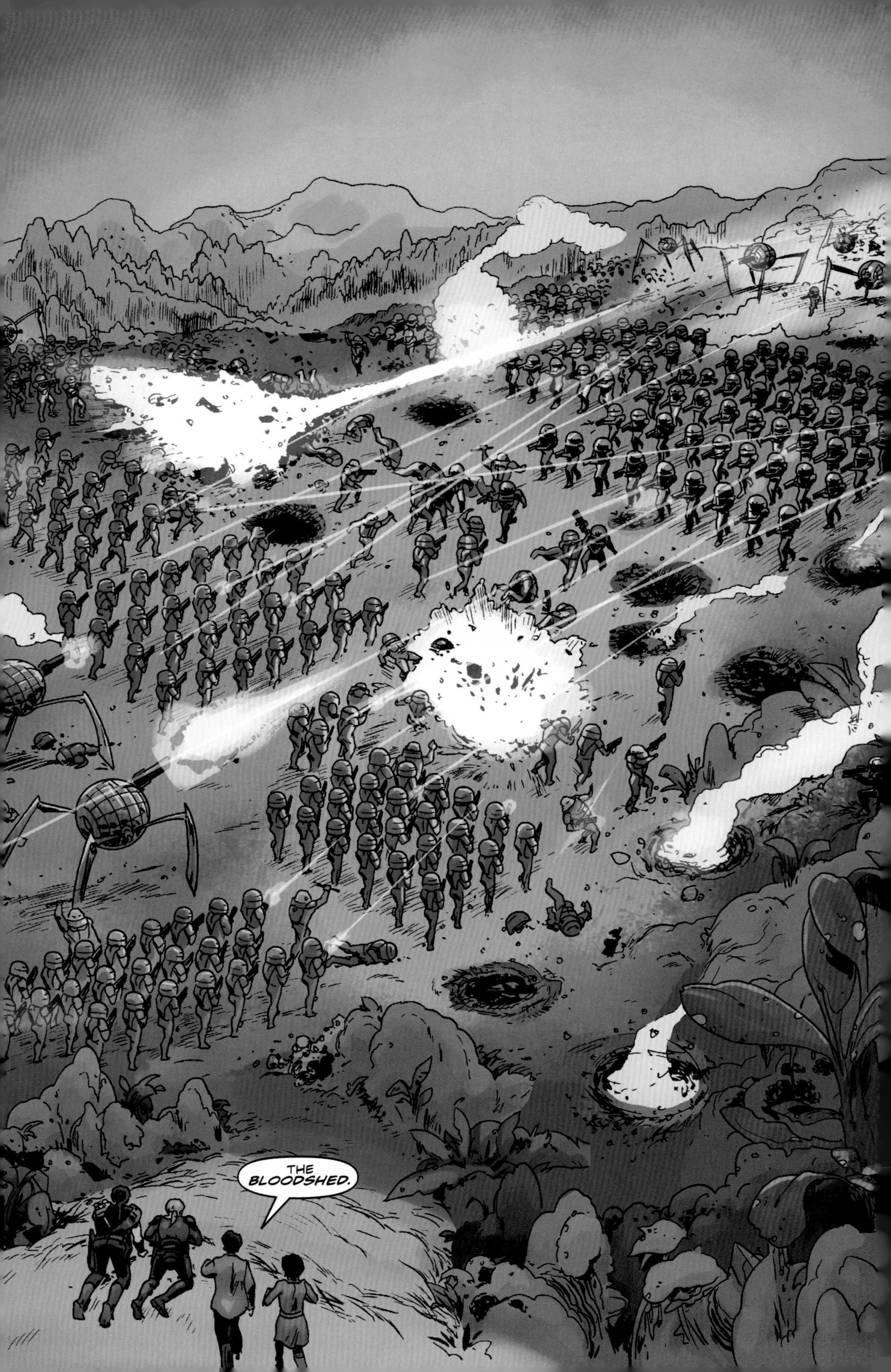
THE BLOODSHED.

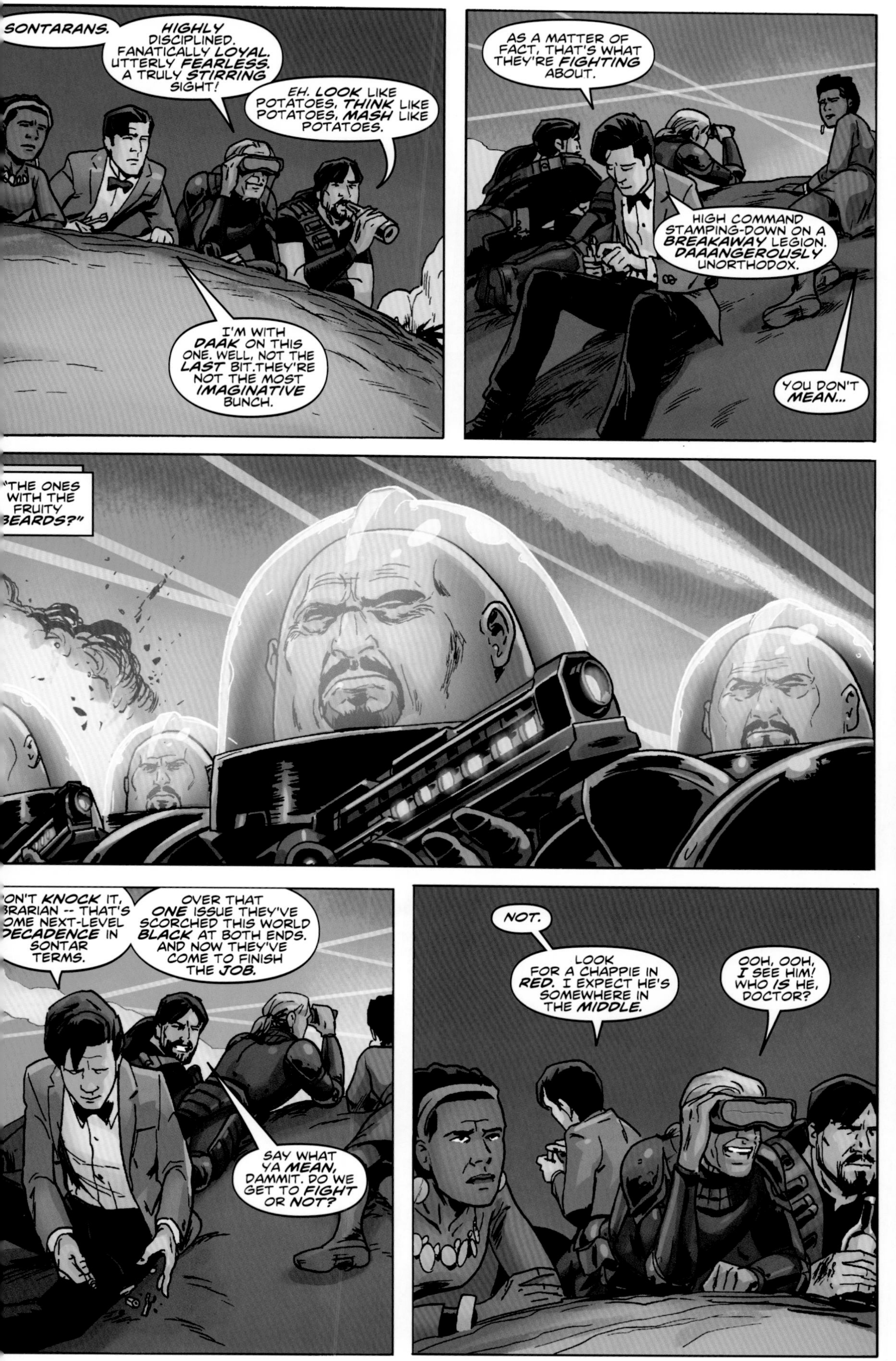
SONTARANS.
HIGHLY DISCIPLINED. FANATICALLY LOYAL. UTTERLY FEARLESS. A TRULY STIRRING SIGHT!
EH. LOOK LIKE POTATOES, THINK LIKE POTATOES, MASH LIKE POTATOES.
I'M WITH DAAK ON THIS ONE. WELL, NOT THE LAST BIT.THEY'RE NOT THE MOST IMAGINATIVE BUNCH.
AS A MATTER OF FACT, THAT'S WHAT THEY'RE FIGHTING ABOUT.
HIGH COMMAND STAMPING-DOWN ON A BREAKAWAY LEGION. DAAANGEROUSLY UNORTHODOX.
YOU DON'T MEAN...
"THE ONES WITH THE FRUITY BEARDS?"
ON'T KNOCK IT, BRARIAN -- THAT'S OME NEXT-LEVEL DECADENCE IN SONTAR TERMS.
OVER THAT ONE ISSUE THEY'VE SCORCHED THIS WORLD BLACK AT BOTH ENDS. AND NOW THEY'VE COME TO FINISH THE JOB.
SAY WHAT YA MEAN, DAMMIT. DO WE GET TO FIGHT OR NOT?
NOT.
LOOK FOR A CHAPPIE IN RED. I EXPECT HE'S SOMEWHERE IN THE MIDDLE.
OOH, OOH, I SEE HIM! WHO IS HE, DOCTOR?

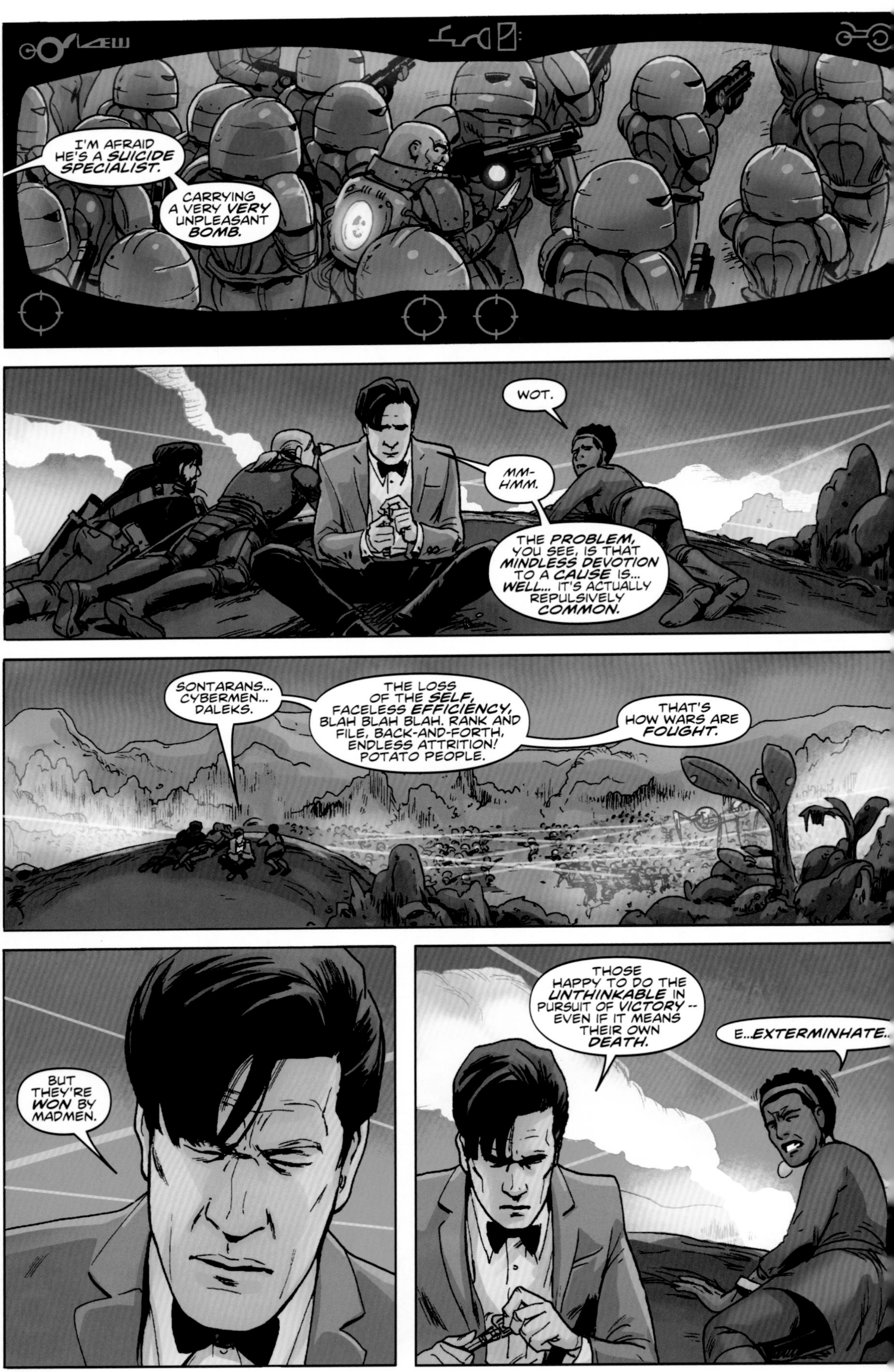
I'M AFRAID HE'S A SUICIDE SPECIALIST.
CARRYING A VERY VERY UNPLEASANT BOMB.
WOT.
MM-HMM.
THE PROBLEM, YOU SEE, IS THAT MINDLESS DEVOTION TO A CAUSE IS... WELL... IT'S ACTUALLY REPULSIVELY COMMON.
SONTARANS... CYBERMEN... DALEKS.
THE LOSS OF THE SELF, FACELESS EFFICIENCY, BLAH BLAH BLAH. RANK AND FILE, BACK-AND-FORTH, ENDLESS ATTRITION! POTATO PEOPLE.
THAT'S HOW WARS ARE FOUGHT.
BUT THEY'RE WON BY MADMEN.
THOSE HAPPY TO DO THE UNTHINKABLE IN PURSUIT OF VICTORY -- EVEN IF IT MEANS THEIR OWN DEATH.
E...EXTERMINHATE...

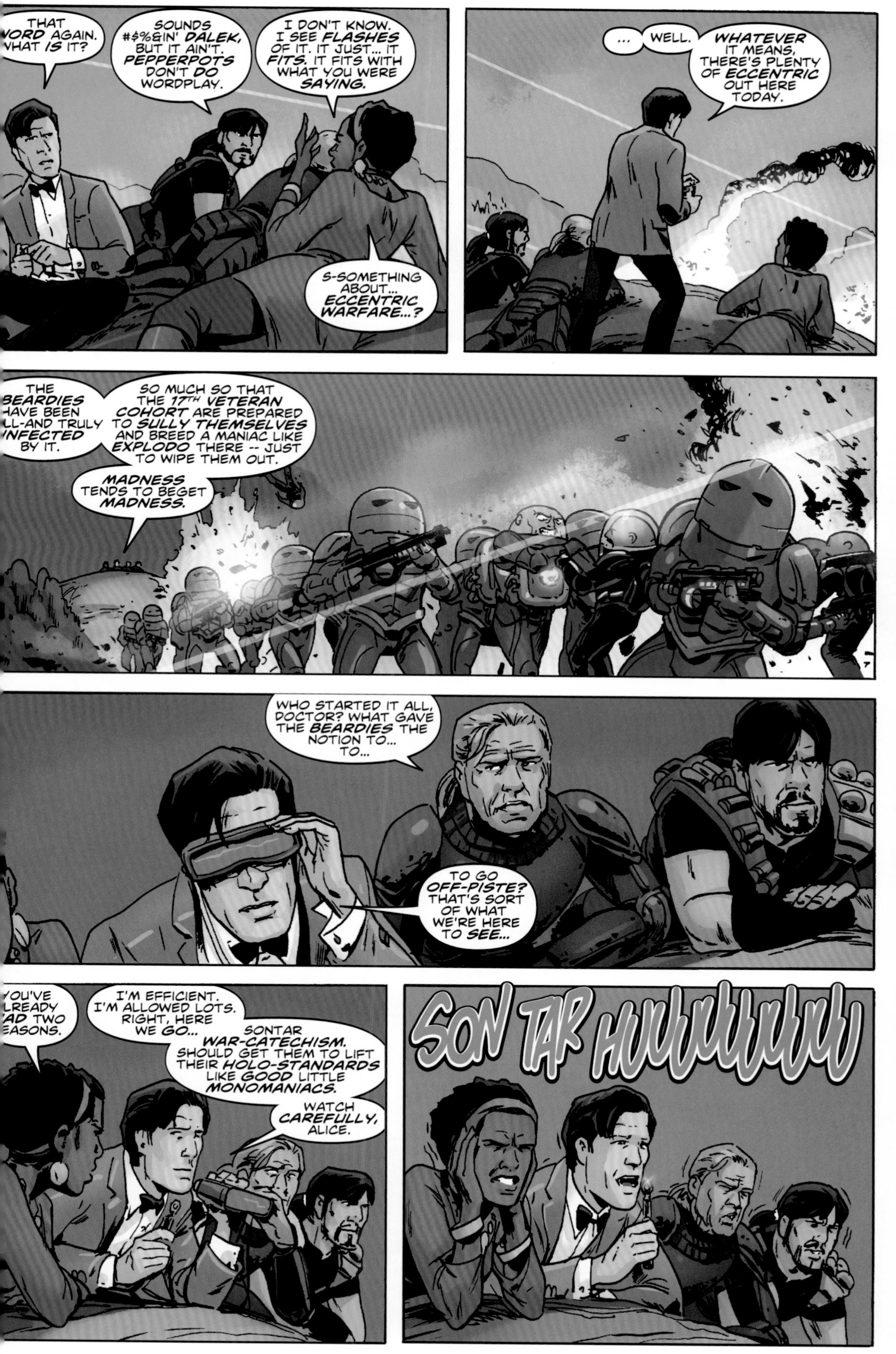
THAT WORD AGAIN. WHAT IS IT?
SOUNDS #$%&IN' DALEK, BUT IT AIN'T. PEPPERPOTS DON'T DO WORDPLAY.
I DON'T KNOW. I SEE FLASHES OF IT. IT JUST... IT FITS. IT FITS WITH WHAT YOU WERE SAYING.
S-SOMETHING ABOUT... ECCENTRIC WARFARE...?
...
WELL.
WHATEVER IT MEANS, THERE'S PLENTY OF ECCENTRIC OUT HERE TODAY.
THE BEARDIES HAVE BEEN ALL-AND TRULY INFECTED BY IT.
SO MUCH SO THAT THE 17TH VETERAN COHORT ARE PREPARED TO SULLY THEMSELVES AND BREED A MANIAC LIKE EXPLODO THERE -- JUST TO WIPE THEM OUT.
MADNESS TENDS TO BEGET MADNESS.
WHO STARTED IT ALL, DOCTOR? WHAT GAVE THE BEARDIES THE NOTION TO... TO...
TO GO OFF-PISTE? THAT'S SORT OF WHAT WE'RE HERE TO SEE...
YOU'VE ALREADY HAD TWO REASONS.
I'M EFFICIENT. I'M ALLOWED LOTS. RIGHT, HERE WE GO...
SONTAR WAR-CATECHISM. SHOULD GET THEM TO LIFT THEIR HOLO-STANDARDS LIKE GOOD LITTLE MONOMANIACS.
WATCH CAREFULLY, ALICE.
SON TAR HUUUUUUUU

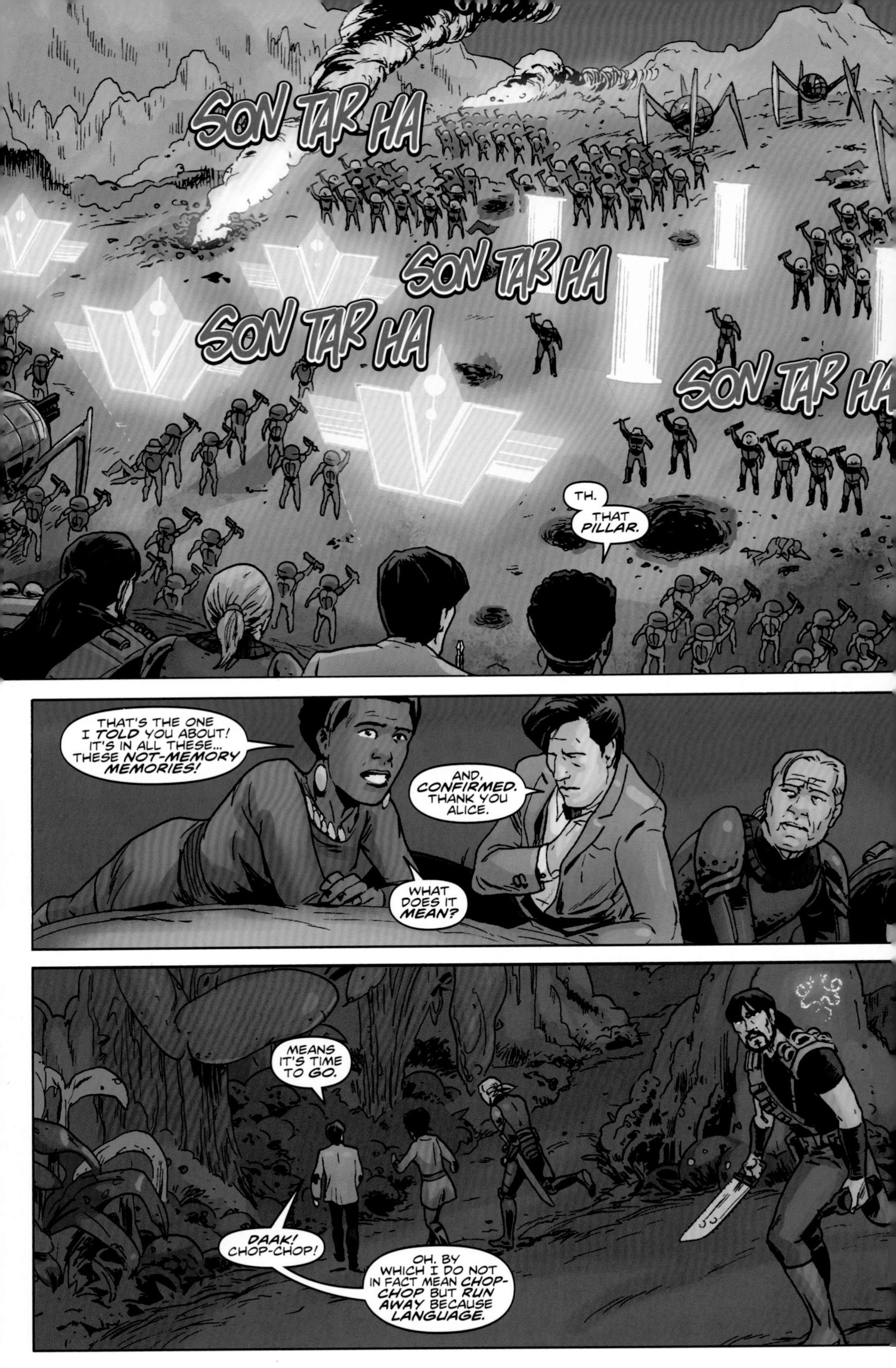
SON TAR HA
SON TAR HA
SON TAR HA
SON TAR HA
TH. THAT PILLAR.
THAT'S THE ONE I TOLD YOU ABOUT! IT'S IN ALL THESE... THESE NOT-MEMORY MEMORIES!
AND, CONFIRMED. THANK YOU ALICE.
WHAT DOES IT MEAN?
MEANS IT'S TIME TO GO.
DAAK! CHOP-CHOP!
OH. BY WHICH I DO NOT IN FACT MEAN CHOP-CHOP BUT RUN AWAY BECAUSE LANGUAGE.

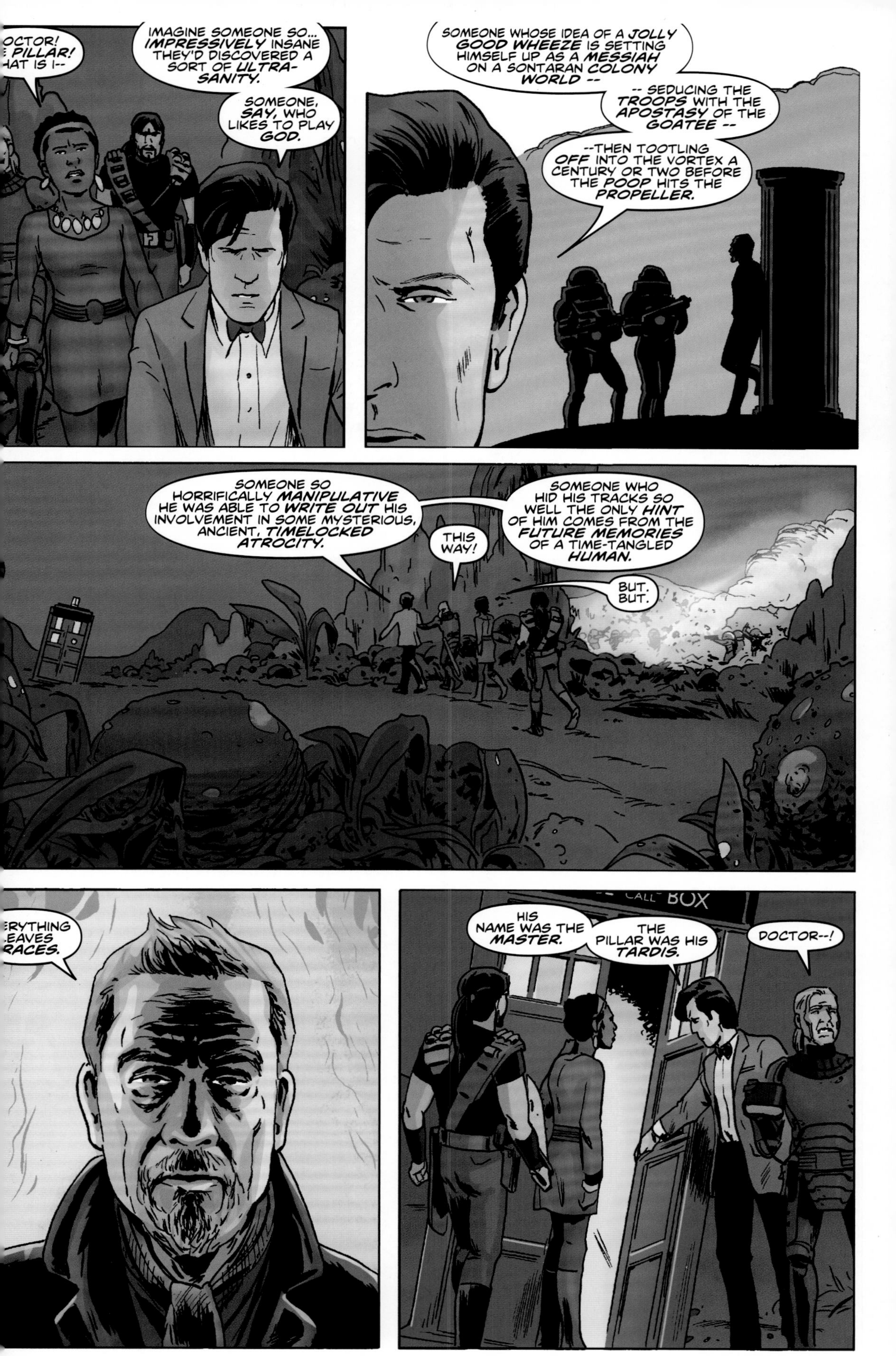
OCTOR! E PILLAR! HAT IS I--
IMAGINE SOMEONE SO... IMPRESSIVELY INSANE THEY'D DISCOVERED A SORT OF ULTRA-SANITY.
SOMEONE, SAY, WHO LIKES TO PLAY GOD.
SOMEONE WHOSE IDEA OF A JOLLY GOOD WHEEZE IS SETTING HIMSELF UP AS A MESSIAH ON A SONTARAN COLONY WORLD --
-- SEDUCING THE TROOPS WITH THE APOSTASY OF THE GOATEE --
--THEN TOOTLING OFF INTO THE VORTEX A CENTURY OR TWO BEFORE THE POOP HITS THE PROPELLER.
SOMEONE SO HORRIFICALLY MANIPULATIVE HE WAS ABLE TO WRITE OUT HIS INVOLVEMENT IN SOME MYSTERIOUS, ANCIENT, TIMELOCKED ATROCITY.
THIS WAY!
SOMEONE WHO HID HIS TRACKS SO WELL THE ONLY HINT OF HIM COMES FROM THE FUTURE MEMORIES OF A TIME-TANGLED HUMAN.
BUT. BUT.
ERYTHING LEAVES RACES.
CALL BOX
HIS NAME WAS THE MASTER.
THE PILLAR WAS HIS TARDIS.
DOCTOR--!

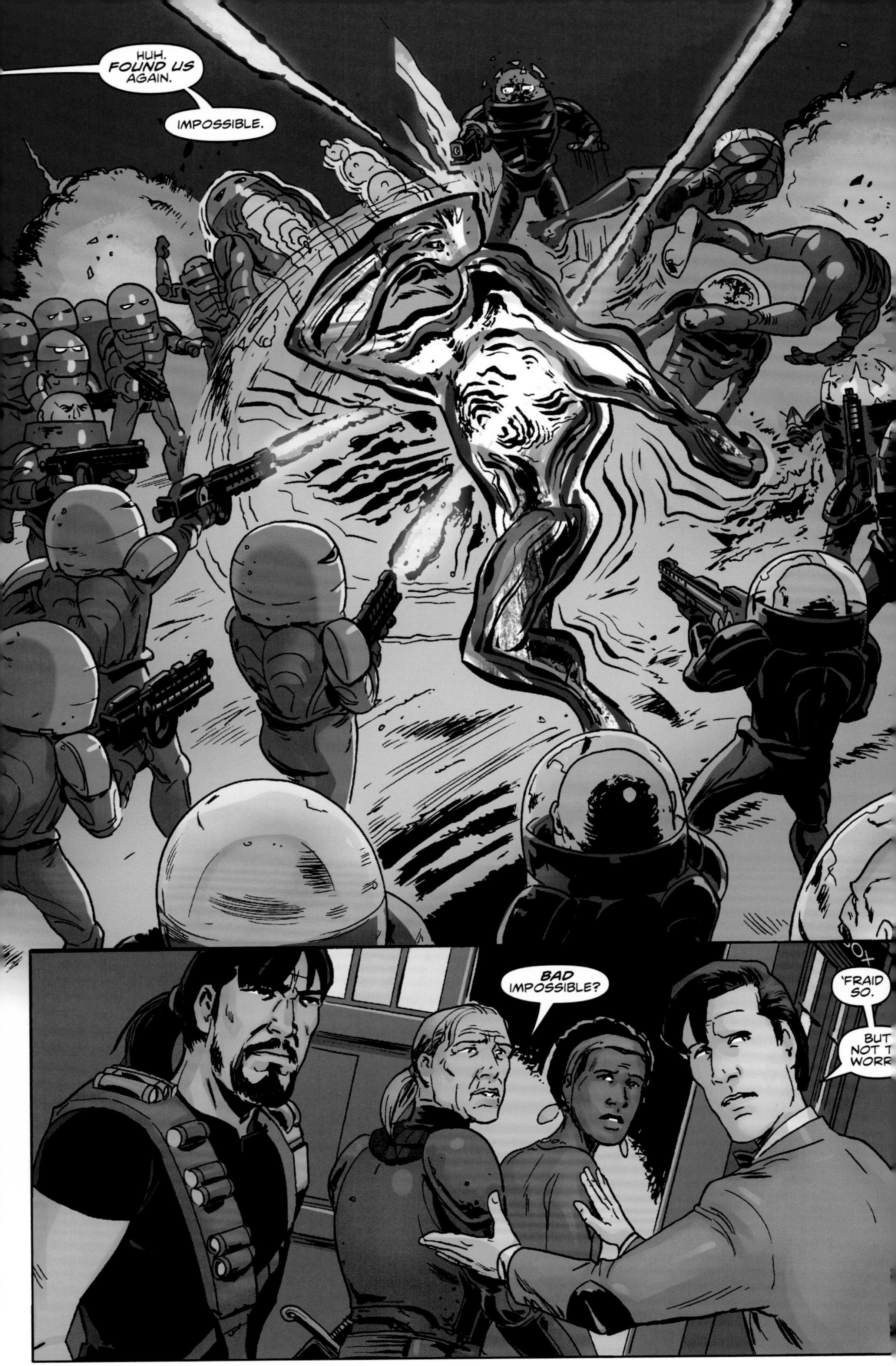
HUH. FOUND US AGAIN.
IMPOSSIBLE.
BAD IMPOSSIBLE?
'FRAID SO.
BUT NOT

IN TEN SECONDS OUR CHERRY-RED *CHUM* GOES *KABLOOIE.*

TAKING THE 17TH VETERAN COHORT, THE BEARDIE-WEIRDIES AND ALL THE *RASSILONIAN TIMEFLIES* IN EXISTENCE *WITH* HIM.

LET'S SEE HOW OUR IRRITATING PURSUER HANDLES A SONTARAN *ESCHATOMIC WARHEAD,* SHALL WE?

THAT'S WHY WE CAME HERE.

FOUR REASONS! OH *VERY GOOD,* DOCTOR.

...YOU WERE JUST COMPLAINING ABOUT THIS CACKLING *NEMESIS* OF YOURS BEING A MANIPULATIVE *SWINE!* AND NOW HERE *YOU* ARE D--

UNFAIR *CALL,* REFEREE. IT'S *CLEARLY* NOT THE *SAME.*

IT'S.

I'M.

I.

I'LL DO A WITTY RIPOSTE LATER, OKAY?

FOR NOW--

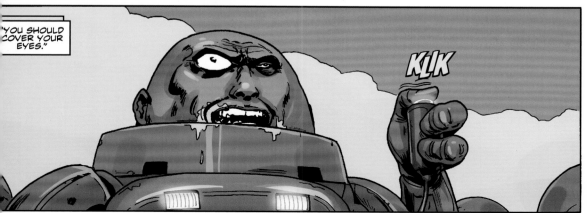

"YOU SHOULD COVER YOUR EYES."

KLIK

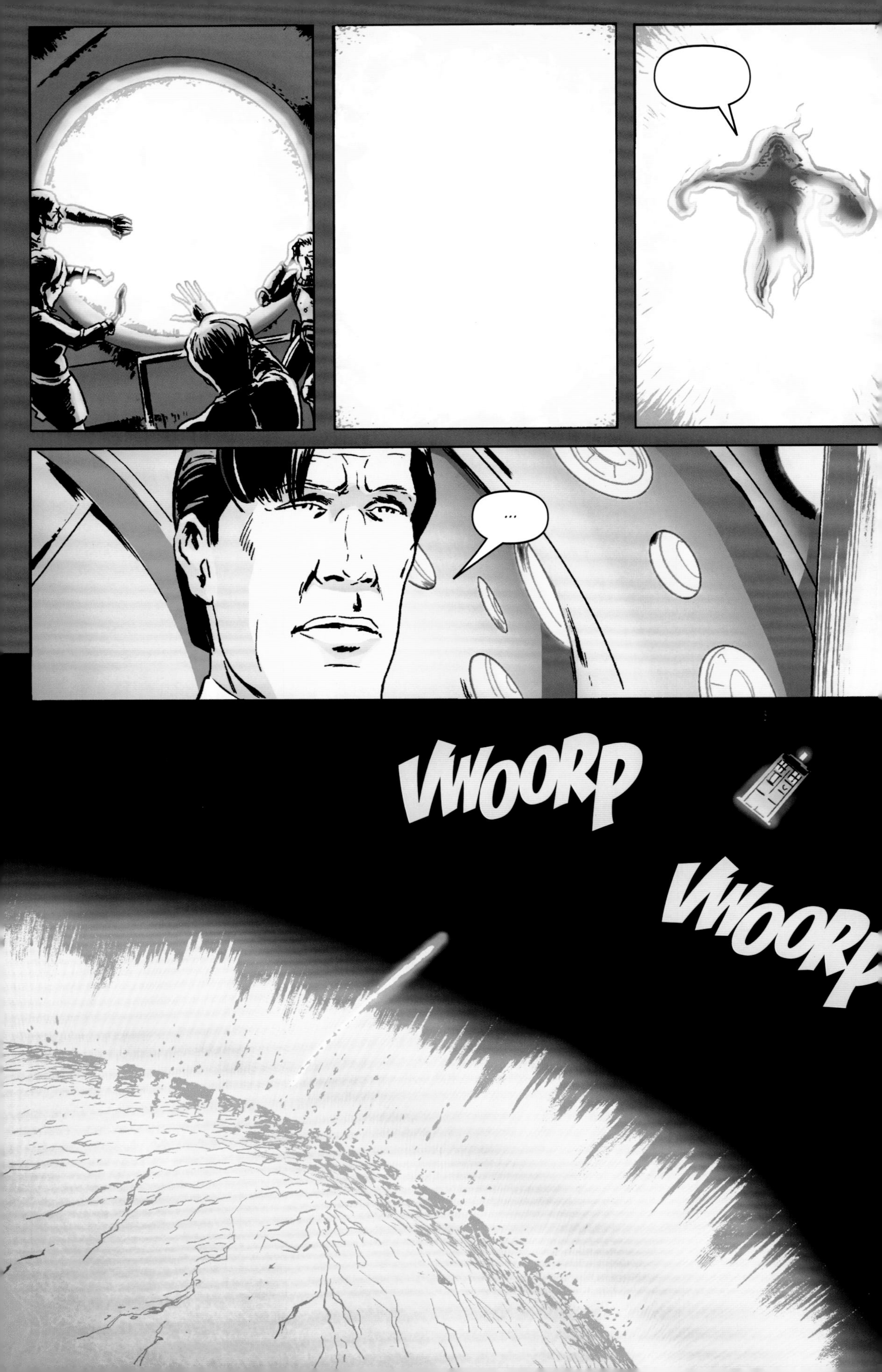
...
VWOORP
VWOORP

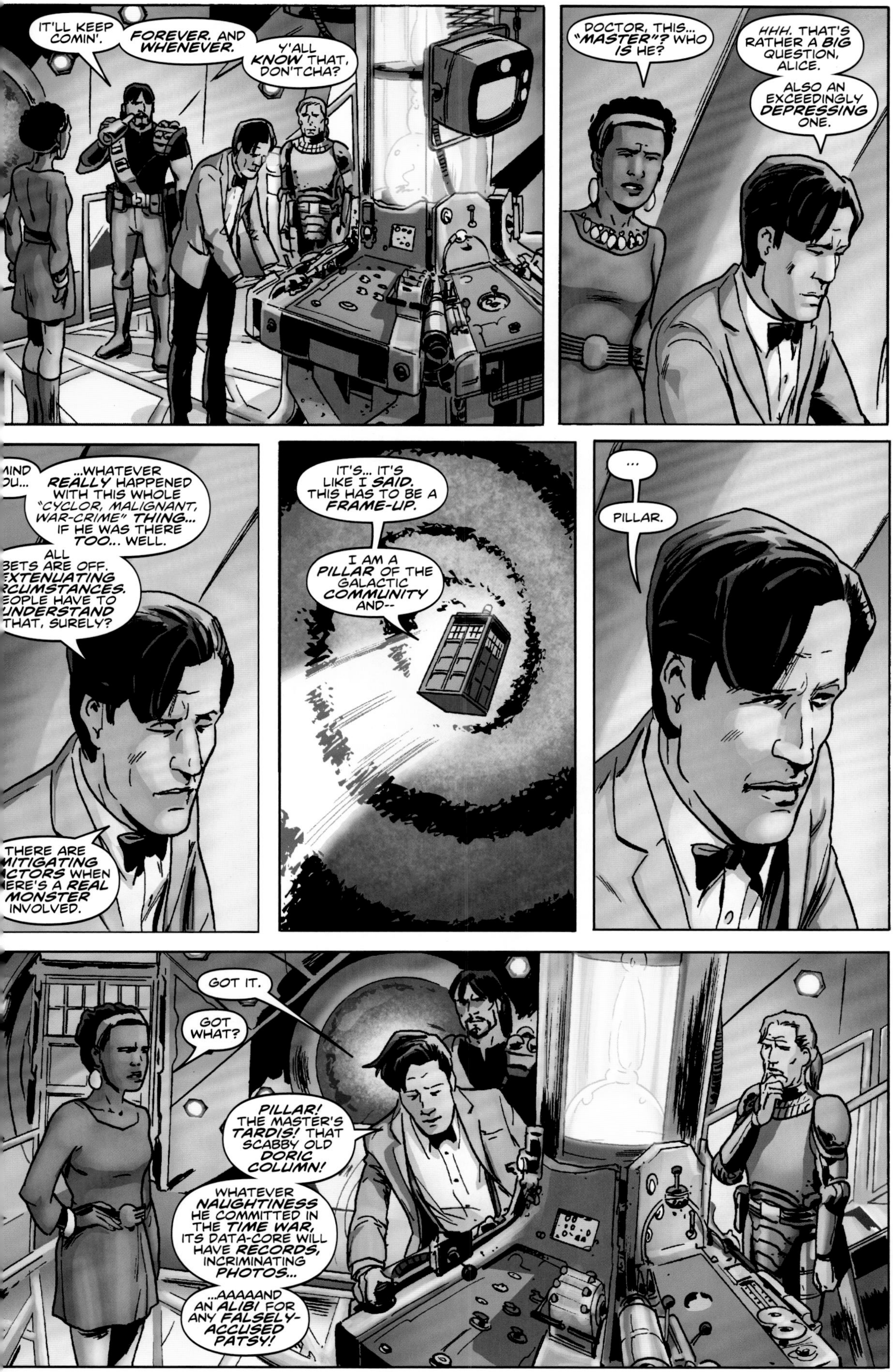
IT'LL KEEP COMIN'.
FOREVER. AND WHENEVER.
Y'ALL KNOW THAT, DON'TCHA?
DOCTOR, THIS... "MASTER"? WHO IS HE?
HHH. THAT'S RATHER A BIG QUESTION, ALICE.
ALSO AN EXCEEDINGLY DEPRESSING ONE.
MIND YOU...
...WHATEVER REALLY HAPPENED WITH THIS WHOLE "CYCLOR, MALIGNANT, WAR-CRIME" THING... IF HE WAS THERE TOO... WELL.
ALL BETS ARE OFF. EXTENUATING CIRCUMSTANCES. PEOPLE HAVE TO UNDERSTAND THAT, SURELY?
THERE ARE MITIGATING FACTORS WHEN THERE'S A REAL MONSTER INVOLVED.
IT'S... IT'S LIKE I SAID. THIS HAS TO BE A FRAME-UP.
I AM A PILLAR OF THE GALACTIC COMMUNITY AND--
...
PILLAR.
GOT IT.
GOT WHAT?
PILLAR! THE MASTER'S TARDIS! THAT SCABBY OLD DORIC COLUMN!
WHATEVER NAUGHTINESS HE COMMITTED IN THE TIME WAR, ITS DATA-CORE WILL HAVE RECORDS, INCRIMINATING PHOTOS...
...AAAAAND AN ALIBI FOR ANY FALSELY-ACCUSED PATSY!

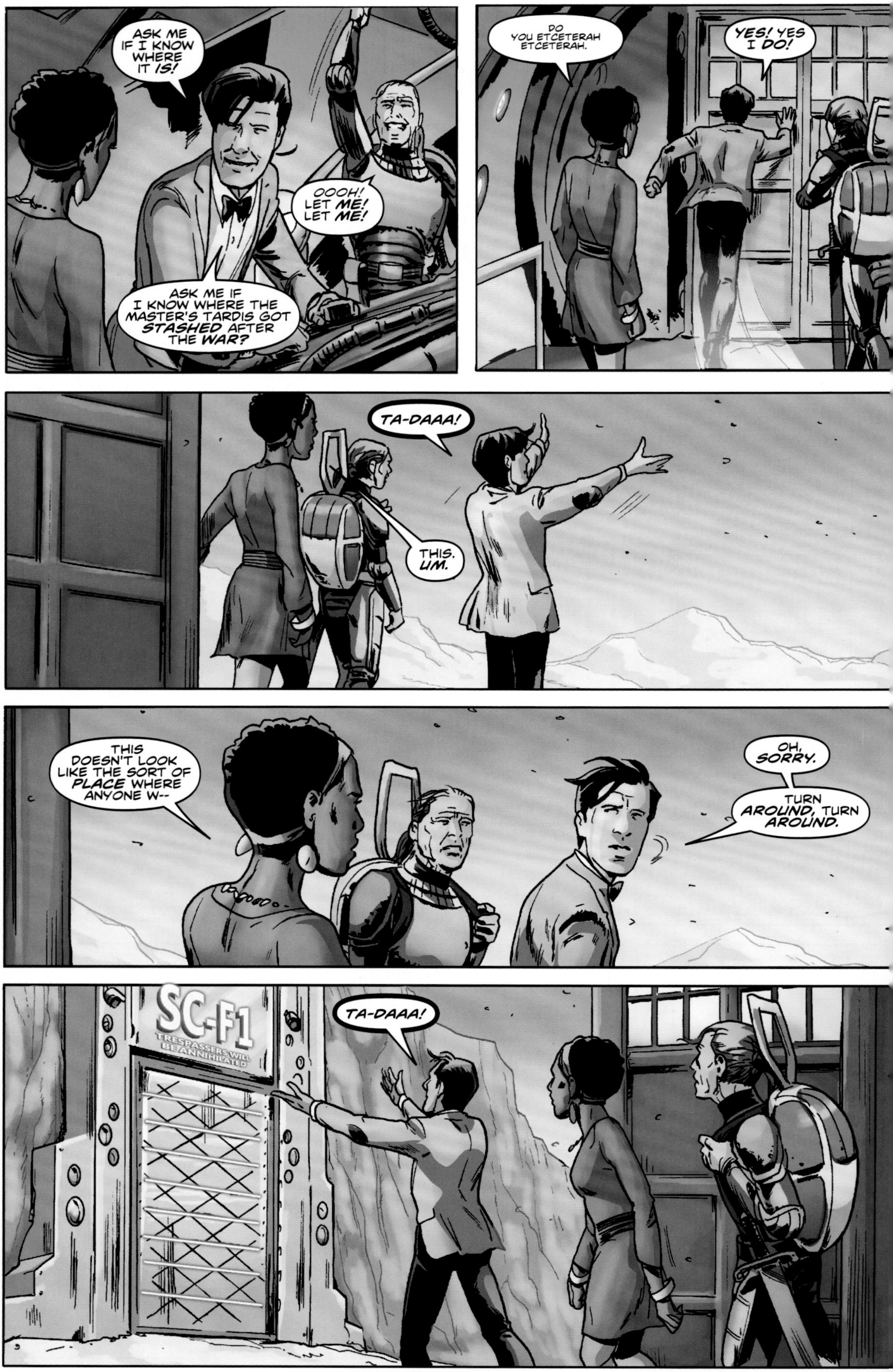
ASK ME IF I KNOW WHERE IT IS!
OOOH! LET ME! LET ME!
ASK ME IF I KNOW WHERE THE MASTER'S TARDIS GOT STASHED AFTER THE WAR?
DO YOU ETCETERAH ETCETERAH.
YES! YES I DO!
TA-DAAA!
THIS. UM.
THIS DOESN'T LOOK LIKE THE SORT OF PLACE WHERE ANYONE W--
OH, SORRY.
TURN AROUND, TURN AROUND.
SC-F1
TRESPASSERS WILL BE ANNIHILATED
TA-DAAA!

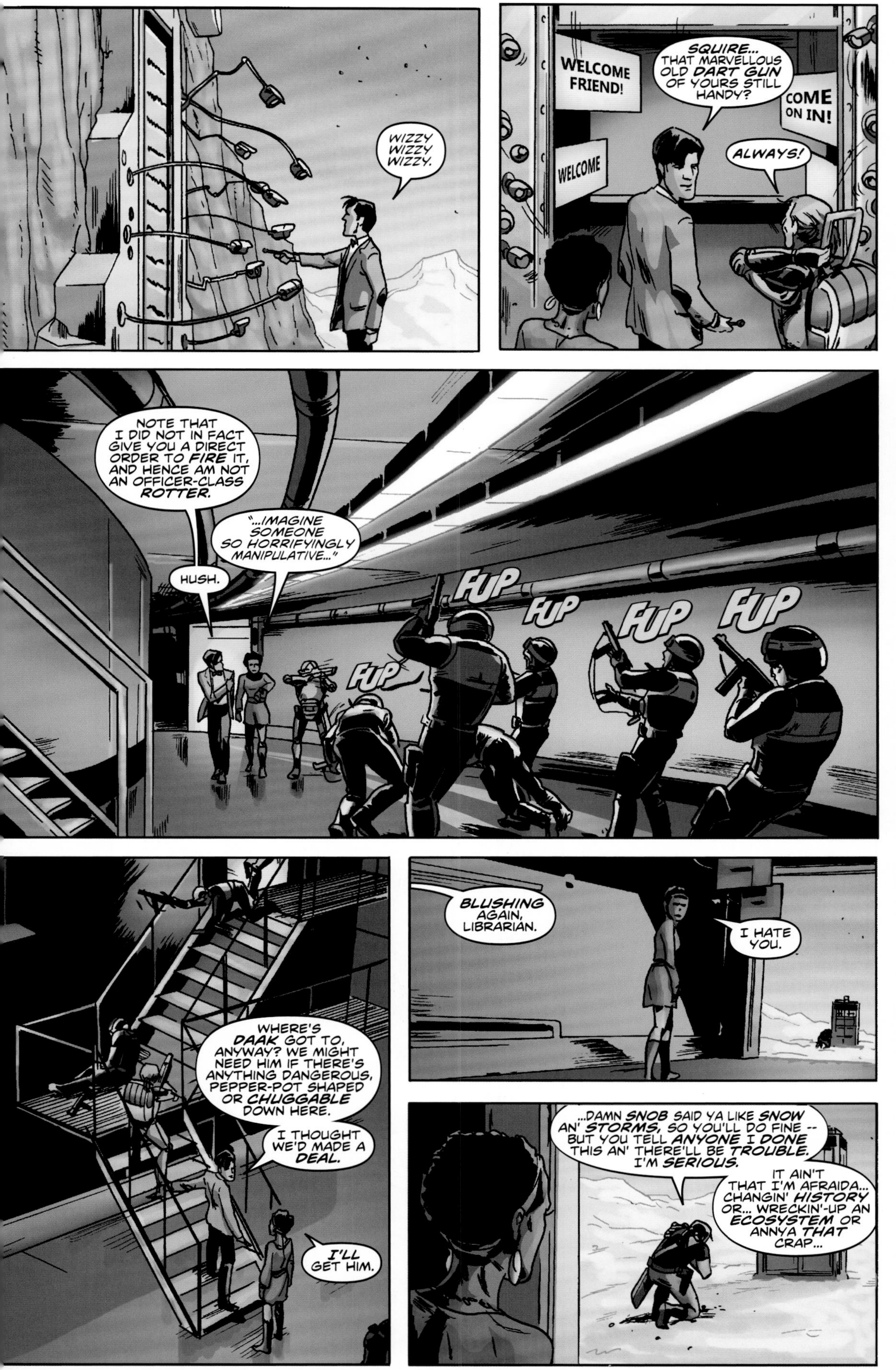

WIZZY WIZZY WIZZY.
WELCOME FRIEND!
SQUIRE... THAT MARVELLOUS OLD DART GUN OF YOURS STILL HANDY?
COME ON IN!
WELCOME
ALWAYS!
NOTE THAT I DID NOT IN FACT GIVE YOU A DIRECT ORDER TO FIRE IT, AND HENCE AM NOT AN OFFICER-CLASS ROTTER.
"...IMAGINE SOMEONE SO HORRIFYINGLY MANIPULATIVE..."
HUSH.
FUP
FUP
FUP
FUP
FUP
WHERE'S DAAK GOT TO, ANYWAY? WE MIGHT NEED HIM IF THERE'S ANYTHING DANGEROUS, PEPPER-POT SHAPED OR CHUGGABLE DOWN HERE.
I THOUGHT WE'D MADE A DEAL.
I'LL GET HIM.
BLUSHING AGAIN, LIBRARIAN.
I HATE YOU.
...DAMN SNOB SAID YA LIKE SNOW AN' STORMS, SO YOU'LL DO FINE -- BUT YOU TELL ANYONE I DONE THIS AN' THERE'LL BE TROUBLE. I'M SERIOUS.
IT AIN'T THAT I'M AFRAIDA... CHANGIN' HISTORY OR... WRECKIN'-UP AN ECOSYSTEM OR ANNYA THAT CRAP...

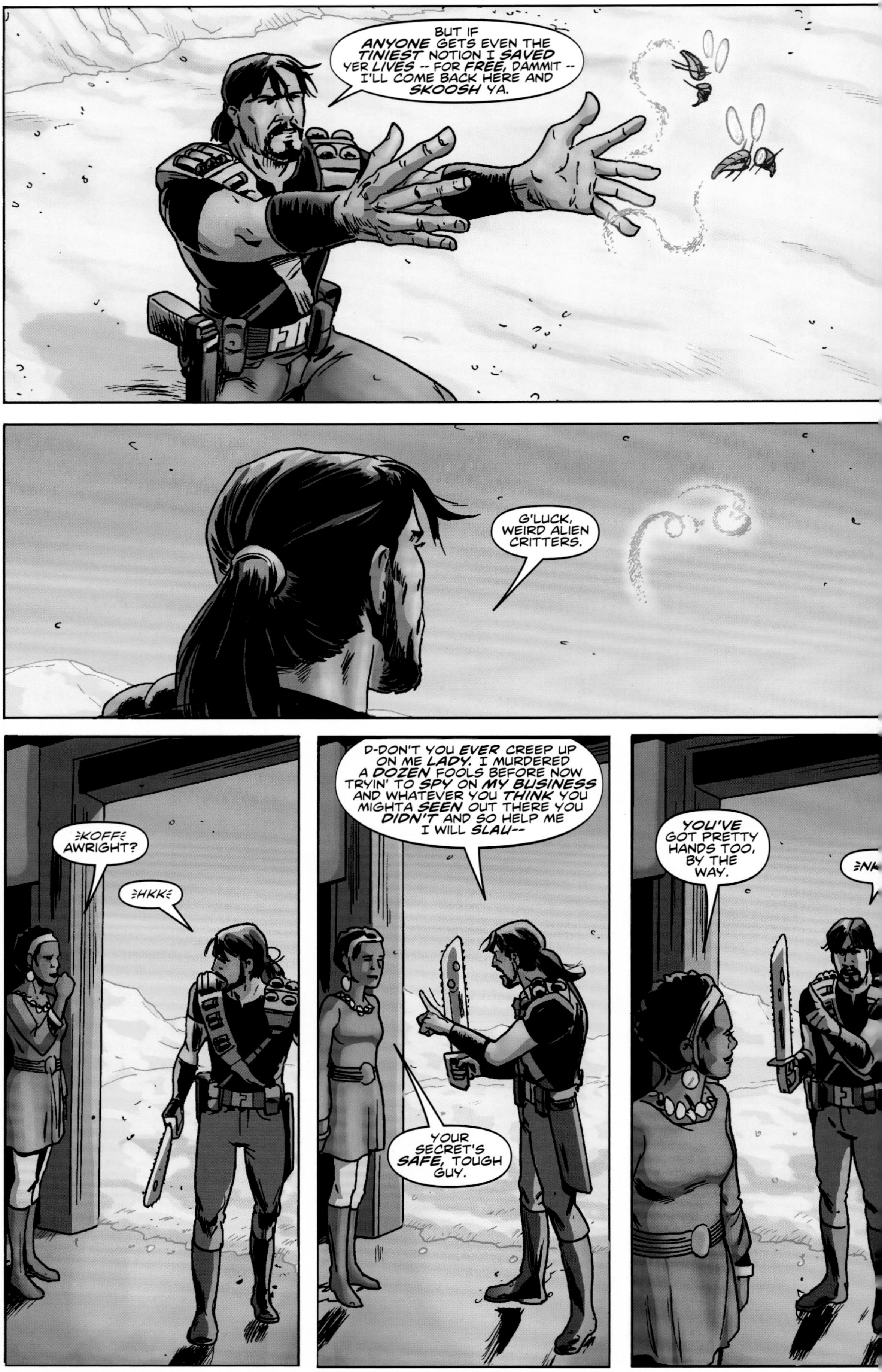
BUT IF ANYONE GETS EVEN THE TINIEST NOTION I SAVED YER LIVES -- FOR FREE, DAMMIT -- I'LL COME BACK HERE AND SKOOSH YA.
G'LUCK, WEIRD ALIEN CRITTERS.
KOFF AWRIGHT?
HKK
D-DON'T YOU EVER CREEP UP ON ME LADY. I MURDERED A DOZEN FOOLS BEFORE NOW TRYIN' TO SPY ON MY BUSINESS AND WHATEVER YOU THINK YOU MIGHTA SEEN OUT THERE YOU DIDN'T AND SO HELP ME I WILL SLAU--
YOUR SECRET'S SAFE, TOUGH GUY.
YOU'VE GOT PRETTY HANDS TOO, BY THE WAY.

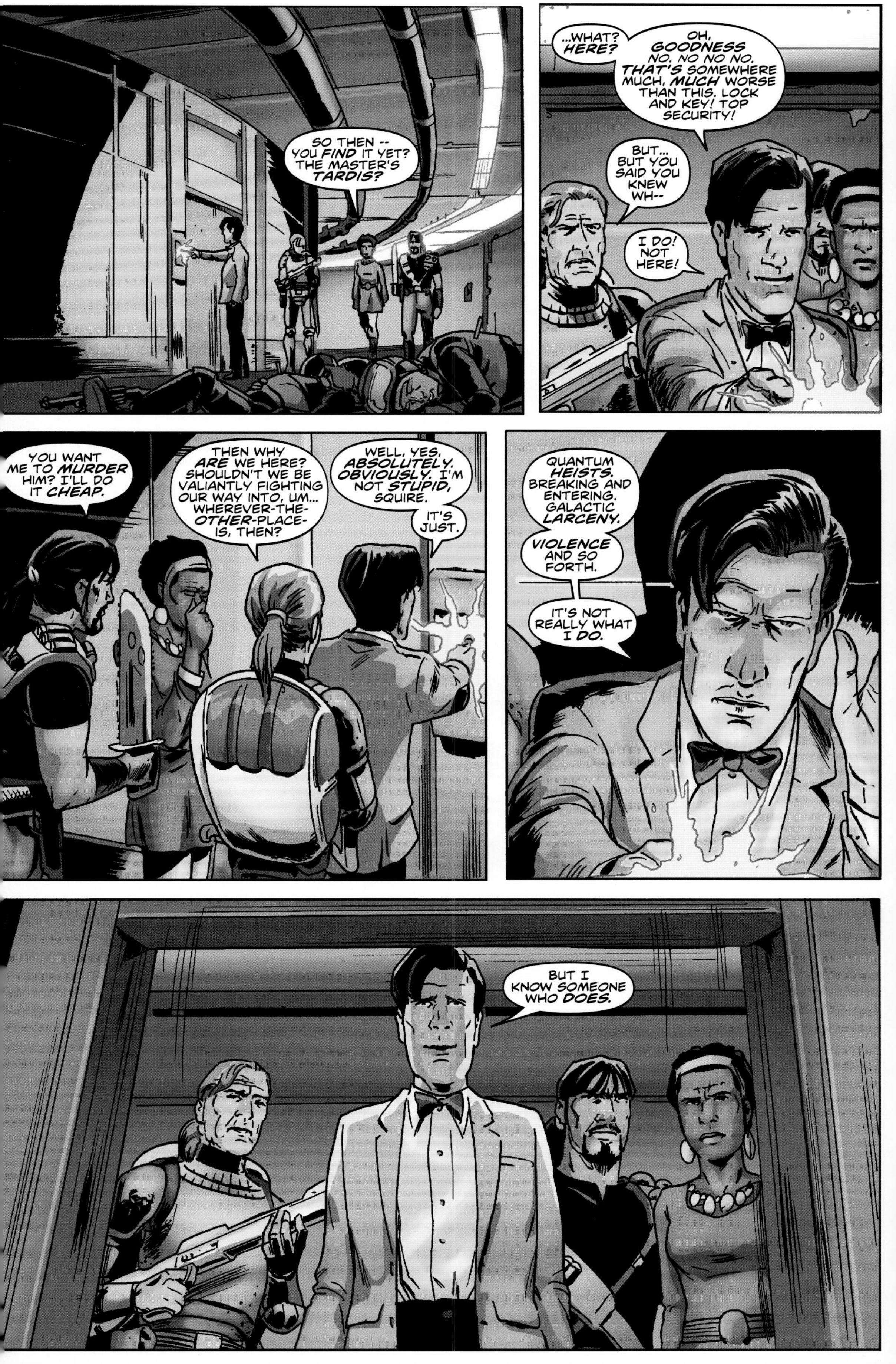
SO THEN -- YOU FIND IT YET? THE MASTER'S TARDIS?
...WHAT? HERE?
OH, GOODNESS NO. NO NO NO. THAT'S SOMEWHERE MUCH, MUCH WORSE THAN THIS. LOCK AND KEY! TOP SECURITY!
BUT... BUT YOU SAID YOU KNEW WH--
I DO! NOT HERE!
YOU WANT ME TO MURDER HIM? I'LL DO IT CHEAP.
THEN WHY ARE WE HERE? SHOULDN'T WE BE VALIANTLY FIGHTING OUR WAY INTO, UM... WHEREVER-THE-OTHER-PLACE-IS, THEN?
WELL, YES, ABSOLUTELY. OBVIOUSLY. I'M NOT STUPID, SQUIRE.
IT'S JUST.
QUANTUM HEISTS. BREAKING AND ENTERING. GALACTIC LARCENY.
VIOLENCE AND SO FORTH.
IT'S NOT REALLY WHAT I DO.
BUT I KNOW SOMEONE WHO DOES.

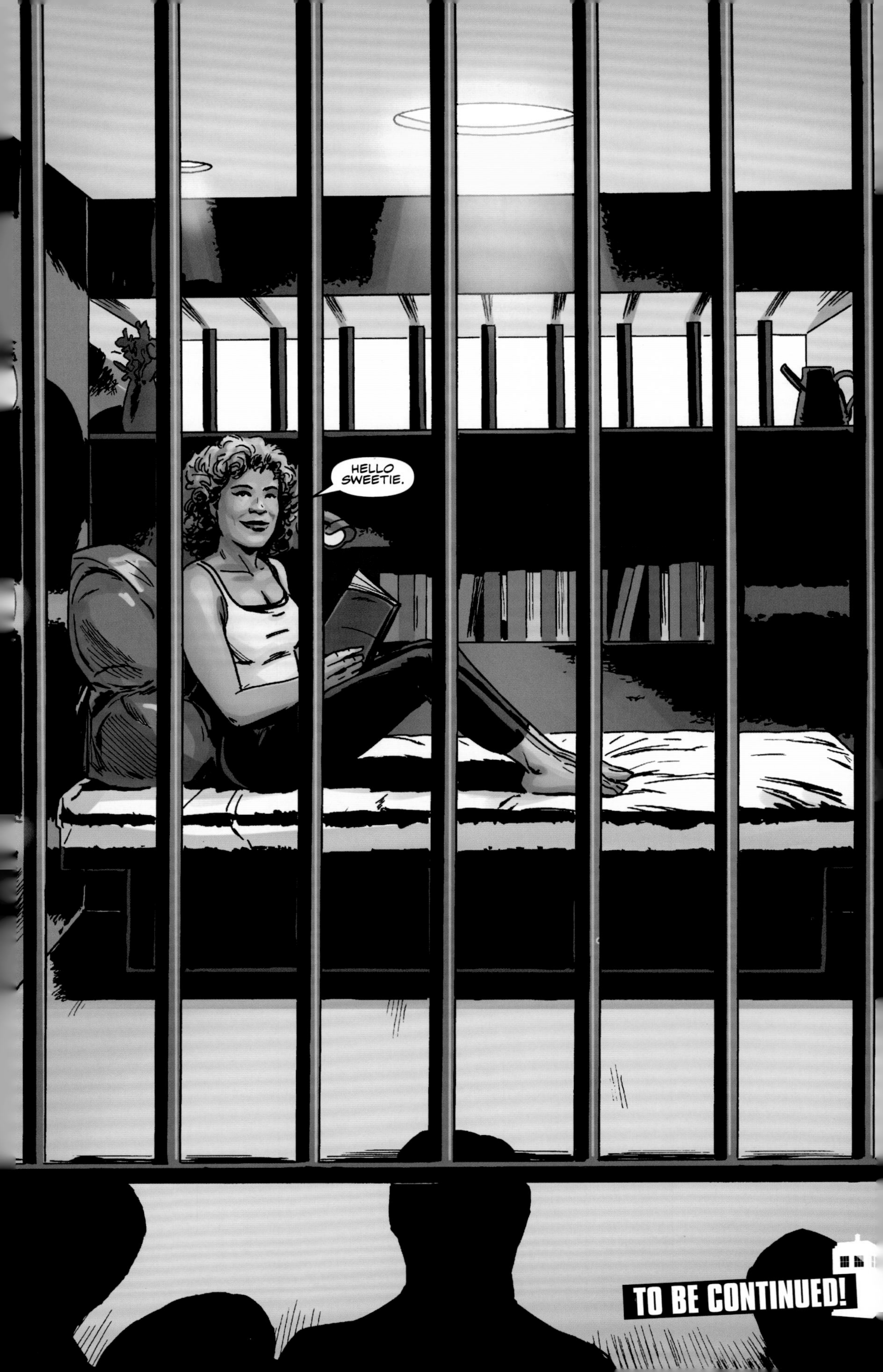
HELLO SWEETIE.
TO BE CONTINUED!

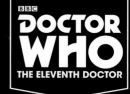

BBC DOCTOR WHO THE ELEVENTH DOCTOR

COVER GALLERY

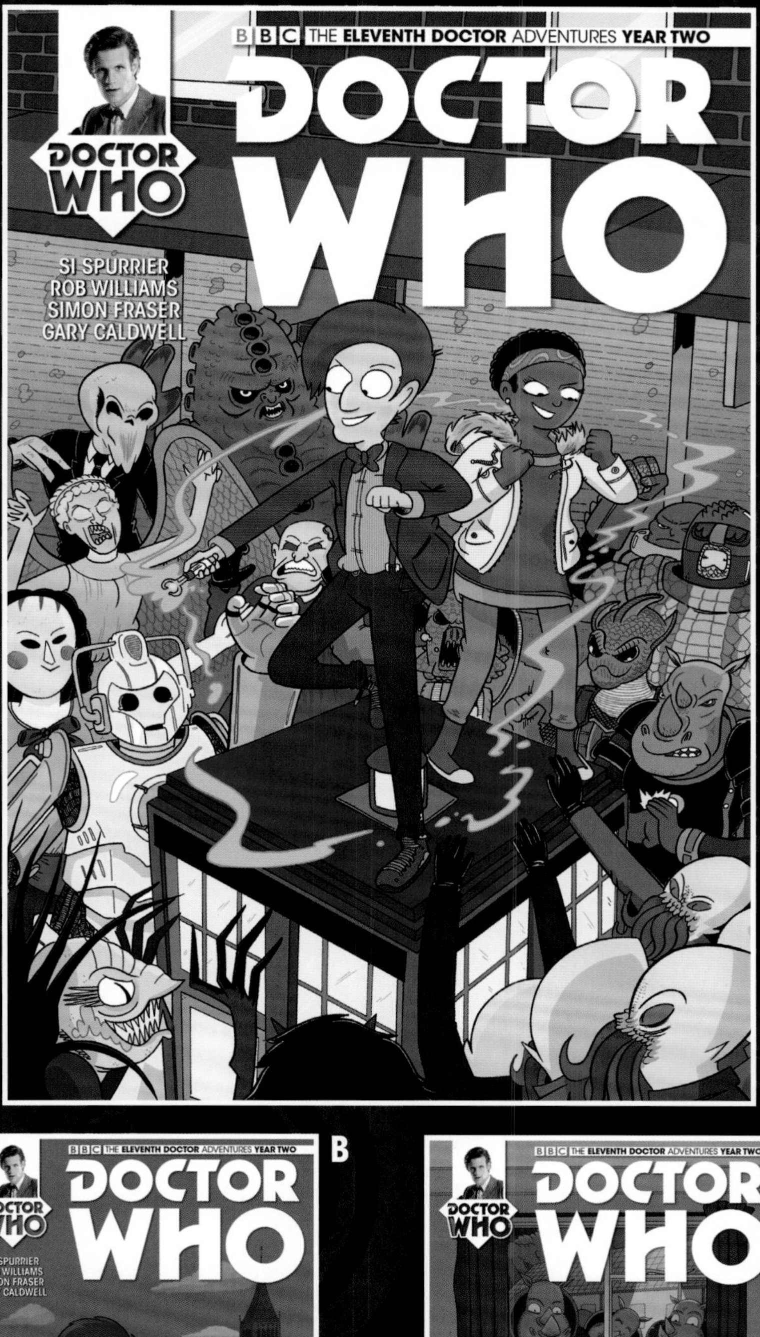
BBC THE ELEVENTH DOCTOR ADVENTURES YEAR TWO
DOCTOR WHO
DOCTOR WHO
SI SPURRIER
ROB WILLIAMS
SIMON FRASER
GARY CALDWELL

A

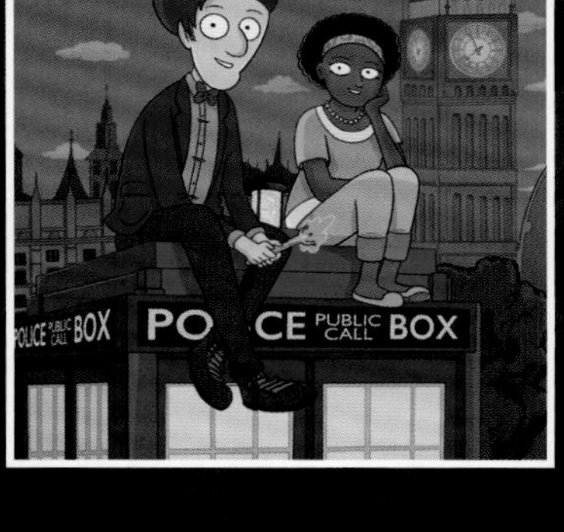
BBC THE ELEVENTH DOCTOR ADVENTURES YEAR TWO
DOCTOR WHO
DOCTOR WHO
SI SPURRIER
ROB WILLIAMS
SIMON FRASER
GARY CALDWELL
POLICE PUBLIC CALL BOX
PO CE PUBLIC CALL BOX

B

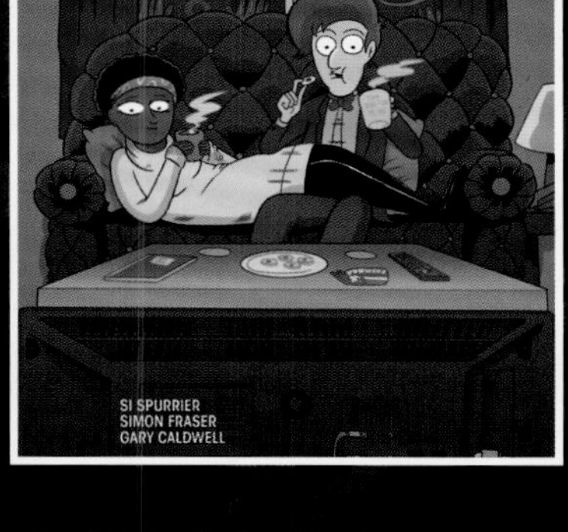
BBC THE ELEVENTH DOCTOR ADVENTURES YEAR TWO
DOCTOR WHO
DOCTOR WHO
SI SPURRIER
SIMON FRASER
GARY CALDWELL

C

ISSUES #2.1 - #2.3

A: #2.1 Cover C – MARC ELLERBY
B: #2.2 Cover C – MARC ELLERBY
C: #2.3 Cover C – MARC ELLERBY

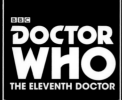

BBC DOCTOR WHO THE ELEVENTH DOCTOR

COVER GALLERY

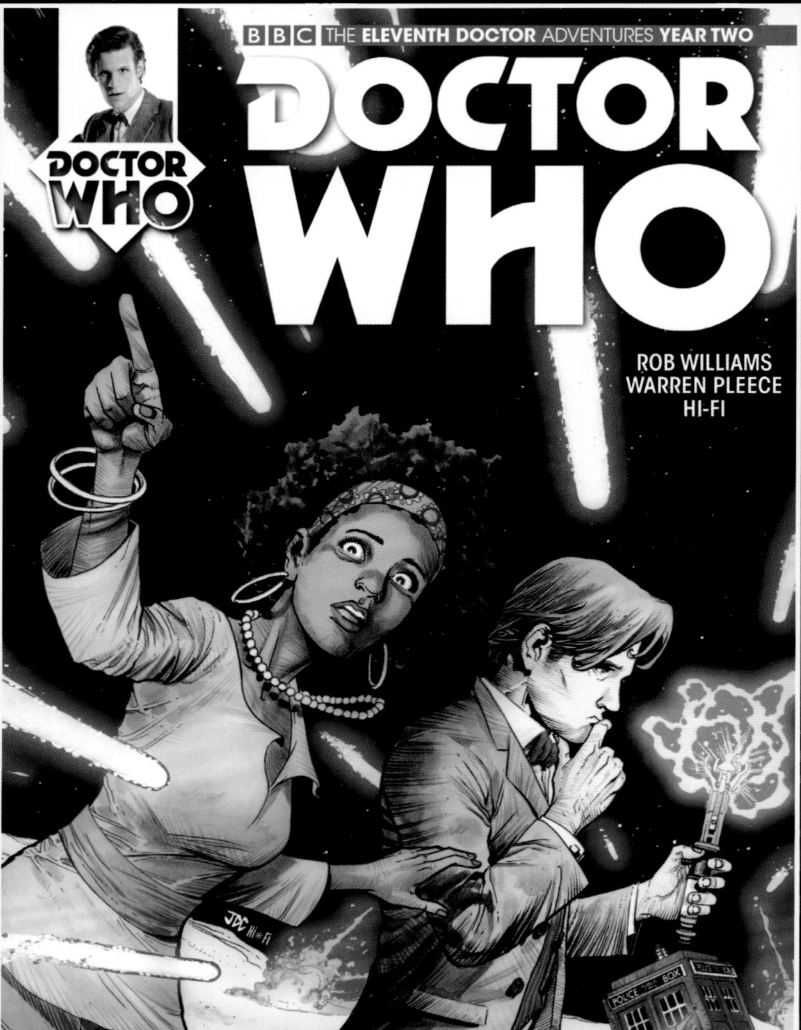

BBC THE ELEVENTH DOCTOR ADVENTURES YEAR TWO
DOCTOR WHO
DOCTOR WHO
ROB WILLIAMS
WARREN PLEECE
HI-FI
POLICE BOX

A

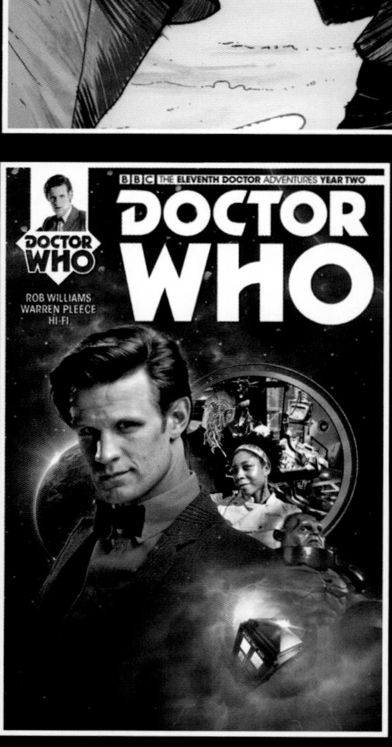

BBC THE ELEVENTH DOCTOR ADVENTURES YEAR TWO
DOCTOR WHO
DOCTOR WHO
ROB WILLIAMS
WARREN PLEECE
HI-FI

B

ISSUES #2.4

A: #2.4 Cover A – JOSH CASSARA & HI-FI
B: #2.4 Cover B – WILL BROOKS

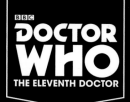

COVER GALLERY

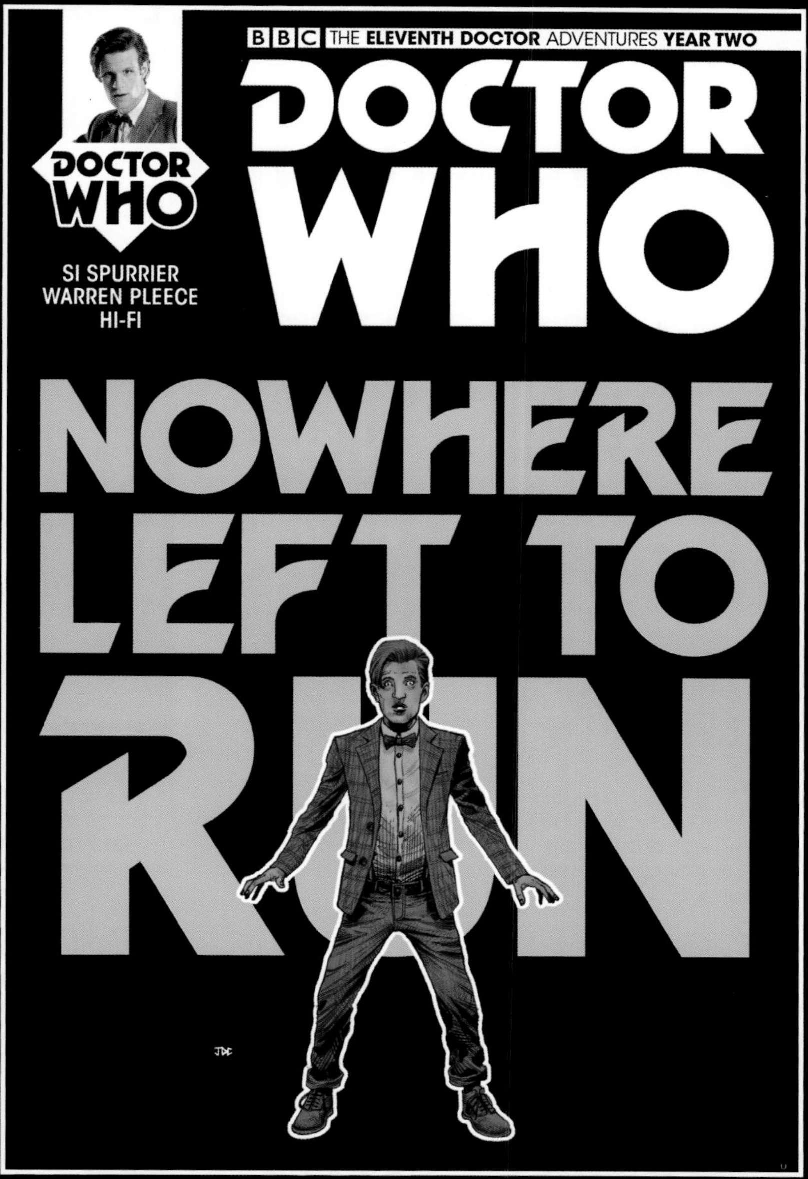
BBC THE ELEVENTH DOCTOR ADVENTURES YEAR TWO
DOCTOR WHO
DOCTOR WHO
SI SPURRIER
WARREN PLEECE
HI-FI
NOWHERE LEFT TO RUN

A

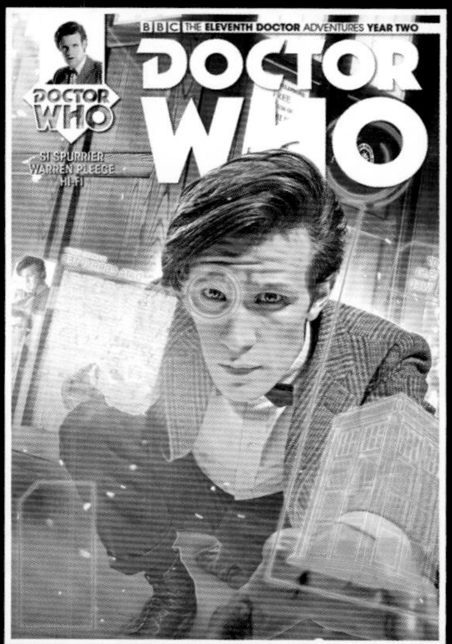
BBC THE ELEVENTH DOCTOR ADVENTURES YEAR TWO
DOCTOR WHO
DOCTOR WHO
SI SPURRIER
WARREN PLEECE
HI-FI

B

ISSUES #2.5

A: #2.5 Cover A – JOSH CASSARA & HI-FI
B: #2.5 Cover B – WILL BROOKS

FOLLOW YOUR FAVORITE INCARNATIONS ACROSS THESE FANTASTIC COLLECTIONS!

DOCTOR WHO: THE TWELFTH DOCTOR VOL. 1:TERRORFORMER

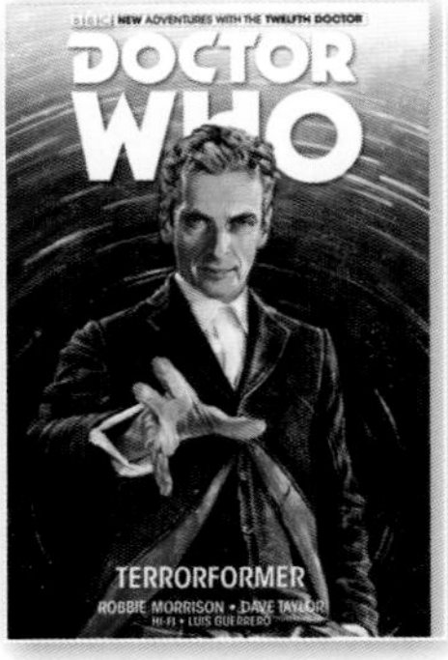
DOCTOR WHO
TERRORFORMER

ISBN: 9781782761778
ON SALE NOW - $19.99 / $22.95 CAN / £10.99
(UK EDITION ISBN: 9781782763864)

DOCTOR WHO: THE TWELFTH DOCTOR VOL. 2: FRACTURES

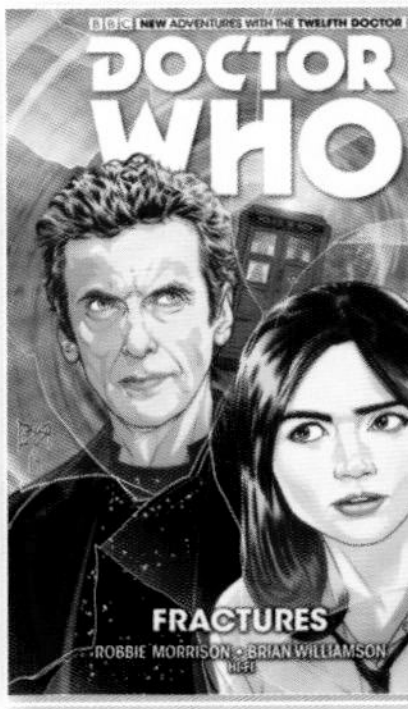
DOCTOR WHO
FRACTURES
ROBBIE MORRISON • BRIAN WILLIAMSON

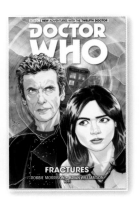

ISBN: 9781782763017
ON SALE NOW - $19.99 / $25.99 CAN / £10.99
(UK EDITION ISBN: 9781782766599)

DOCTOR WHO: THE TWELFTH DOCTOR VOL. 3: HYPERION

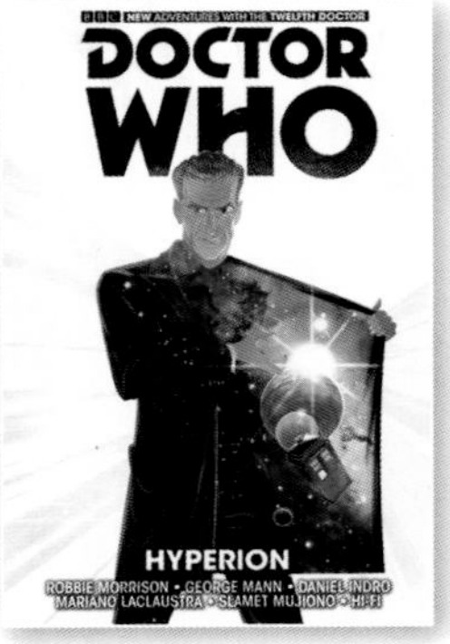
DOCTOR WHO
HYPERION
ROBBIE MORRISON • GEORGE MANN • DANIEL INDRO
MARIANO LACLAUSTRA • SLAMET MUJIONO • HI-FI

ISBN: 9781782767473
ON SALE NOW- $19.99 / $25.99 CAN / £10.99
(UK EDITION ISBN: 97817827674442)

DOCTOR WHO: THE TWELFTH DOCTOR VOL. 4: THE SCHOOL OF DEATH

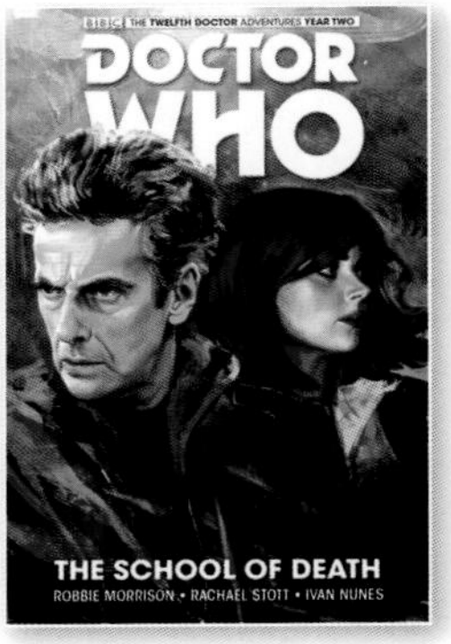
DOCTOR WHO
THE SCHOOL OF DEATH
ROBBIE MORRISON • RACHAEL STOTT • IVAN NUNES

ISBN: 9781785851087
COMING SOON - $19.99 / $25.99 CAN / £10.99
(UK EDITION ISBN: 9781785851070)

DOCTOR WHO: THE TENTH DOCTOR VOL. 1: REVOLUTIONS OF TERROR

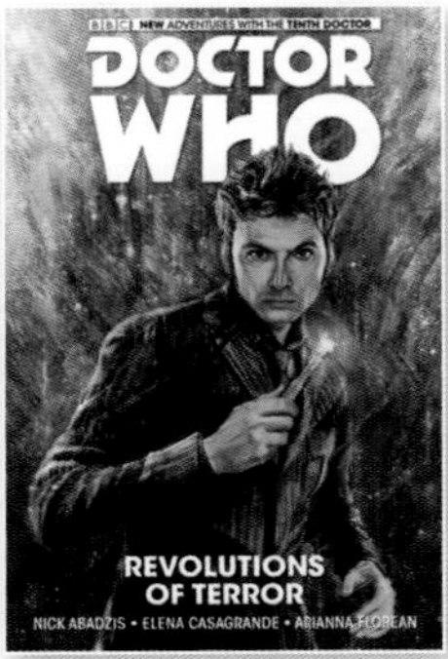
DOCTOR WHO
REVOLUTIONS OF TERROR
NICK ABADZIS • ELENA CASAGRANDE • ARIANNA FLOREAN

ISBN: 9781782761747
ON SALE NOW - $19.99 / $22.95 CAN / £10.99
(UK EDITION ISBN: 9781782763840)

DOCTOR WHO: THE TENTH DOCTOR VOL. 2: THE WEEPING ANGELS OF MONS

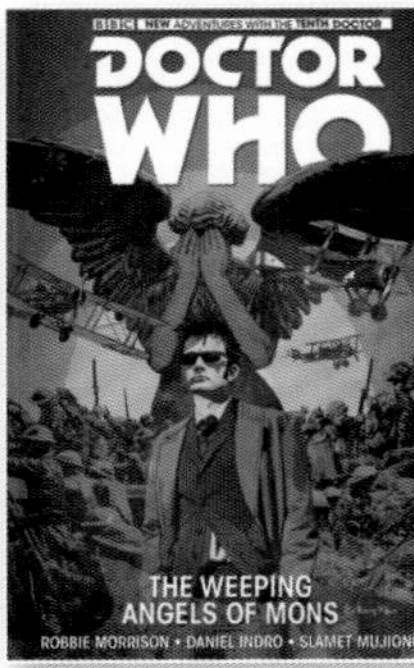
DOCTOR WHO
THE WEEPING ANGELS OF MONS
ROBBIE MORRISON • DANIEL INDRO • SLAMET MUJIONO

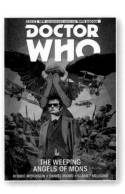

ISBN: 9781782761754
ON SALE NOW - $19.99 / $25.99 CAN / £10.99
(UK EDITION ISBN: 9781782766575)

DOCTOR WHO: THE TENTH DOCTOR VOL. 3:THE FOUNTAINS OF FOREVER

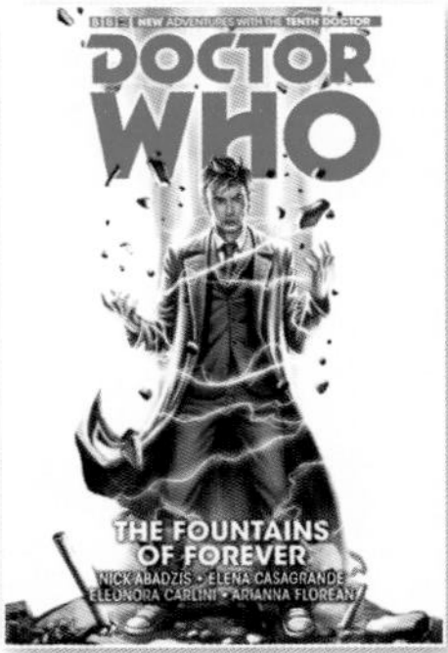
DOCTOR WHO
THE FOUNTAINS OF FOREVER

ISBN: 9781782763024
ON SALE NOW - $19.99 / $25.99 CAN / £10.99
(UK EDITION ISBN: 9781782767404)

DOCTOR WHO: THE TENTH DOCTOR VOL. 4:THE ENDLESS SONG

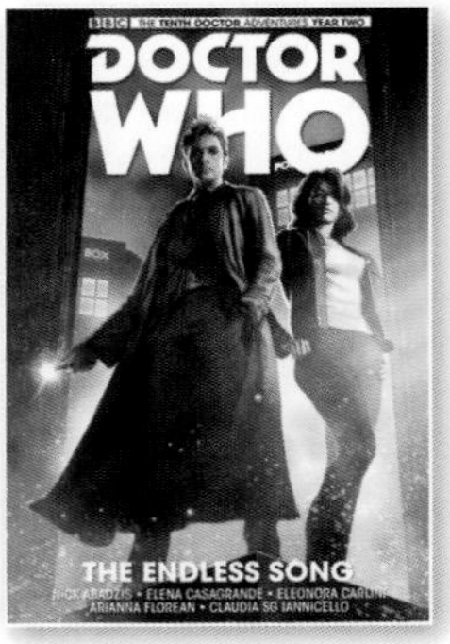
DOCTOR WHO
THE ENDLESS SONG

ISBN: 9781782767411
ON SALE NOW - $19.99 / $25.99 CAN / £10.99
(UK EDITION ISBN: 9781782767459)

For information on how to subscribe to our great Doctor Who titles, or to purchase them digitally for your favorite device, visit:

WWW.TITAN-COMICS.COM

TITAN COMICS

COMPLETE YOUR COLLECTION!

DOCTOR WHO: THE ELEVENTH DOCTOR VOL. 1: AFTER LIFE

BBC
NEW ADVENTURES WITH THE ELEVENTH DOCTOR
DOCTOR WHO
AFTER LIFE
AL EWING • ROB WILLIAMS • SIMON FRASER • BOO COOK
GARY CALDWELL • HI-FI

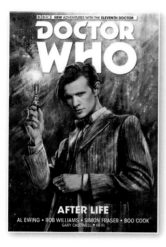

ISBN: 9781782761747
ON SALE NOW - $19.99 / $22.95 CAN / £10.99
(UK EDITION ISBN: 9781782763857)

DOCTOR WHO: THE ELEVENTH DOCTOR VOL. 2: SERVE YOU

BBC
NEW ADVENTURES WITH THE ELEVENTH DOCTOR
DOCTOR WHO
SERVE YOU
AL EWING • ROB WILLIAMS • SIMON FRASER • BOO COOK • WARREN PLEECE
GARY CALDWELL • HI-FI

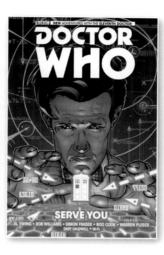

ISBN: 9781782761754
ON SALE NOW - $19.99 / $25.99 CAN / £10.99
(UK EDITION ISBN: 9781782766582)

DOCTOR WHO: THE ELEVENTH DOCTOR VOL. 3: CONVERSION

BBC
NEW ADVENTURES WITH THE ELEVENTH DOCTOR
DOCTOR WHO
CONVERSION
AL EWING • ROB WILLIAMS • SIMON FRASER • BOO COOK • WARREN PLEECE
GARY CALDWELL • HI-FI

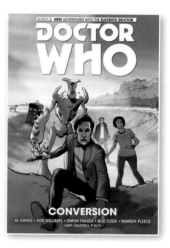

ISBN: 9781782763024
ON SALE NOW - $19.99 / $25.99 CAN / £10.99
(UK EDITION ISBN: 9781782767435)

DOCTOR WHO: THE NINTH DOCTOR VOL. 1: WEAPONS OF PAST DESTRUCTION

BBC
NEW ADVENTURES WITH THE NINTH DOCTOR
DOCTOR WHO
WEAPONS OF PAST DESTRUCTION
CAVAN SCOTT • BLAIR SHEDD

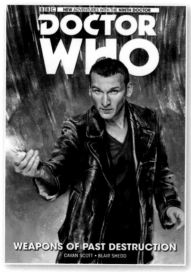

ISBN: 9781782763369
ON SALE NOW - $19.99 / $25.99 CAN / £10.99
(UK EDITION ISBN: 9781782761056)

DOCTOR WHO EVENT 2015 FOUR DOCTORS

BBC
A DOCTOR WHO COMICS EVENT
DOCTOR WHO
PAUL CORNELL I NEIL EDWARDS
FOUR DOCTORS
WITH IVAN NUNES AND COMICRAFT

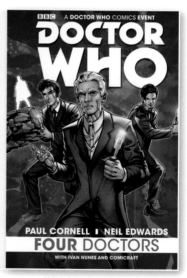

ISBN: 9781782765967
ON SALE NOW - $19.99 / $25.99 CAN / £10.99
(UK EDITION ISBN: 9781785851063)

AVAILABLE IN ALL GOOD COMIC STORES, BOOK STORES, AND DIGITAL PROVIDERS!

BIOGRAPHIES

Si Spurrier has written often for *2000 AD* and *Judge Dredd Magazine*, and continues to produce ambitious work in both prose and comics. He is best known for writing titles such as *X-Force* and *X-Men: Legacy* for Marvel, and his creator-owned titles *The Spire* and *Six-Gun Gorilla* at BOOM!, *Cry Havoc* at Image, and *Numbercruncher* at Titan Comics.

Rob Williams began his comics career with *CLA$$WAR*, and now writes stunning work for *2000AD (Judge Dredd: Titan, Low Life, Trifecta, Ichabod Azrael)* DC (*Martian Manhunter*), Vertigo (*Unfollow, The Royals*), and Titan, which also publishes his creator-owned success *Ordinary*. He lives in Bristol, UK.

Simon Fraser is a world-traveling artist, born in Scotland, now based in New York City. Best known as the co-creator of *Nikolai Dante for 2000AD*, Fraser has drawn for *Judge Dredd, Grindhouse, Family, Hell House* and his own series, *Lilly MacKenzie*.

Warren Pleece is a comic artist and graphic novelist of over 20 years experience – working for *2000AD*, DC, Dark Horse and many more – on titles such as *True Faith, Hellblazer, The Invisibles, Deadenders* and *Incognegro*. He lives in Brighton, UK.

Gary Caldwell has been coloring Simon Fraser's work for over twenty years, as Simon's right-hand man. Based in Scotland, he quietly knocks his pages out of the park every time.

Hi-Fi Colour Design was founded in 1998 by Brian and Kristy Miller and provides digital color for comic books, toys, video games, and animation, and tutorials on color through masterdigitalcolor.com.

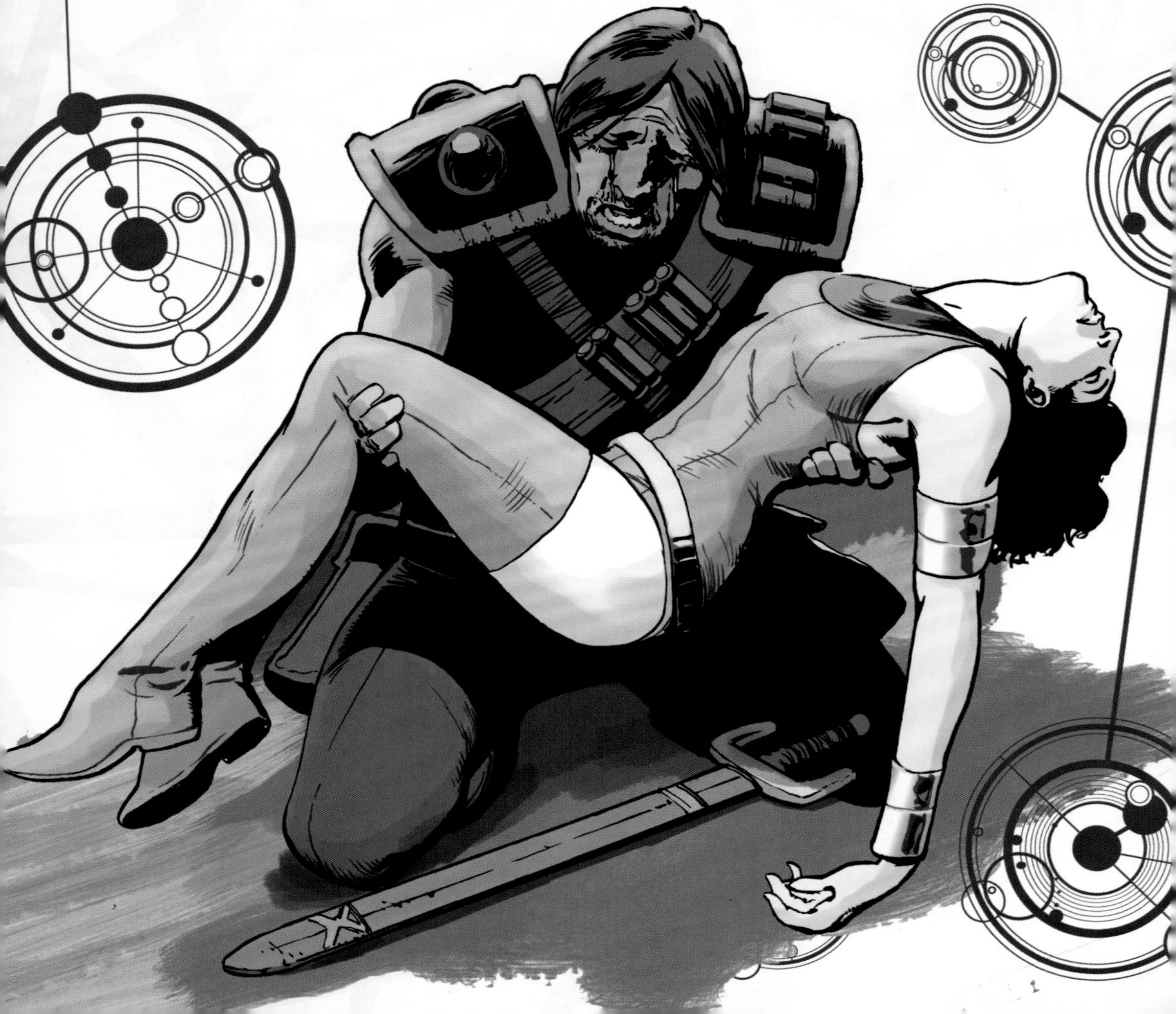